# THE DE PREE LEADERSHIP CENTER

The De Pree Leadership Center provides opportunities for individuals and organizations to think reflectively about issues surrounding the intersection of faith and leadership toward the goal of leading for positive transformation. We help organizations become places of realized potential by drawing on the person-centered principles of acclaimed business executive Max De Pree. Through our work we strive to engage others in building a leadership ethos of commitment to the optimal development of all.

The rich legacy built by De Pree shapes our content-rich programs, which offer participants fresh perspectives and creative learning opportunities. Faculty, facilitators, and adjunct presenters work collaboratively with organizations to create high-impact results for all participants. We offer both public and custom-designed events, including seminars, leadership briefings, workshops, executive retreats, roundtable discussions, and mentoring in the United States, Australia and Pacific Rim countries, the United Kingdom, and other locations around the world.

De Pree Leadership Center
135 N. Los Robles, Suite 620
Pasadena, California 91101
626-578-6335

# FAITH IN LEADERSHIP

*How Leaders Live Out Their Faith in
Their Work—and Why It Matters*

Robert Banks

Kimberly Powell

*Editors*

o

*Foreword by*
Max De Pree

Jossey-Bass Publishers
San Francisco

TCF Manufactured in the United States of America on Lyons Falls Turin Book. This paper is acid-free and 100 percent totally chlorine-free.

**Library of Congress Cataloging-in-Publication Data**

Faith in leadership : how leaders live out their faith in their work, and why it matters / Robert Banks and Kimberly Powell, editors ; foreword by Max De Pree.
    p. cm.
    Includes bibliographical references and index.
    ISBN 0-7879-4586-2
    1. Leadership—Religious aspects—Christianity.  2. Work—Religious aspects—Christianity.  I. Banks, Robert.  II. Powell, Kimberly.

BV4597.53.L43 F35 1999
248.8'8—dc21                                 99–052720

FIRST EDITION

*HB Printing* 10 9 8 7 6 5 4 3 2 1

# CONTENTS

## PART THREE
## Vital Issues for Faith and Leadership

## PART FOUR
## Faith-Based Leadership in Action

# FOREWORD

*LEADERSHIP* IS A HOT WORD these days. We live in difficult times, with things breaking down and changing too fast; we may feel uncertain or lose our way. When this happens we start to look for help. We call for leaders to step in—or step out, in some cases—and deal with difficult situations. The *"L* word" is also being tossed around frequently because those in charge of our venerable institutions, both public and private, have often failed us: they have either lacked the courage to do what was needed or used their positions to serve their own interests rather than to fulfill their proper responsibilities. Thus we continue our search for women and men of integrity to assume these leadership positions.

Coincidentally, another hot word today is *spirituality*. When life becomes difficult, we look for guidance and strength. When we feel that others have let us down, we search for something or someone greater than ourselves to depend on. Instead of experiencing anxiety and perplexity, we hunger for trust; we desire vibrant faith.

These two tendencies—the call for leadership and the search for faith—are two sides of one phenomenon with a complex relationship. Our hope that we will find help from capable leaders to solve our current problems is itself a form of faith and occurs precisely because we have lost faith in our existing leaders. We are once again realizing that leadership involves more than a charismatic personality or particular skills; rather, leadership is about character. Character does not emerge from nowhere but springs from deeply held convictions. In other words, if leaders are to do what is required of them and to withstand the inherent pressures in their positions, then their character must be anchored in faith.

At the deepest level, then, faith and leadership go together. It is just that for a time we lost sight of this. Our culture of religious pluralism raises new questions, challenging long-held beliefs about faith and leadership, either as distinct terms or two interconnected aspects. One of the hallmarks of sound leadership is the ability to ask questions, especially questions that get to the heart of the matter. Over the last two decades, we have seen writers grappling with issues such as the connection between leadership, power, and service; management and vision; and profit and compassion. Others have explored the connection between leadership as a science and an art and the connection between formal and informal types of leadership. This book raises a potentially divisive question that we have tended to avoid: what is the connection between people's personal convictions and their public responsibilities? The link between these two was once taken for granted, but over the years it has become suspect, even taboo. Some of the contributors to this book approach this experientially and others more generally, some from within large organizations and others from smaller ones. In all cases, this blend of the public and private adds substance to the main question the book seeks to address.

Another hallmark of leadership is its willingness to define reality. One of the strengths of this book is that it seeks to do just that. In various ways the contributors explore both the need and the quest for faith in leadership today from their unique vantage points. Leadership is also about an openness to diversity. It welcomes and courts a range of opinions, creating space for them to be heard. Leadership listens carefully to what is said and then seeks to discern what is most valuable for the greater good. Cohesion for this particular work stemmed from the common faith its contributors share, despite very different expressions of that faith. Sometimes these subtleties lie below the surface; sometimes they are in plain sight. Whatever their specific religious backgrounds—be it evangelical, mainline Protestant, Catholic, nondenominational, or Orthodox—their contributions, at their best, open up a conversation rather than present a series of discrete issues.

Several authors draw on the wisdom of the past—whether biblical, historical, or familial—to enhance our understanding of the present. Other contributors employ metaphors, create analogies, or tell stories. But enough has been said to indicate not only the value of this collection on faith and leadership but also the way it has sought to embody its theme by tackling it in a faithful way and, in doing so, exercising its own style of leadership. May it encourage many of you, its readers, to do the same.

*November 1999*                                    MAX DE PREE
*Holland, Michigan*

# PREFACE

THERE IS A NEED for a book on the role of faith in the lives of leaders in the workplace. Some attention has been given in the literature on leadership to the roles of vision, care, and compassion, but this attention has reflected only the virtues of hope and love, leaving unexplored the vital role of faith, the third of the three key virtues in the spiritual life. Apart from the occasional biography or autobiography of a Christian leader in the business world, or the rare larger survey (such as Laura Nash's 1994 book *Believers in Business*), little has been written about the importance of faith in the lives of leaders.

Christians who hold leadership positions in today's great variety of workplaces struggle with issues of integrity, trust, and risk. They seek wisdom and balance, fairness and justice. At conferences and seminars, voices call out from podiums and urge leaders to find the true way. But these exhortations are often nothing more than thinly veiled pop psychology: all dressed up, and going nowhere.

The ambiguity of this book's title will not escape the observant reader. Is the book about faith's impact on leadership, or is it about having faith in effective leadership? We intend to leave this question with no definitive answer, for both possible meanings are at issue today. We want to encourage more faith on the part of leaders who are striving to make a difference: their efforts depend, in part, on a stronger connection between faith and leadership.

It seemed to us that in the absence of absolutes, and in an organizational context where cross fire and ambiguity undermine trust, the starting point for our examination of faith in the workplace had to be a focus on resurgent virtues. These virtues, which can motivate elegant action, must be supported by a continuous commitment to practicing faithfulness and to learning the gifts of humility and vision; then and only then will leaders have the confidence and faith necessary for taking the risks that will move them out of the arena of the expected and into the arena of the exceptional. Moreover, those of us who are Christian leaders may find ourselves facing threats if we are not astute in facing the vital issues involved in bringing faith into the workplace. For example, we must consider vulnerability, so often called for and yet fearfully shunned. We also cannot ignore the struggle to find the right balance between expressing our truest selves in our workplaces, as people of faith, and being sensitive to those who are not so compelled or so oriented.

Therefore, to explore these matters faithfully, and to discover their impact on how people function in the workplace, we invited the perspectives of a diverse group of contributors who have strong Christian convictions. In their day-to-day lives as consultants, educators, and practitioners who also happen to belong to religious denominations all along the theological spectrum, they express their convictions in very different ways. In this volume, these lively practitioners and practical thinkers have moved in highly imaginative and constructive ways toward the initiation of a discussion that will be an important one for our understanding of faith's importance in the workplace.

## Contents

The discussion contained in this volume covers three broad, primary themes—virtues, practices, and vital issues for faith in leadership—that are examined in the first twelve chapters. In the book's final two chapters, these themes are examined through two examples, the first a personal account of the importance of faith in the workplace and the second an in-depth case study of an organization that measures itself against its highest ideals. Because faith is a slippery matter, difficult to describe adequately, we are fortunate to have these two examples.

## Acknowledgments

Every contributor to this volume was willing to go beyond the requirements for meeting deadlines and moving this work along. We are, to say the least, humbled by their example and encouraged by their enthusiasm. We are also deeply grateful to our colleagues at the De Pree Leadership Center, all of whom gave us the freedom to explore this topic and encouraged us to maintain our faith in its importance. In many meaningful ways, they gave us the gift of focus that we needed to complete this project. We are especially thankful for the talents of our assistant, Sara Schwarz, who enthusiastically stepped up to the demands of the details and provided invaluable assistance in compiling the annotated guide to organizations, videos, and publications found at the end of the book. To you, Sara, we acknowledge our indebtedness.

*November 1999*                             ROBERT BANKS
                                            Sydney, Australia

                                            KIMBERLY POWELL
                                            Kansas City, Missouri, U.S.A.

*To women and men who improve our world
by integrating their faith and work,
creatively and consistently*

## PART ONE

# RESURGENT VIRTUES FOR FAITH-BASED LEADERSHIP

# MOVING FROM FAITH TO FAITHFULNESS

*Robert Banks*

Robert Banks has served as executive director of the De Pree Leadership Center at Fuller Theological Seminary, Pasadena, California, where he was also Homer L. Goddard Chair of the Ministry of Laity. He is also the author or coauthor of several books on faith and work, public ethics, and leadership and is coeditor (with R. Paul Stevens) of *The Complete Book of Everyday Christianity: An A-to-Z Guide to Following Christ in Every Aspect of Life.* He was recently named director and dean of the newly established Macquarie Christian Studies Institute, Sydney, Australia.

○

THE EXPRESSION *RESURGENT VIRTUES* describes important aspects of the leader's character that have, or should have, significant ramifications for his or her daily practice in the workplace. This chapter explores the meaning of the word *faith* and its connection with its cognate term *faithfulness,* focusing especially on why a gap has developed between these two and how the gap can be closed. (Because trust is part of what is involved in faith, there is a link between this chapter and Chapter Three, which has more to say about the responsibility of managers in general; that chapter gives more attention to structural issues, and so it extends what is in view here.)

In the workplace, the word *faith* generally denotes a belief of some kind—in a supreme being, a cause or a goal, another person, a method or even a technique—and it is an attitude that seems to come more naturally to some people than to others. *Faithfulness* is mostly associated with a certain kind of behavior, such as consistency (as when a manager says, "She's been a faithful employee" or when a lawyer asks a witness, "Have you been faithful to your wife?" or when the leader of a volunteer organization comments, "He's always been a faithful supporter"). Sometimes a person is said both to have faith and to exhibit faithfulness; when the two characteristics are not united in one person, the person may seem to have faith in the religious sense but is not regarded as displaying faithfulness in his or her everyday dealings. This is what is described in biblical language as the character of a hypocrite (James 2:17).

We observe this disjunction too often today, which is why we are often cautious about firms that have the word *Fidelity* in their names, or about mission statements that discuss what a company "believes," or about advertisers who ask us to "trust" certain products. We are not always sure whether these faith-related words will be followed up by faithful action, and we look for evidence to verify the promises that these words contain. Our skepticism, fanned by the high incidence of marital or financial faithlessness among religious celebrities and the higher than usual divorce rate of pastors, even reaches into the church.

## Disjunction Between Faith and Faithfulness

My main interest in this chapter is the responsibility of faith-based leaders in for-profit and nonprofit organizations to reintegrate faith and faithfulness in their workplaces. If I focus more in what follows on personal than on structural expressions of faithfulness, it is for reasons of space, although I will provide some examples of structural expressions. When I use the word *faith*, I have in mind a combination of what is covered by the terms *belief, trust,* and *commitment,* for faith involves rational, emotional, and volitional components. The classic theological understanding of faith is that it is more a gift from God than a human capacity. This understanding of the word is a far cry from the way it is used in popular speech, even among religiously minded people. In that context, it tends to refer simply to having confidence in someone or something, often when there are no grounds for such confidence, and it is regarded as more inherent in some people than in others, or as a capacity that anyone can summon up.

In the marketplace arena, alongside more general statements about the move away from a faith-based view of life in modern societies, there has been increasing recognition of the disappearance of trust in and among organizations (Fukuyama, 1995). By comparison to the days of the so-called organization man, the same is the case with respect to loyalty in and to the company (Whyte, 1956). In the mid-1980s, the centrality of faithfulness, which overlaps in part with trust and loyalty, is also linked with integrity and credibility. This is readily evident in Farley (1986), especially in the section titled "The Way of Fidelity," and it is explored more fully in Diehl (1987). Grosman (1989) investigates the diminishing incidence of corporate loyalty, a theme followed up in Reichheld (1996). De Pree (1992, 1997) has also written about faithfulness.

Some have suggested that the disjunction between words and actions, beliefs and practices, is due to cities' and organizations' growth in size. They argue that this growth has created a distancing effect whereby those in leadership positions are too isolated from the branches of organizations to see the implications of their own actions. In other words, they argue, there are too few links of an organic kind to create the kind of culture where faithfulness flourishes and where employees' trust, loyalty, and commitment are returned (Grosman, 1989). Others have found or suggested that companies in smaller towns or cities seem to have a better chance of creating the kind of culture that encourages and rewards faithfulness. There is some evidence for this idea, but there may also be evidence to the contrary, as when intense loyalty is generated by a large global company that uses franchises. Overall, however, three reasons can be identified for the disjunction between faith and faithfulness: a movement toward faith as a personal and individual matter, a shift from vocations to careers, and the growing preoccupation with financial gain and tangible results.

## Movement Toward Individual Faith

Over the last two centuries, as a by-product of modernity, we have seen a steady movement toward individual faith. As the public realm (which includes work) gradually became separate from the institutional church (which was increasingly a private realm), people began to think of faith as primarily a personal matter, a shift that took place as part of the wider movement to separate private and public life. In the post-Puritan period, for example, many people began to draw a firm boundary between their work and their religious commitments; they attended to each but focused on one primarily during the week and on the other around the edges of the day and on Sunday. Voluntary associations (frequently established by religious-minded people) bridged this gap, but over time these associations, too, tended to become separated from their faith-based origins. This tendency became more pronounced with the growth of individualism and the weakening of absolutes. It resulted in the equation of faith with personal conviction, and of morality with personal values.

This shift has left a legacy of mostly silent believers, who no longer talk about their faith in public settings. They may occasionally talk about their values, but mostly with no reference to the bases of these values in a religious worldview. Apart from their inner attitudes and personal relationships, they do not see faith as having much effect on what they do in the workplace, whether as leaders or as followers. Their faith may come through more in their work with voluntary organizations, but in many cases it is legally and culturally more difficult to express a strong connection between faith and work. (Chapter Ten further explores fear of expressing one's faith.) The danger here is that the leadership goals, methods, practices, and styles of these people will lose some of its distinctive edge.

## Shift from Vocations to Careers

There has been a profound shift from following a call or vocation to pursuing a career. Whenever someone has a strong sense of vocation, it forms a bridge between religious beliefs and public activities. This sense of vocation enables faith to be carried more fully into one's conduct at work and into workplace structures. When the emphasis shifts from calling to career, however, the link between a person's private and public worlds is weakened. Work becomes a personal expression rather than a divine commission, a means of personal achievement rather than of public obedience, an arena for individual fulfillment rather than social transformation.

Until relatively recently, people in the nonprofit sector generally had a sense of calling or vocation rather than career ambitions, and so the nonprofit sector was often a place where the connection between faith and faithfulness could remain strong, but this is not necessarily true today. Some people do manage to keep their private and public selves connected, despite this change in how work is viewed. As a rule, though, personal agendas and preferences take precedence over public ones; the two are more often separate and in conflict. Pursuing a career leads a person in and out of various positions and institutions, and this mobility exacerbates the situation.

## Preoccupation with Gain and Results

There is a growing preoccupation with financial gain and tangible results, and especially with short-term gains rather than long-term effectiveness. Where the quest for financial success dominates everything else, it is all too easy for people to cut corners—not just moral corners but others as well, thus affecting organizational culture, the aspirations and needs of employees, and the organization's social and economic responsibility to the wider community. Concentration on the bottom line and a short-sighted view of the future frequently result in a divorce between goals and values, means and ends, people and processes, words and actions. (Of course, too little attention to the bottom line creates a different set of problems.) Just to complicate the matter, sometimes even the achievement of a competitive advantage or unexpected profits will lead a firm to shred loyalty by shedding employees.

The purposes of a business include not just making a profit but also helping workers grow as people. The firm that works hard to find employees who enhance its people-sensitive culture will create value for customers. Faithfulness to employees becomes visible in financial benefits, relative organizational stability, identification and use of employees' gifts, employees' sense of worth and achievement, roles for employees in decision making, and incentives for employees to come up with creative ideas. Faithfulness also means cultivating a physical and operational environment conducive to faithfulness, as well as enabling employees to share in the profits that come to the company.

Where all of this is standard operating procedure, there is stronger loyalty between employees and the company: image and reality, ideals and practice, statements and behavior go hand in hand to a greater extent. It is precisely because nonprofit organizations still exhibit many of the practices just listed that they can offer a model to for-profit institutions.

## Understanding Faithfulness

In considering how to move beyond simply having faith to being faithful, I will start with what is self-evident and move on to what is usually overlooked. Faithfulness in the workplace involves more than maintaining a consistent personal relationship with God and talking about one's faith with others. Diehl (1987) asked a number of mainline religious people in the workplace for a definition of faithfulness. Most defined it in terms of belief in or commitment to God, with the emphasis on the private dimension of the relationship; some respondents connected faithfulness with following the example or standards of Christ, or with asking what Christ would do in a given situation. If Diehl had asked a group with a more charismatic or fundamentalist orientation, he probably would have been told that being faithful entails sharing one's personal relationship with Christ with others. At any rate, few of the people that Diehl interviewed made a connection between faith in God and faithfulness to others in any broader sense. Of course, there are appropriate times and settings in the workplace for sharing something about one's faith; this is one part of being faithful, especially when such sharing arises organically out of the work that people are doing together. It is also true that asking about Christ's life or standards is a way of determining what faithfulness involves. Nevertheless, sharing our worldviews and beliefs, and focusing solely on the example of Christ, is not primarily what faithfulness involves, nor is it how faith is discerned, however great a role such sharing or such a focus may play in the workplace.

Leaders in particular have an obligation to be the voice of those in the workplace who often have little or no voice at all. In so doing, they exhibit faithfulness to their core convictions by calling into question the good faith of the institutions for which they work, thereby calling the institution back to its core convictions and basic mission. To take a stand against an institution in this way, to call it into question, generally takes character. Many people in the workplace want leaders who operate not merely according to the dictates of company policy, cultural correctness, or whim but according to sound character. For character to take root, a person must first have principles, and principles must form into habits.

The importance of internalized priorities and values being developed into regular habits is once again being recognized (Bellah, 1996; Covey, 1989). Too often, however, it sounds as if developing the right kinds of principles and habits at work is simply a matter of trying harder. But if principled and habitual behavior has any connection with faith, then there is a problem with this kind of thinking: according to the Bible, faith is a gift rather than an achievement, a gift that is not arbitrary but rather is requested. The principles and habits discussed in most popular books do not go deep enough. It is fine to talk about the need for fairness, honesty, dignity, service, excellence, potential, and growth; as Covey suggests (1989, p. 34), these are not "unique to any specific faith or religion" but "are a part of [almost] every enduring religion, as well as enduring philosophies and ethical systems." But they do not cover the full range of Christian qualities. For example, justice involves more than fairness, goodness more than honesty, and sacrifice more than service. The reason why all these qualities are not in the forefront is because they go beyond normal aspirations and ways of operating.

In the biblical writings, faithfulness is always expressed within an existing *relationship*; it is not extended to an idea or a cause. Similarly, it is never just an attitude or a feeling but is always manifested *in action*. It is not sanctioned by law or rules but is freely undertaken. It is offered, whether in a dramatic or minor way, to someone who needs it (and who is thus placed in a dependent position) by one who has the capacity to help. All human faithfulness ultimately depends on the conscious acknowledgment or unconscious influence of God's faithfulness, and it tends to manifest itself most in a person's life where there has been an ongoing experience of it in a variety of settings and circumstances. This understanding of faithfulness is confirmed by the testimony of people today, in a variety of settings (Diehl, 1987).

In addition to offering these general statements about the nature of faithfulness, the biblical writings are realistic enough to indicate that the mere exercise of faithfulness is not the simple answer to every difficult situation. There is no formula that is appropriate to all occasions. The biblical writings take the complexities of life and work into account—for example, if the strategy of expressing faithfulness fails to bring about good, the failure does not necessarily stem from disloyalty—but the writings do not endorse the view that it is enough if people expressing faithfulness have their hearts in the right place. The writings also exhibit the awareness that arrangements that have been made sometimes cannot remain unchanged. Sometimes it is right to modify them, although never in a way that subverts their basic intent or allows anyone to discard a relationship lightly. This kind of modification happened even in the case of Jewish Law, as indicated by the various editions of the Mosaic codes in the books of Exodus and Deuteronomy (Sakenfeld, 1985).

## Faithful Leadership in Action

Just as institutions, situations, and problems differ, so do courses of action. Confronted with the challenge of exhibiting faithfulness, a company in a relatively homogeneous culture can respond in ways that a large corporation in a multicultural environment cannot. An organization, whether large or small, that is still family-owned, and that resonates with its founders' values, provides opportunities and challenges that are different from those found in a company that has been set up primarily on more pragmatic grounds, by people who have formed a pact to work together for certain limited ends. An organization providing customer service as a unified package over several years is in a different position from one that deals with discrete products and that has rapid turnover in customers. A consultancy that challenges organizations to undertake a paradigm shift in how they operate is under a greater obligation than its counterparts to model, through its own governance and practices, what it is advocating. Despite these differences, however, there are a number of areas in which leaders and institutions can exhibit similar forms of faithfulness.

## Organizational Mission

Every organization has a mission. Sometimes an organization's mission statement is in writing, and sometimes it is not. Sometimes it is clear, and sometimes it is confused. Sometimes it is clear from the beginning; sometimes it requires time for experiment and feedback.

Organizations that are successful have a clear sense of their collective identity. Those that exhibit faithfulness, whether they are for-profit or nonprofit organizations, have a clear commitment to creating value for employees or members, partners or allies, customers or clients. If this commitment does not exist, it must become a reality, but the only effective way of making this happen is to persuade investors and supporters that this is the way to proceed.

In a way, stating a mission is an act of faith—not necessarily of religious faith, but of faith nevertheless. (See Chapter Twelve for a slightly expanded view of faith.) At the beginning of an organization's life, there is no guarantee that it will fulfill its stated mission. It may promise to do so, but this promise is also an act of faith. Even when the institution has a demonstrated track record, that does not guarantee it will continue to perform consistently in the future.

Having a mission is an act of faith in another sense as well: it is an expression of a commitment not just to do but to be something, to be the kind of organization that can do what it claims. This is quite an undertaking, and no one involved in an enterprise should take it for granted. It is not enough to have done the homework, gathered the resources, and taken possession of the know-how. A body of people has to cohere well enough, long enough, and effectively enough to bring the mission to fulfillment. Use of the word *faith* in these two respects is not improper, especially when we take into account that most business start-ups fail and that many voluntary organizations survive only for a few years.

Where does faithfulness enter in? It is important for those in leadership positions, at whatever level, to "keep the faith" that is enshrined in the organization's mission. What does this mean in practice? Leaders must continue to believe that what they have embarked on is achievable, and they should seek to operate in a way that is consistent with the parameters of the mission. This does not mean that they should downplay unanticipated difficulties or hurdles or pretend they do not exist, but they should maintain the viability of the mission and continue to uphold it, and this is especially true for those leaders who are anxious or unclear about it. Leaders should behave, relate, and operate in ways that reflect the character of the mission. For example, if the mission puts customers first, then leaders must put employees first. If the mission promises extraordinary service to its customers, then leaders must provide the same to the organization's stakeholders. If the mission states a commitment to quality and value-added products, then leaders must create a culture and an environment with the same characteristics (thus, if wage cuts are being made, leaders must include themselves among those who suffer the consequences).

## Promises

Over a period of time, the leaders of organizations will tend to make a range of promises to those who work with and for them. These promises may be large or small, explicit or implicit, personal or collective, strong or weak. Like many politicians' promises, these may be met with skepticism; as many cultural critics have lamented, there seems to be a growing disparity, in private as well as public life, between the promises that leaders and institutions make and the promises that they keep. This disparity is due in part to the changing definition of what a promise is: nowadays, most people seem to regard a promise as the expression of a hope rather than as the creation of an obligation. The disparity is also due to the move away from a principle-based ethic and toward a situational, fulfillment-oriented one whereby it is enough, in order to break a promise, to say that external circumstances or personal aspirations have changed. According to De Pree (1997, p. 127), "At the heart of fidelity lies . . . promise keeping." This statement applies as much to a leader's external relations with providers, partners, agents, customers, and the wider community as it does to his or her internal relations with stockholders, superiors, peers, subordinates, and their families.

A leader should not make private and public promises (whether to people inside or outside the organization) that contradict each other. When a personal agenda is dressed up as a promise that is then broken, the integrity of the leader and the organization will suffer. A leader also should not make casual promises. Followers, for example, cannot afford such a leader, for someone is bound to take these casual promises seriously and be severely disappointed should they be broken, especially in a period of reorganization or in a difficult business climate. At such times, when people's feelings of uncertainty are more intense and their hopes are higher, the leader will be held more accountable for keeping any promises that have been made.

I am not suggesting that all promises be regarded as absolute. There are both conditional and unconditional promises. The fulfillment of promises depends on both parties' keeping their part of a bargain that has been reached, or on jointly acknowledged circumstances, but sometimes there are circumstances completely beyond the control of those who have made and received promises—an unexpected buyout, for example. But such circumstances do not necessarily absolve the person who has made the promise from all obligation; much depends on how hard he or she has fought to honor previous commitments, and on how well prepared he or she has been to suffer the consequences of keeping those commitments.

As much as possible, faithful leaders will seek to keep their word. Every time they break their word, something tends to die in their organizations, in the wider culture, in their followers, and in themselves. Faithful leaders will not make light use of their own shifting goals in excusing themselves from fulfilling their responsibilities. They will seek to honor their promises as much as possible despite altered circumstances. Even when they have legitimate reasons to break their promises, they will look for some way to partially honor their pledges.

## Mistakes

We all make mistakes. The best leaders know this, factor it in to their calculations, and get on with the business of doing the best they can. This does not mean, however, that they overlook others' mistakes and fail to hold them accountable. As De Pree comments (1997, p. 127), "truth-telling" is at the heart of faithfulness in the workplace, and sometimes telling the truth means that a leader must circumspectly identify unwelcome realities, which some may not want made public.

Less effective leaders often have little tolerance for mistakes committed by those working for them. They expect near perfection, and they make life difficult for their subordinates when this level of perfection is not forthcoming, often because they unknowingly make many mistakes themselves and are unconsciously looking to their subordinates to compensate. The trouble with expectations, however, is that they evoke judgment when they are not met, and they act in the way the law tends to do: it takes only one infraction for condemnation to come crashing down on the offender's head. Subordinates then develop a sense of the boss keeping a scorecard of failures for use against them in the future.

Faithful leaders do not work this way. They have hopes for (rather than expectations about) the performance of the people around them, hopes that are not amorphous or static but clear and always rising. Faithful leaders are also continually on the lookout for ways to minimize mistakes, and for ways to learn the most from any that are made. They are aware that the future does not belong to those who make the fewest mistakes but rather to those who make and learn from the most adventurous ones. Leaders who have hope for others' performance do not lose faith in people who make typical mistakes. They do not tolerate or ignore mistakes, nor do they fail to hold people accountable, but they are less interested in condemning others than in forgiving them and helping them improve their performance. In this way, they demonstrate that they continue to place their faith in their subordinates—not less faith than before, and not a half-hearted faith. They continue to exhibit full faith, and in so doing they show that they are acting in a genuinely faithful way.

## Job Security

Once upon a time, mostly as an unwritten understanding, it was possible for some organizations to hire people for life. In a more stable society, with less emphasis on individualism and a stronger sense of class, lifelong employment by the firm and lifelong loyalty to the firm were common. But times have changed, and this arrangement is now the rare exception. The number of jobs that the average person will cycle through in the course of a lifetime keeps growing. Job shift has replaced job security. Serial relationships with several firms are the rule rather than a permanent arrangement.

How do leaders in an organization exercise faithfulness in such a climate? In most cases, it is no longer possible to promise secure, long-term advancement. Does this mean that leaders can only make short-term, provisional promises? That they must initially lay out a best-case scenario and appraise employees of more difficult realities only when they hit? That they should merely forecast, as honestly as they can, what the short- or medium-range future looks like on the basis of current trends?

Making short-term, provisional promises involves only a minimal commitment to workers, and it often gets only a minimal commitment in return. Laying out a best-case scenario puts leaders in danger of promising more than they can deliver and usually leads workers to feel let down or betrayed. Faithful leaders can go farther. They can commit themselves to building or maintaining an organization that will last, whatever changes may have to take place along the way. This approach may involve the employee's making a long-term commitment to the organization instead of looking for another position as soon as difficulties or opportunities appear. Beyond this baseline, leaders can design procedures that allow others to express their ideas for creating long-term futures for themselves in the organization and to influence decisions that will foster this goal.

One possibility here, as exemplified at Herman Miller, Inc., is to grant workers a share in the company's profits, especially any portion of the profits that flow directly from their own suggestions. In earlier times, Herman Miller was generally able to promise job security and appropriate advancement. When Max De Pree became CEO, he took an additional step: he promised training for any employee who suffered from a cutback, to help make him or her more marketable; he assisted the former employee in finding a new position; and he assured the former employee of a salary until he or she received an offer relatively close to the level that he or she had enjoyed at Herman Miller. This was a creative, responsible reformulation of the principle of loyalty, adapted to a more volatile, unpredictable marketplace.

Another example is provided by Charles Ambler's response to his consultant's call for either downsizing or a merger with Ambler's largest competitor in his wholesale grocery business in Ontario, Canada. Ambler believed in his obligations: to the original vision of the company, to the service of his long-term senior employees, and to the wider community of which the company was an integral part. Therefore, he placed the dilemma before his managers and other employees, to see what wisdom they could contribute. This move brought an extraordinary outpouring of commitment on their part to help the company survive. Employees voluntarily agreed to part-time rotations and salary reductions, and they bought shares in the company to increase its cash flow. Within a year, the company, boosted by significant employee ownership, had turned the corner and become fully competitive once again.

## Nurturing Faithful Leadership

Faithful leadership does not come merely from gaining knowledge about it. You cannot acquire it by taking a set of seminars or a course (although these certainly may help you toward a better understanding of what is involved).

Faithful leadership is not a skill or even an art. It radiates from a person's spiritual and moral center. Its fundamental components are integrity in all things, an attitude of service, a concern for justice and equity, and a willingness to be vulnerable (De Pree, 1992). These are qualities that spring from a deep well of basic convictions and commitments. If these qualities become habits, in the very best sense of the term, they are primarily habits of the soul and heart. How does a person or an organization nurture these qualities and characteristics? The usual programs for education, training, and mentoring are not enough. I suggest two approaches, one indirect and the other direct.

## Indirect Approach

A few years ago, a well-known national figure was talking about the kind of leadership that will be required in the next century. This sort of leadership, he said, will not come from those who operate on the basis of institutional power or formal qualifications. Some of its most important characteristics and capacities will require would-be leaders to place themselves into settings (such as voluntary associations) where, initially, they will hold no positions, where their qualifications will not matter, and where there will be few tangible rewards. In those settings, they will generally only begin to earn others' respect and trust, by serving the associations' aims and purposes faithfully over a period of time. This will be one way for people to learn and cultivate some of the qualities involved in faithful leadership.

We live in a society in which relationships that traditionally had a covenantal character (binding two parties unconditionally for a particular purpose or length of time) have been steadily replaced by contractual relationships of limited duration, with built-in conditions. This trend is noticeable even in marriage, friendship, and the church. Most workplace obligations do properly have a contractual character, but not all do, and even those obligations that do are more likely to be honored by people who know something about the art of keeping covenants. This means that those leaders who are already in covenantal relationships "for better or for worse, for richer or for poorer, in sickness and in health" with spouses, families, friends, and fellow believers are more likely to be the ones who will develop the characteristics required for faithful leadership in the marketplace.

## Direct Approach

The opportunity to observe how a more experienced leader handles issues related to faithfulness is a wonderful asset, especially if such a leader is willing to invest time in younger or emerging leaders. We can also learn from our peers who seek to practice faithfulness, and we should not forget what we might gain from observing how subordinates in positions of leadership handle this challenge; sometimes they know more about consistency and loyalty than those to whom they are responsible. We can also learn from other role models whose stories we come across in books, journals, and magazines.

Where leadership is more of a collegial or team affair, we can learn from those working with us about how to identify, handle, and evaluate issues related to faithfulness. Group wisdom has much to offer, even when people tackle issues in different ways. Tackling situations in pairs rather than alone, whenever working in pairs is possible, we can reduce the learning curve and improve our responses. When there is no agreement on the best course of action, observing how others deal with issues gives us an opportunity to see the strengths and weaknesses of different approaches.

There is also great benefit in being a member of an informal group, whether inside or outside the organization, with people at a level similar to one's own. When trust builds in such a group, there is an opportunity to discuss questions related to faithfulness, raise particular instances of it as case studies, and ask for help with our individual struggles in this area. Some groups meet casually for breakfast or lunch on a regular basis; others, like Bill Diehl's Monday Connection group in Allentown, Pennsylvania, have monthly meetings at a local restaurant that begin with breakfast and are followed by presentation of a case study and then by general discussion, so that each member has the opportunity to feature his or her own issues and stories (see Diehl, 1987). One of the participants in Diehl's group is a local pastor who acts as a kind of scriptural and theological consultant. Adding prayer to the mix, not just prayer of a general kind but rather prayer that is specifically focused on the issue at hand, immeasurably deepens the value of the exercise.

To what extent can the same effect be obtained by belonging to one of the burgeoning number of virtual networks and other on-line fellowships and associations? We should not dismiss them, as some tend to do, just because they do not have a face-to-face character; some existing covenantal relationships are already being technologically assisted through use of the phone and e-mail. But there is something irreplaceable about regular face-to-face meetings. They contain more reality checks and operate at more complex levels. They require more of us, and we receive more from them.

## Conclusion

I have argued that leaders should take faithfulness as well as faith more seriously and seek to integrate them more completely in the workplace. Doing so will increase their capacity to live by faith, and to be faithful as well as full of faith. It will also bring with it a decided individual advantage: not only does it develop a greater degree of integration and integrity, it also creates an advantage for others in the organization; it leads to a clearer understanding of organizational goals and values, a better sense of morale, a higher degree of trust, and a higher rate of retention. As De Pree says (1997, pp. 127, 129), "Trust grows when people see leaders translate their personal integrity into organizational fidelity" and when followers see "that leaders can be depended on to do the right thing."

Integrating faith and faithfulness into the workplace also generates significant growth potential for the organization. As De Pree states (1997, p. 129), "Leaders who keep their promises and followers who respond in kind create an opportunity to generate enormous energy around their commitment to serve others." In for-profit organizations, authentic faithfulness tends to spill over into improved loyalty from suppliers and customers, greater cost advantages through superior productivity, and stronger and longer-term commitment from investors (Reichheld, 1996). In nonprofit organizations, it creates greater buy-in of members, more vigorous initiative and effort, and more permanent financial support.

Authentic faithfulness also offers more advantages to the wider community. An organization that models how faithfulness can realistically function tends to increase the amount of trust, and therefore of social capital, in society overall and to present a model of organizational fidelity from which other institutions can learn. Here and there, strengthening the link between faith and faithfulness may also make others inside and outside the workplace receptive to discovering or recapturing the fundamental role of faith in life generally: "Above all, we make our choices trusting in God's great loyalty—loyalty that forgives our misunderstandings . . . that forgives our lack of steadfastness, . . . and loyalty that in the end despite all odds will bring the world round right" (Sakenfeld, 1985, p. 42).

REFERENCES

Bellah, R. N., Madsen, R., Sullivan, W. M., Swindler, A. and Tipton, S. M. *Habits of the Heart* (rev. ed.). Berkeley: University of California Press, 1996.

Covey, S. *The Seven Habits of Highly Effective People: Powerful Lessons in Personal Change.* New York: Simon & Schuster, 1989.

De Pree, M. *Leadership Jazz.* New York: Doubleday, 1992.

De Pree, M. *Leading Without Power: Finding Hope in Serving Community.* San Francisco: Jossey-Bass, 1997.

Diehl, W. *In Search of Faithfulness: Lessons from the Christian Community.*
    Philadelphia: Fortress, 1987.

Farley, M. A. *Personal Commitments: Beginning, Keeping, Changing.*
    San Francisco: Harper San Francisco, 1986.

Fukuyama, F. *Trust: The Social Virtues and the Creation of Prosperity.*
    New York: Free Press, 1995.

Grosman, B. A. *Corporate Loyalty: A Trust Betrayed.* New York: Penguin,
    1989.

Reichheld, F. F. *The Loyalty Effect: The Hidden Force Behind Growth, Profits
    and Lasting Value.* Boston: Harvard Business School, 1996.

Sakenfeld, K. D. *Faithfulness in Action: Loyalty in Biblical Perspective.*
    Philadelphia: Fortress, 1985.

Whyte, W. H. *The Organization Man.* New York: Simon & Schuster, 1956.


### ADDITIONAL READINGS

Collins, J. C., and Porras, J. I. *Built to Last: Successful Habits of Visionary
    Companies.* San Francisco: Harper San Francisco, 1994.

Covey, S. *Principle-Centered Leadership.* New York: Simon & Schuster, 1990.

# 2

# INTEGRITY AND THE ART OF COMPROMISE

*Richard Higginson*

Richard Higginson is director of the Ridley Hall Foundation and professor at Ridley Hall, Cambridge, England. He fosters the connection that people in business, the professions, and public life seek in integrating their faith with their work. He is the author of *Called to Account,* of *Transforming Leadership: A Christian Approach to Management,* and of *Mind Gap.*

———o———

INTEGRITY IS A FASHIONABLE QUALITY to espouse in the organizational world today; few words are mentioned more often in corporate mission statements. This widespread corporate endorsement of integrity raises many problems. The most obvious one—the gulf that can develop between a laudable ideal and actual practice—is one to which even the best-intentioned organization can succumb.

But there remains the fundamental question of what the term *integrity* means. Certainly, when I have asked businesspeople what they understand by the term, they have struggled to come up with a simple definition. Do the writers of mission statements have a clear understanding of the word? Do employees have the same understanding? If a disparity exists, what is done to resolve it?

If people cannot come up with a simple definition of integrity, that does not mean that they lack an authentic sense of what it is. Rather, it means that the word *integrity* is a rich one with many dimensions. The word in its many dimensions is well worth exploration. In this chapter, as I explore this word, I hope to draw attention to subtle aspects of integrity that are often neglected or undetected.

## Five Layers of Integrity

The following sections discuss integrity in terms of five layers, or areas of meaning. These areas are concerned with high moral standards, personal consistency, justifiable goals, public conduct, and congruence between private and public life.

### Layer 1

The first layer of meaning attached to the word *integrity* has to do with high moral standards. Two more specific qualities often come to mind when integrity is mentioned: fairness and honesty. Kouzes and Posner (1993), for example, writing about international research conducted among employees about the characteristics they most admired in leaders, report integrity as one of the top three characteristics cited. For most of these employees, it meant being honest—a habit of being straight with people so that they know where they stand. This kind of honesty was also thought to extend to situations in which speaking truthfully causes pain (either to the speaker or to the listener) or entails a measure of cost.

Further confirmation that honesty and integrity are closely allied in popular understanding is provided by Collins and Porras (1996), who studied the core ideologies of visionary companies and found that of the eighteen successful, long-term companies whose records they analyzed, four could be identified as having honesty and integrity as core values. A similar understanding of the word *integrity* is implied in the writings on business ethics compiled by Rae and Wong (1996), who also draw attention to the fact that ethics in the workplace means more than personal honesty. Indeed, people or organizations with integrity tend not to be utilitarian in outlook; they will not readily justify dubious means in support of desirable ends. Integrity, understood in this way, is certainly a penetrating, demanding trait of character.

### Layer 2

The second layer of meaning attached to the word *integrity* has to do with personal consistency. Leaders who are consistent do not surprise people with their moral decisions; they do not say one thing one day and something radically different the next. This essential constancy, being "all of a piece," is fundamental to the understanding of integrity set forth by Bennis and Nanus (1985), who argue that the welcome consequence of consistency is the creation of trust.

But the importance of consistency is equally illustrated by the behavior of people whom we consider to be poor examples of leadership. In Britain, for example, the controversial publisher Robert Maxwell was a notorious example of inconsistency. Biographies written about him since his death (see, for example, Davies, 1992) describe the delight that Maxwell seemed to take in making unexpected decisions, to keep people on their toes and enslaved to him. He apparently thought nothing of letting people down by canceling engagements at the last minute. A leader who makes unpredictable, arbitrary decisions spreads confusion and fear among the ranks.

## Layer 3

The third layer of meaning for the term *integrity* is uncovered through reflection on tyranny. It may be said of certain tyrannical leaders that they are relatively honest about the nature of their goals and unerringly consistent in the means used to pursue them. Adolf Hitler, a notable example of a tyrant, publicized his views on Aryan supremacy early in his political career when he wrote *Mein Kampf*. If integrity is defined—inadequately, in my view—as living a life true to one's convictions, then Hitler can hardly be faulted. But most of us would balk at calling him a leader with integrity: we see his underlying convictions as fatally flawed or morally warped. Therefore, the implication is that integrity must involve ends as well as means. It assumes the basic defensibility and desirability of the goals that an organization and its leaders are pursuing. If these goals cannot be justified, then integrity is called into question.

## Layer 4

The fourth layer of meaning for the word *integrity* has to do with the public conduct of an organization and its leaders. Organizations are bound to come under critical fire from time to time. Those whose integrity is suspect tend to react in one of two contrasting ways. In the first case, they keep their heads down and say as little as possible; these leaders are notable for its invisibility, for hiding behind a "not available" from secretaries or a "no comment" from press officers. In the second case, organizational leaders respond in a highly defensive way and fail to engage seriously with the criticisms that are being made. In both cases, what is open to question is whether these leaders and their organizations are demonstrating appropriate sensitivity to real concerns about the issues at hand.

An interesting contrast to these two reactions was provided recently by the example of the Royal Dutch/Shell Group. During 1995, Shell was involved in two major controversies, one over its attempted disposal of the Brent Spar oil platform in the North Sea, with predicted environmental damage, and the other over its involvement in the Ogoni area of Nigeria and its alleged failure to use its influence with the Nigerian government to prevent the execution of political protesters. The criticism provoked by Shell's actions (or inaction) caused a great deal of soul-searching within the company. Traditionally, Shell has been a highly inscrutable company with a culture in which, by Shell's own admission, openness has not necessarily been encouraged. Since 1995, however, a change appears to have been taking place. Shell has entered into a continuing dialogue with most of its critics. It has produced a report (Royal Dutch/Shell Group, 1998) that sets out the company's point of view but admits the complexity of many of the issues it faces and invites readers to contribute their own views and suggestions. On the issue of Brent Spar, Shell defends the original disposal plan but admits that it failed to consult widely enough. On the issue of Ogoni, Shell argues that its policy of long-term capital investment means that its commitment is to a people and a country rather than to the government of the day, but the company acknowledges that a moral tension exists when the current government is a particularly dubious one. The events of 1995 remain controversial, but Shell deserves praise for its subsequent interactions with the public. The company has made a plausible case and listened carefully to its critics. These are important marks of integrity.

## Layer 5

The fifth layer of meaning for the word *integrity* follows naturally from the preceding four. The word suggests, logically enough, a life that is well integrated—what Covey (1992, p. 298) calls "inside-out congruence," whereby discrete parts are interconnected and belong together. Indeed, the words *integrity* and *integration* have a common root.

Initially, integrity may appear to be just one quality or virtue among others, but this final layer of meaning hints at more. As Solomon (1992, p. 168) convincingly argues, "Integrity is not so much a virtue itself as it is a complex of virtues, the virtues working together to form a coherent character, an identifiable and trustworthy personality." Integrity describes the whole, and so the secular world is apt to describe integrity in this sense as *wholeness,* whereas those of a religious disposition may prefer the term *holiness.* Whichever term is preferred, to say that someone is a person of integrity is one of the highest compliments that can be bestowed.

With this understanding of what integrity is, there are two clear implications: first, integrity wages war on the blind spots and doublethink by which so much reprehensible behavior is justified; and, second, integrity tolerates no split between public and private behavior. As Thomas Jefferson said, anyone who assumes a public trust becomes public property. Of course, this idea should not be taken to justify the nastier types of media intrusion into individuals' lives. Nevertheless, public figures should be living in such a way that there is nothing in their personal lives of which they are ashamed: if there are no skeletons in the closet, then journalists will come to accept that it is pointless even to open it.

## Integrity in the Bible

The view of integrity sketched out so far is one to which many people, not just men and women of faith, might give assent, but there is also good reason to think that this view is consistent with a biblical understanding. In the Bible, words translated as *integrity* do not appear with great frequency. When they do, they are very instructive.

The heaviest concentration of such occurrences appears in the so-called wisdom literature of the Old Testament—for example, "The integrity of the upright guides them, but the crookedness of the treacherous destroys them" (Prov. 11:3). Here, the implication is that integrity contributes to one's success. Even if integrity brings no financial reward, scripture insists, "Better the poor walking in integrity than one perverse of speech who is a fool" (Prov. 19:1). Presumably, then, integrity has something to do with plain speaking.

In the Psalms, integrity is often used as a parallel word for *righteousness* or *uprightness* (for instance, see Pss. 7:8, 25:21). Psalm 26 uses the word twice: "Vindicate me, O Lord, for I have walked in my integrity" (Ps. 26:1), and then, after pointing to a contrast with "those in whose hands are evil devices, and whose right hands are full of bribes," makes the plea "But as for me, I walk in my integrity; redeem me, and be gracious to me" (Ps. 26:1). According to Kidner (1973, p. 118), the basic meaning of the word *integrity* is "wholeness, usually in the sense of whole-heartedness or sincerity, rather than faultlessness." It is interesting that the psalmist twice paints the scene of walking in one's integrity, the picture perhaps being that of a path or a channel, a settled groove within which the good person operates, or of a godly ambience or atmosphere surrounding everything that he or she does. Integrity becomes the air one breathes or the ground one treads.

Psalm 85, meanwhile, points to the idea of integrity in a corporate or social context. Here, *integrity* or *wholeness* could be an alternative rendering of the Hebrew word *shalom,* usually translated as *peace.* The psalm also contains a wonderful passage that looks forward to a time when heaven and earth will be in perfect partnership:

> Steadfast love and faithfulness will meet;
> righteousness and peace will kiss each other.
> The Lord will give what is good,
> and our land will yield its increase.
>
> —Psalm 85

This is integrity in an ultimate sense: God and human beings acting together in harmony, with the human qualities of faithfulness and peace responding to the divine attributes of love and righteousness. Both the psalmist's and the prophets' vision of *shalom* means much more than the mere absence of war. It is a state of concord that is grounded on right relations vertically (between God and people) and right relationships horizontally (among people).

What are the implications for leadership? There is no doubt that the Old Testament depicts God as looking, often in vain, for the highest standards of integrity in Israel's leaders. In particular, they are expected to seek after the welfare of their people rather than after their own needs. Great leaders in the Old Testament, such as Nehemiah and Daniel, display their integrity by refusing to lower their standards or betray their convictions in the face of pressure and opposition.

In the New Testament, the searching challenge of Jesus' teachings makes clear that God's rule extends over the whole of our lives: there is no possibility here of a private/public split. His diatribe against the Pharisees condemns those who are like whitewashed tombs—beautiful on the outside but full of filth within (Matt. 23:27). In the Sermon on the Mount, Jesus' disciples are challenged, not just at the level of their purity of action but also at the levels of their motives, intentions, and inner feelings (Matt. 5:21–28).

## Obstacles to Integrity

"Integrity is all very well as an ideal," it may be said, "but. . . ." Precisely: we need to take stock of that *but.* It is salutary to step back for a moment from these statements of lofty ideals and infuse the discussion with some solid realism. This kind of realism is required with respect to three different but interrelated areas: human failings, organizational culture, and complexity.

## Human Failings

Leaders, like everyone else, need to be realistic about themselves. Few people are as well integrated as they would like to be. Foibles, inconsistencies, and other flaws of personality mar our lives. We fall short— sometimes by a long way—of our highest hopes and aspirations.

Leaders, then, take part in the common human struggle against sin and temptation. A leader who is renowned most of the time for her kindness, patience, and good humor may occasionally bewilder others (and disappoint herself) by giving vent to a sudden, uncontrolled loss of temper. A leader who loves his wife and is profoundly committed to the sanctity of marriage may still lapse into adultery when confronted by sexual temptation on a work-related trip far away from home. Leaders who pride themselves on treating all their staff members fairly and objectively can find their judgment marred by loathing or prejudice when someone simply rubs them the wrong way.

A visiting speaker at the college where I teach asked some of our students who were training for ordained ministry to share some of the things they hoped to see happening in the churches to which they would soon be going. The answers were predictably worthy: people growing in faith, a high level of mutuality and interdependence in relationships, evidence of the gifts and fruit of the Holy Spirit, a community with an open and welcoming attitude toward outsiders. Then the speaker asked them to make a list of saboteurs—the things inside them that might subvert or frustrate the fulfillment of these high ideals. The students came up with such items as "a yearning for power," "doing the right things for the wrong reasons," "wanting to be noticed," "the desire to be popular with everyone," "avoiding conflict at all costs," "dwelling on one's own inadequacies," and "interpreting everything as an attack on oneself." These are all common pitfalls of leadership.

The point is clear, and it applies to leadership in the marketplace just as much as it does to leadership in the church. We carry all kinds of baggage that can get in the way of our ability to realize our fine objectives. Forces of disintegration block the way to our becoming the rounded, well-integrated people we are in our dreams.

One way of exploring the darker side of human existence is to do so in terms of Carl Jung's theory of the shadow archetype. O'Neil (1995) argues that the leader often has a shadow, which personifies everything that the leader refuses to acknowledge about himself or herself, but which is constantly making its presence felt. The shadow may consist of a painful but suppressed memory, or private aspects of our lives that cause us shame, or even a wild dream that has little prospect of ever being realized. O'Neil recommends that the leader make time to face up honestly to the shadow and seek either to resolve the tensions that emerge or to draw on the shadow as something potentially positive.

There is much that is helpful in the Jungian approach. What Christians will miss from the analysis is a frank acknowledgment of human sin (not just our own), which has left its mark on our personalities. Acknowledgment of sin can actually be very liberating whenever it is the prelude to repentance, to the assurance of forgiveness, and to the healing work of the Holy Spirit. Drawing on this divine resource, believers who are in positions of leadership can learn techniques for managing stress, can avoid obvious places and occasions of temptation, and can search for positive qualities in people who are difficult to like. Through the experience of being loved, by God and by other people, we in turn become better equipped to love others—to relate to them neither aggressively nor defensively but with the appropriate balance of confidence and humility that is, again, perhaps characteristic of the person who has integrity.

In short, there can be a healing process—it is possible to grow into a state of increasing wholeness—but in this life the healing is never total; two steps forward are often punctuated by at least one step backward. Leaders need to be honest about their failings and vulnerabilities and about the fact that integrity remains an ideal, a constant but always elusive aspiration. As Campbell (1986, p. 12) rightly says, "the person of integrity is first and foremost a critic of self, of tendencies to self-deception and escape from reality, of desire for a false inner security in place of the confrontation with truth which integrity demands."

## Organizational Culture

Another obstacle to integrity can be the intractability of the organization itself. The fact is, most corporate cultures settle for something less than the lofty ideals that they proclaim in public. Mission statements sometimes have the feel of an empty shell or a hollow promise: there is a major gulf between what the organization says and what it does. Usually, however, this does not mean that the company code is being openly flouted; it is more that the code is diluted and qualified, and that one is taking one's lead from something rather different: the prevailing culture of that part of the organization in which one works.

Many practices in organizational life fall short of the yardstick of integrity but are nonetheless solidly entrenched as customs. For example, small groups often conspire to cheat their own organizations. Manual workers know how to drag their feet over a particular task in order to earn extra money working overtime. Managers collude in making unreasonable claims for expenses on overseas trips. Jackall (1988), investigating the occupational ethics of American managers at work, observed what went on behind desks and out in the field more than he listened to companies' public professions of ethical stances. The results were very revealing. Jackall's study portrays a world in which managers, pursued by an all-consuming desire for promotion and by a nagging anxiety about how they are viewed by those who matter in the company, become adept at manipulating appearances, hiding their true thoughts and feelings in the interest of "getting along," and ensuring that they get credit when things go well and avoid blame when things don't.

All this has serious implications for the person with integrity, particularly one who aspires to leadership. The prevailing culture may be so at odds with the individual's make-up that it is difficult for him or her to rise in the organization. Practicing a different code of behavior creates social distance, which is likely to be a barrier to making the needed connections with peers and with those who are in a position to advance one's career.

Some might suggest that the answer is to go along with the accepted practices while making one's way through the ranks, and then to attempt radical reform of the culture upon attaining a position of influence. But this strategy cannot and will not do. It would be a contradiction of the very idea of integrity if someone were to discover a sudden enthusiasm for it only upon reaching the dizzying heights of power. Moreover, such a person would have no moral authority with which to persuade others to do things differently. In any case, the appetite for integrity would probably have long since disappeared, having been dormant for such a long period.

It is better to operate within the organizational culture while showing a readiness to question it. An instructive example from the Bible is Daniel. To serve in the administration of Nebuchadnezzar, Daniel and his friends were prepared to accommodate themselves somewhat to the Babylonian court. They were educated for three years, learning "the language and literature of the Babylonians" (Dan. 1:4–5). This education involved their absorption in a completely alien world of thought, one characterized by astrology, polytheism, and spiritual dualism, and yet it was only by immersing themselves in this foreign culture that they could be equipped to serve God in it. They passed their tests with flying colors: "as for these four youths, God gave them learning and skill in all letters and wisdom" (Dan. 1:17). Even at this stage of their apprenticeship, Daniel and his friends showed that they were prepared to be different, but it is noteworthy that they were selective in doing so. One might have expected them to object to the new names given them by the chief eunuch (Dan. 1:7), on the ground that some of these names incorporated references to the foreign deities and were therefore marred by idolatry. It was not on this issue, however, but on the question of food that they chose to raise an objection, for Daniel believed that it was important to observe the Israelite dietary laws. In a sense, the question of the specific issue on which Daniel took a stand is not important; what is important is that he did take a stand, and at an early stage, showing that his ultimate loyalty was to his God and not to the Babylonian king. He set down a marker. Similarly, Christians who aspire to leadership in today's world have to be thoroughly acquainted with their chosen areas and prove their competence by passing examinations and showing their mettle. Once they have become aspiring leaders, working in unsympathetic organizations, they too, like Daniel, need the courage to set down their own markers and the wisdom to know which issues warrant their doing so.

## Complexity

Organizational life offers many dilemmas that have no easy answers. Ethical complexity is all around, and so leading with integrity is often a matter of walking through a moral minefield.

There are many instances of such complexity. Elsewhere (Higginson, 1996), I have used the example of improper payments, a recurring problem for many organizations that are doing business across cultures, particularly with countries in eastern Europe, the Middle East, Asia, and Africa. The payment of outright bribes can be declared unequivocally to be wrong, but there are various intermediate forms of payment that are more ambiguous. These range from generous acts of hospitality to commissions paid to agents. It takes some carefully nuanced moral distinctions to identify a corporate policy of integrity in this area.

An example of the subtleties involved in moral integrity was offered by a friend of mine, a former officer in the British army. He described to me a year-long process of training a group of young people to become army officers. The training entailed a very high degree of group cohesion, and the completion of the training, with the successful trainees' subsequent commissioning as officers, was built up as something that had great symbolic importance. It was depicted as a major rite of passage for each individual, and there were high expectations of professional competence on the part of all who would be commissioned.

Near the end of the training, one of the would-be officers began to perform erratically. He started to show signs of having an infection of the inner ear; he became wobbly on his feet and found it difficult to coordinate his actions. As the date for his commissioning approached, the possibility emerged that he had a longer-term problem than a mere infection—that he might be suffering from a chronic illness. Nevertheless, he was duly commissioned as an officer, even though by that time he could hardly walk.

After his commissioning, the new officer was diagnosed as suffering from a serious terminal disease that was related to his having taken growth hormones. His health continued to deteriorate. He never actually functioned as an officer, but his status as an officer meant that his salary continued to be paid, and that the army took responsibility for his medical care. He died in a military hospital in his late twenties, having spent the last two years of his life in an ever-deepening coma.

The question that plagued my friend was whether the army had acted with integrity in commissioning this man as an officer. The case can be argued both ways. The argument in favor was that the army owed this individual a commission because, in training, he had done all that was asked of him, and his commissioning was a way of expressing personal support. This decision was consistent with the concept of mutual loyalty—between the institution and its members—which had played a major part in the officers' training. The man never took active command, but his brave battle against disease made him an inspiration to his peers and to the people who would have been his subordinates.

The argument against his commissioning is that the position of officer is meant to be an active one, not simply an honor or a reward for training undergone. Would it not have been a greater display of integrity to acknowledge the reality of this trainee's increasing disability and apply the rules that required physical fitness of all those to be commissioned? Not commissioning this individual would have been consistent with the view that the army's primary duty is to society, to be an efficient fighting force.

The arguments both ways are finely balanced, as my friend well appreciates. His greatest concern had to do with the fact that what was done was never articulated; some in the army clearly had questions about the validity of the decision, but these questions were left unanswered. Therefore, the action may be seen as falling short of what was discussed earlier as the third layer of integrity: a justifiable goal. Here too, however, a defense can be offered: that the authorities were reluctant to state their reasons, for fear of establishing a precedent that might prove unhelpful. Transparency in decision making remains a laudable ideal, but I would not advocate making it an absolute rule. The moral virtue of being frank in public sometimes needs to be balanced against the way information in the public domain can be misused and cited out of context.

## The Place of Compromise

In this chapter, I seek to demonstrate that challenges to integrity abound in the real world. But one mark of leaders with integrity is precisely that they face up to this fact. Integrity is not a matter of having a squeaky-clean reputation and avoiding the hard choices. It is about confronting those choices conscientiously and courageously.

In all this, it needs to be remembered that leaders do not fulfill their tasks simply by acting ethically. They are assumed to have basic competence in the core functions of their organizations. They are expected to be able to meet, or to facilitate the meeting of, certain corporate goals—for instance, to provide a better service, or to increase market share. In meeting goals, integrity needs to be accompanied by astuteness.

Being astute does not mean disparaging or toning down high moral sentiments. It means couching them in a context of realism. Astute leaders rightly seek to turn situations to their organizations' advantage, financially or otherwise. In so doing, they draw on a variety of tactical skills. They know when to encourage and when to rebuke (see, for example, Titus 2:15), how to outthink and outpace the competition, how much is appropriately revealed in a delicate negotiation, and how deeply to cut when decisive money-saving measures have to be made. But if astuteness is to be distinguished and saved from plain sharp practice, it needs to be shot through with the qualities of integrity, described earlier.

This point leads to a discussion of the place of compromise. For many people, compromise is a negative term. It suggests settling on a course of action that is morally tainted: an abandonment of principle for the sake of expediency. And, clearly, many compromises are nothing better than that and are therefore deserving of criticism. But there is a more positive way of viewing compromise. Sometimes, for example, a compromise is an attempt to do justice to two or more different moral claims, both or all of which are valid. Whatever the precise position one adopts in the "stakeholder" debate (see Rae and Wong, 1996), it is now generally acknowledged that companies are responsible to a range of different groups: stockholders, employees, customers, suppliers, and the wider community. Much of the time, there is no serious conflict among the interests and expectations of these different groups in relation to the company; when corporate fortunes are booming, all can be satisfied, and generally at the same time. When times are hard, however, clashes of interest are likely to occur. For instance, a company facing the need to cut costs may have to choose between reducing stockholders' dividends, making some staff positions redundant, narrowing the product range for customers, delaying payment to suppliers, or slowing down a process of complying with environmental-protection regulations. Often it will be appropriate to spread the burden of cost, and compromise then takes on the character of a search to balance the interests (and maintain the confidence) of different groups rather than the complete abandonment of one group in favor of another. (This is an entirely reasonable goal, of course, but sheer financial reality often constrains an organization to the point where it cannot honor the legitimate moral claims represented by different groups as fully as it would like to.)

## Serpents and Doves

When Jesus sent his disciples out on a missionary journey, he did so with an intriguing message: "Behold I send you out as sheep in the midst of wolves; so be wise as serpents and innocent as doves." The danger that wolves posed for sheep is obvious, but the juxtaposition of images in the second half of the statement makes a startling contrast.

Why does Jesus associate serpents with wisdom? Probably because of Genesis 3:1: "Now the serpent was more subtle than any other wild creature that the Lord God had made." The word for *subtle* can also be translated as *shrewd*: the implication is that Jesus' followers need a worldly wisdom, an awareness of the cunning stratagems of others, and astuteness in knowing how to counter them. And why does Jesus associate doves with innocence? It may be because doves are white, a symbol of purity.

To be both serpentlike and dovelike appears to be a blatant contradiction, but this is the blend of attitudes that Jesus commands of his disciples. He warns them both to be on their guard against persecution and to be faithful and unsullied in the face of evil. Jesus' words are not relevant only to first-century Christian missionaries. They have something to say about every Christian's vocation to live in the world. The challenge is to act in a way that both shows familiarity with the world's way of operating and refuses to be dragged down by it.

Jesus' words are particularly salutary for those who find themselves in leadership positions. Problems occur when leaders emphasize one of the two images, serpent or dove, to the neglect of the other. "Wise as serpents, innocent as doves" evokes idealism tempered by realism, principles laced with shrewdness, integrity married to astuteness: precisely the qualities that leaders need. Leaders help no one by being naive, and yet they are required to maintain purity of thought, speech, and action. Leadership is indeed a demanding vocation.

## Conclusion

Walking the fine line demanded by integrity, and keeping one's balance through the wise use of compromise, is truly an art. Leaders with faith have the solid foundation of scripture to shape their wisdom and guide their intuition. Nevertheless, although many of the areas where integrity can have an influence are clearly demarcated, there are often no prescriptions for subtle choices. Each day, every day, leaders usually must rely on strong instincts in choosing wisely among the courses of action before them.

REFERENCES

Bennis, W., and Nanus, B. *Leaders: The Strategies for Taking Charge.* New York: HarperCollins, 1985.

Campbell, A. *Rediscovering Pastoral Care.* London: Darton, Longman & Todd, 1986.

Collins, J. C., and Porras, J. I. *Built to Last: Successful Habits of Visionary Companies.* San Francisco: Harper San Francisco, 1994.

Covey, S. *The Seven Habits of Highly Effective People: Powerful Lessons in Personal Change.* New York: Simon & Schuster, 1989.

Davies, N. *The Unknown Maxwell.* London: Sidgwick & Jackson, 1992.

Higginson, R. *Transforming Leadership: A Christian Approach to Management.* London: SPCK, 1996.

Jackall, R. *Moral Mazes: The World of Corporate Managers.* New York: Oxford University Press, 1988.

Kidner, D. *Psalms 1–73.* London: IVP, 1973.

Kouzes, J. M., and Posner, B. Z. *Credibility: How Leaders Gain and Lose It, Why People Demand It.* San Francisco: Jossey-Bass, 1993.

O'Neil, J. R. *The Paradox of Success: When Winning at Work Means Losing at Life.* New York: McGraw-Hill, 1995.

Rae, S. B., and Wong, K. L. *Beyond Integrity: A Judeo-Christian Approach to Business Ethics.* Grand Rapids, Mich.: Zondervan, 1996.

Royal Dutch/Shell Group. *Profits and Principles: Does There Have to Be a Choice?* London: Shell External Affairs, 1998.

Solomon, R. C. *Ethics and Excellence: Cooperation and Integrity in Business.* New York: Oxford University Press, 1992.

ADDITIONAL READING

McLoughlin, M. "The Ethics of Shrewdness." *Faith in Business Quarterly,* 1998, 2(2), 12–17.

# 3

# REBUILDING TRUST IN THE FRACTURED WORKPLACE

*Carlton J. Snow*

Carlton J. Snow is professor of law at Willamette University in Salem, Oregon, where he teaches courses in business and dispute resolution. He is a permanent arbitrator for United Airlines, the United States Postal Service, the Internal Revenue Service, and the Department of the Army.

———— o ————

RELATED TO THE ISSUE of faithfulness—indeed, overlapping with it—is the role of trust in the workplace. Trust is also one dimension of some of the other virtues considered in this volume (for example, integrity; see Chapter Two). As we shall see, trust is connected with vulnerability (although I am more interested in trust as a personal characteristic than as an aspect of the internal work environment or of the external circumstances surrounding the workplace). What I say in this chapter also lays a partial basis for remarks to come later, on the role of humility (see Chapter Five). Here, I focus on the importance and function of trust between leaders and followers and, more broadly, between managers and their subordinates. In so doing, I am not ignoring the distinction commonly drawn between leaders and managers; rather, I am recognizing that there is some overlap between the functions of leadership and management, and that leaders require the help of managers in accomplishing their goals.

Trust is an elusive abstraction. Like the air we breathe, trust is taken for granted, drawing little attention to itself until the atmosphere goes bad. At the same time, trust, elusive though it is, is a concept that has practical importance: the issue of trust is central to the development and continuation of a productive work experience, and an examination of trust is useful because it illuminates the interdependence necessary to work. Nevertheless, an exploration of trusting behavior at work must be undertaken without denial of the current decline in trust of modern institutions and leaders, and without denial of the deep cynicism about their trustworthiness.

From a Christian perspective, there is another side to any discussion of trust. The word *trust* is a central term in the lexicon of faith, and the experience it describes is at the heart of the believer's relationship with God. The word refers to the sense of present and future confidence in God, even though we do not know everything we would like to know about God's character or methods of operation. Trust is not blind faith, as its critics sometimes suggest, for it is based on God's giving evidence to people of the kind of person He is, as well as evidence of how He works out His divine purposes.

The trust that this process engenders is not a purely vertical affair, however, affecting only the relationship between human beings and God. It is also intended to be both a model for and an impetus to the development of trust between human beings. Where this impetus is present, personal relationships as well as institutional arrangements reap the benefits. To both domains it adds an element necessary to their full and proper functioning. In the discussion that follows, we shall see more of the connection between this theological dimension of trust and the form it takes in the workplace.

## Trust as Risk Taking

Trust, in keeping with its basic religious meaning, generally involves placing confidence in another person, or in an institution, without having complete information. The fact of incomplete information thus requires a person who may be inclined to trust also to become a risk taker. This involves not so much what has so often been described as a leap of faith into the unknown as a step of faith, which goes beyond the evidence of our minds and emotions. Such a step calls on a person's capacity to trust—as, for example, in being willing to forgive past wrongs, or as in accurately assessing risk, the reliability of new information, and the question of whether any basis for suspicion exists. Because so many variables affect the establishment of trust, it would be as misleading to propose a fool-proof formula for trusting as it would to require scientific evidence for the existence of God. To suggest a course of action for building trust, it is more useful to examine the components of the process of trusting.

The term *trust,* in popular usage, means a reasonably assured reliance on someone's good character or ability, as well as the placement of reasonable confidence in people or in an organization. The person who trusts may also rely on principles and systems of knowledge—on the principles of aerodynamics, for example, when he or she enters an airplane. Whether trust is invested in a person, an organization, or a set of principles, it helps people deal with uncertainty and unpredictability. For example, competent longtime employees generally trust their employers not to terminate them merely because there may be people with more recent training who can do their jobs better, and employers trust employees not to give away company secrets to competitors.

Trust in the workplace engenders cooperation, whereas distrust generates a risk-averse work environment. Leaders who build trusting relationships have an advantage. First, being trustworthy gives one the right to have one's messages heard, and so communication and understanding are enhanced. Second, as Fukuyama argues (1995, p. 26), "if people who have to work together in an enterprise trust one another because they are all operating according to a common set of ethical norms, doing business costs less." Third, some economists (for example, Sako, 1992) believe that the degree of trust among workers is closely correlated with an organization's productivity. The presence of trust has these effects because trust is a basic building block of effective relationships, a fact for which there is not only an empirical but also, from a Christian point of view, an ultimate theological foundation. This explains why low trust is a primary trait of unsuccessful organizations, as well as why trust has to be genuine, not merely apparent, in order to fulfill its proper function. Employees are not fooled by schemes that are designed to foster trust but that actually thwart employees by favoring narrow managerial objectives. It is immeasurably more difficult to reestablish lost trust in the workplace than to build it in the first place.

## Trust as Social Capital

Work has become a social exchange, and trust can be its by-product. Most employees today work in groups; indeed, *partnering* and *teamwork* are buzz words in the modern workplace. But cooperative behavior does not necessarily express trust, which is of an emotional nature; cooperation may be calculated only to serve personal objectives. Team members certainly can cooperate on the basis of self-interest, but this kind of work group will require far more regulation and managerial supervision (and therefore operational expense) than will a group organized on the basis of trust.

By contrast, working on the basis of trust is not only more profitable but also more satisfying and more effective. When trust is based on shared norms and values, it gives managers an opportunity to mold a work group in a way that will function for a common purpose. In such a work environment, trust can emerge as a sort of social capital. The term *capital* generally refers to money or property devoted to the production of goods, or calculated to produce income. Trust should be viewed as nonphysical capital—that is, as an asset that fosters the cooperation of social organizations and individuals for the benefit of society. Work groups rich in the social capital of trust make the work experience more productive and personally enriching and ultimately more effective and profitable.

An element of this mix is information, which enables workers to do their jobs. When the information in an organization becomes unreliable or flows inconsistently, workers face unpredictable circumstances and often resort to self-protective behavior. Employees' individual self-interest then comes to rule the day as creativity and risk taking are undermined by self-protection. Risks are carefully calculated in terms of what is best for the individual employee, with little regard for the interests of the work group or the employer. Employees become wary of making positive suggestions, for fear that leaders will feel criticized and retaliate, or they work strictly by the book, with no enthusiasm for doing anything even slightly out of the ordinary. In this situation, they tend to distrust their co-workers, and a rising spiral of distrust is set in motion, undermining the group's collective accomplishment.

Suppose, for example, that the managers of a group of two thousand state troopers enact work rules that make expectations clear. If the troopers nevertheless perceive that the rules, although fair, are actually being applied in an arbitrary way, it is highly probable that trust as social capital among the state troopers will be replaced by distrust, because a group reaction of trust or mistrust generally overrides individual employees' relationships with managers, becoming the collective response of a work unit.

Therefore, to help overcome the problem of unpredictability, employees must be able to trust the information that flows back and forth, always imperfectly, between themselves and their leaders. This is because employees choose whom they will trust, and they make that choice on the basis of what they perceive as evidence of trustworthiness or untrustworthiness. In a workplace characterized by unpredictability, rational interactions in a context of incomplete information combine with the collective emotional reaction of a group and produce, almost imperceptibly, a general attitude, whether of trust or mistrust. This reaction can be intense, and if workers conclude that their initial trust has been betrayed, the result may be a general sense of outrage, which can go far beyond any particular incident, eating away at the foundations of a work group's relationship with an employer. In these circumstances, a single dispute, poorly handled, may become emblematic of the group's relationship with the employer.

Trust begets trust. An abundance of trust provides a foundation on which to base collaboration, and collaboration in turn encourages individuals to accept collective responsibility. When collective efforts are embedded in shared values and a shared vision of the future, economic and interpersonal opportunism at work are discouraged, and good-faith performance is encouraged.

## The Decline of Trust

People trust less today. For many years, business and political leaders have ranked low as trustworthy sources of information. A decade ago, less than half of all respondents to a Lou Harris & Associates survey believed management to be "honest, upright, and ethical." In 1991, only one-third of hourly workers surveyed in a study believed that their employers treated them with dignity and respect, and fewer than half trusted their top managers. Research (Lipset, 1995) also suggests that cynicism is a significant attitude among workers in the United States.

Even when workers receive no explicit guarantees of fairness from management, they still expect equitable treatment, and trust erodes when they are not treated with fairness and respect. Active mistrust is fostered by managers who lie to employees, or who are perceived as acting deceitfully or primarily on the basis of their own interests. Employees also mistrust supervisors who are viewed as incompetent or unpredictable. Fear of supervisors like these is often a by-product of this mistrust, and fear, instead of motivating workers, undermines their effectiveness and loyalty.

When leaders and others in managerial positions sense an attitude of mistrust from workers, they may use threats. A leader or a manager who relies on threats may succeed in accomplishing some short-term goals, but he or she cannot reasonably expect to accomplish long-term objectives. The more coercive the style of control from the top, the greater the likelihood that trust in the organization will be undermined.

The consequences will be a higher degree of alienation among workers, a greater focus on self-interest, a tendency to reject social authority, and efforts by individual employees to insulate themselves from vulnerability. It is not reasonable to expect workers to trust institutional systems when they feel no emotional bond with an organization. They are disinclined to trust their superiors when external manifestations of trustworthiness (such as responsiveness to employees' needs) are lacking, or when promises have not been kept.

Indeed, keeping promises is an important aspect of building trust, and this truth has a firm basis in the biblical tradition. It was through the offer, maintenance, and renewal of promises to the people of Israel that God built up a faithful response from many among them, and it was because God kept his promises—at times in the face of repeated betrayals by the people, and ultimately at great cost to Christ—that their trust in their divine Father was built up so securely. God's behavior, as Robert Banks points out in Chapter One, provides a model for any faith-based leader or manager. Leaders who do not keep their promises violate a moral norm. They erode the community's confidence and values by offending accepted notions of community bonds, and in this way they threaten the general trust underlying the authority of the organization. As leaders of a work community, in particular, strive to honor their promises and to act in a context of reasonable expectations based on those promises, it becomes more possible for them to nurture organizational trust. By contrast, alienation and spiraling mistrust seem inevitable in the absence of shared goals or binding promises between workers and managers.

## Sources of Trust

Trust is not self-generating. It is a response to action on the part of others. In the workplace, practices devised by leaders and implemented by managers induce institutional trust.

Central to explaining how workplace practices influence trustworthiness is the mapping of an organization's internal communication patterns. The greater the amount of authentic communication, the higher the likelihood that an atmosphere of trust will develop. The ease of communication at work is as important as the amount of communication. In most American workplaces, for example, information is shared on a need-to-know basis, but a more open pattern of sharing information will engender greater trust. At the minimum, the information shared with workers should be reliable, accurate, timely, and sufficient to respond to employees' concerns. Ideally, this information should provide employees with a rational basis for advancing the mission of the employer and for fostering their individual commitment to high-quality performance.

The perceptions of leaders are also a source of trust. Followers' views of the authority figures in an organization will have a significant impact on their capacity to trust. The extent and perception of leaders' honesty will be directly related to the level of trust within the organization. Leaders committed to generating an atmosphere of trust avoid not only impropriety but also even the appearance of impropriety. To the extent that facts about leaders' private lives are public, any substantial incongruities risk undermining perceptions in the workplace of their trustworthiness.

Leaders sometimes unwittingly distort followers' perceptions of them and create self-fulfilling prophecies. Starting with the presupposition that workers will be most productive if they are rigorously monitored, they encourage overseers to supervise workers closely and may even install surveillance systems to ensure workers' loyalty. Yet it is freedom from close supervision that manifests an employer's trust of workers and reduces the need for bureaucratic work rules. Rigorous monitoring feeds an atmosphere of distrust in the workplace by implicitly supporting a "them and us" mentality. For example, employers often discourage workers and supervisors from fraternizing, on the basis of the unarticulated assumption that a supervisor cannot be loyal both to workers and to upper-level managers. Nevertheless, an open system of communication and information sharing and the absence of intrusive monitoring are what will help people in the work community view one another as supportive colleagues, and this collegiality in turn will help create a more productive workplace.

Another source of trust within an organization is found in the way leaders and their associates show respect for an individual's human dignity. Thousands of grievances filed by workers are caused by supervisors who issue "orders" and "directives" instead of participating in discussions and consultations with workers. For example, one manager announces for the first time, in an open staff meeting, that a specific worker's position must be reduced from full-time to three-quarters-time; another, more secure manager explains the existence of budgetary problems in the department that will require reductions in staff and invites remedial suggestions. By attempting to solve the problem with the workers instead of issuing commands, the second manager not only shows respect for individuals but also makes the specific resolution of a problem more important than an impersonal, formulaic solution. This approach to solving the problem provides an opportunity to explore workers' disagreements, and it fosters the advancement of shared community goals. As it defuses defensive behavior, this approach also promotes an atmosphere of trust, and it gives leaders and followers a chance to forgive each other for past misunder-standings. Thus, an important source of trust is a deep respect for human dignity and the courage to manifest it (Mouw, 1989).

## Suggestions for Developing Trust

How leaders deal with conflict in the workplace is crucial to the building of trust. Stopping work, filing a grievance with an arbitration board, entering a complaint in a court of law, and simply turning the other cheek are all methods of handling conflict, and some are more productive than others.

Creative solutions to conflict rarely come out of violence or litigation. Less damage is done to a relationship when conflict is resolved in a con-text of trust. A dispute decided in arbitration or in court ultimately does reach a final determination, but solutions that flow from a relationship of trust or from negotiation are less destructive and usually do not produce a spiraling cycle of aggression, as litigation and arbitration increasingly tend to do. It is no longer rare for a prevailing party, a judge, or an arbi-trator to be subject to aggression, sometimes even of a physical kind, from a disappointed party after a decision has been made; the same risk is run by organizational leaders whose decisions breach relationships of trust.

Successful completion of a workshop in negotiation should be a job requirement for everyone moving into a leadership position. In the pres-ence of conflict, issuing orders is a corrosive approach to the exercise of power. Effective conflict resolution is found in two-way communication. Many leaders, however, view discord as organizational pathology; they fear conflict and all too quickly issue orders that are not to be challenged, or they make aggressive use of silence to compel compliance. It is not sur-prising that complaints resulting from these courses of action can con-sume twenty times the effort and resources that initially would have been required by proper communication in the first place. The willingness to negotiate shows a leader's respect for others' dignity and may increase fol-lowers' commitment to the organizational enterprise.

Although the workplace should not be seen as a debating society, an initial commitment to talking differences through ought be the general rule, with the demand for obedience only as a secondary, backup position. This is precisely how the most illustrious of the early Christian leaders, the apostle Paul, operated in the work that he set in motion and in the churches that he founded. With his associates, his approach was strikingly collegial; with his followers, it was strongly consultative. Indeed, he had a very high estimate of the capacity that his associates and followers alike had for reaching an understanding of what needed to be done. Only as a last resort did he ever "pull rank," and even then he sought to avoid the formal use of power. In fact, he was a prime exemplar of the leader as "walk-around educator."

Most people everywhere yearn to be able to trust; surveys about the qualities sought in leaders regularly rank trustworthiness at the top of the list. Although workers desire more economic benefits, they do not seek to run organizations. Instead, they long for leaders whom they can trust to make decisions that are equitable, competent, and rooted in the shared values of an organization. But even as workers search for people with integrity whom they can serve, they are less trusting of institutional authority (Daft and Lengel, 1998).

What leaders need are strategies for increasing trust. One such strategy is to loosen managers' controlling grip. In public employment, for example, legislators regularly call for public servants (such as probation officers or juvenile counselors, and especially teachers) to be held accountable for results. Generally, this approach means extensive evaluation of the workers themselves, or perhaps (in the case of teachers) evaluation of students on the basis of standardized tests, but this kind of formal evaluation reflects a desire to make organizational goals conform to a rigid standard. Many employers, in addition to using excessively critical performance evaluations as a tool for exercising control over employees, have adopted more intrusive practices in the workplace, such as surveillance by cameras, use of listening devices, and e-mail monitoring. In the process of doing so, they are undermining workers' motivation and their trust in the institution.

Instead of using a fear-based model whose premise is strict monitoring, leaders should consider the appropriateness and benefits of participatory decision making. Once again, Paul's approach to leadership sets a good biblical precedent. Time and again, even when confronting major crises in the fledgling church or crises of confidence in himself, Paul insisted that the people not only listen to him but also work things out together, keeping his viewpoint in mind (see Cor. 1:5). Paul knew that people who help to make decisions that affect their lives are more likely to implement those decisions effectively. Mistrust and a sense of powerlessness are often the results when people are asked to implement poorly understood decisions, whereas the development and management of consensus in a work group can both increase organizational clarity and support a shared evaluation of performance.

In Chapter Nine, Shirley J. Roels discusses the place of vulnerability in the leader's life. She has in mind the uncertainty and unpredictability that leaders experience as a consequence of organizations' internal workings or of the external circumstances affecting their operations. This is a kind of vulnerability over which the leader has no control. But there is another kind of vulnerability to which the leader can be voluntarily open. It involves the willingness to share decision-making responsibility with others.

This kind of vulnerability is important in a leader, who in order to be effective must be willing to trust and, sometimes, to risk the slings and arrows of detractors and to listen to followers' criticisms. As De Pree (1992, pp. 220–221) has observed, "vulnerable leaders trust in the abilities of other people; vulnerable leaders allow the people who follow them to do their best."

One barrier that leaders often put up to effective communication is the personal perception that they are people of action, people who make decisions. But the leader committed to building trust recognizes that a key part of communication is listening. Active listening on the part of the leader frees followers to talk more fully about their individual needs and interests but also about the needs and interests of the organization. If communication is the heart of building trust, then listening is its life blood. The leader who learns to listen not only for facts but also for feelings can do much to reduce suspicion in the workplace.

An effective manager, for example, must be open to learning from workers. Managers who listen only to other managers risk missing opportunities as group insecurity fosters conformity and consensus. Managers who walk around and make themselves accessible to individual workers, as well as to other managers, are able to balance a tendency toward uniformity in group decision making and help avoid the inclination of groups to suppress dissent. This kind of managerial openness toward those with less organizational status and little power requires a humble spirit and a deep commitment to honoring civility amid diverse viewpoints. In pursuing this level of openness, a Christian leader is doing—and only doing—what was already modeled by Christ, who through his incarnation entered fully into the lives and concerns of all kinds of people, many of whom had little status or power.

If institutional trust is to thrive, the company or administrative agency must have importance for the individual members of a work group, and the group itself must also matter to them. One way of making the larger organization or group matter to individuals is to empower it to protect individual workers from undue risk in the workplace. As workplace risks come to be shared by the members of a group, the individuals in the group establish relationships of mutual cooperation in order to accomplish the institutional goals. Trust within the work group is encouraged by leadership practices that reduce skepticism, secrecy, and dishonesty.

If organizational leaders are attempting to rebuild trust after there has been a breach in the organization's relationship with its employees, then the rebuilding process will probably be a slow one, with progress seen only after there have been many opportunities for employees to interact with the larger organization; workers will first need to test the credibility of leaders' new commitment to institutional trustworthiness. Rebuilding trust is a substantial challenge to any leader. Reorganizing management is no panacea, for the reorganization itself may be perceived as reflecting a lack of integrity and may therefore prove ineffective. A more prudent approach would be to improve communication patterns in the workplace, examine workers' anxieties, and introduce systems designed to improve the quality and accuracy of the information that flows through the organization. As leaders manifest integrity and honesty, and as the workplace environment becomes more predictable, the rebuilding of trust should become a viable goal.

Communication methods also deserve attention. There is danger in virtually total reliance on electronic media for organizational communication. The impact on organizational connectedness of such technology as e-mail is unclear, but it seems reasonable that discourse via e-mail is not the equivalent of frequent face-to-face contact. An electronic forum can, arguably, draw the people in an organization closer together, but it can also fragment work groups (and add to alienation in society, for as socializing with neighbors has decreased, work-based social interconnectedness has increased). Will opportunities to nurture trust in the workforce be undermined as electronic technology loosens social connections between followers and leaders? The isolation that may stem from the use of new technologies can be overcome with sufficient social capital in the broader society, but organizational leaders must be adept at perceiving the shared norms and codes of behavior that enable trust to become generalized among members of the workforce.

## Conclusion

Leadership is not a series of acts. It is a process. Good leaders show followers the way by how they live their lives. They show their commitment to building relationships of trust by how they interact with and show respect for workers. The building of trust demands that we deal with our own internal shadows instead of denying their existence while insisting that others be more responsible. As leaders make themselves more accessible and adopt a more constructive view of workers, institutional trust almost inevitably will increase: "When trust permeates a group, great things are possible, not the least of which is a true opportunity to reach our potential" (De Pree, 1997, p. 23).

The concept of trust is ambiguous but socially important. Followers and leaders, workers and managers, need to place confidence in each other and in their organization in order to be effective. People in the United States generally have an expectation that workers and managers will be competent in their jobs, and that each side will deal with the other in a context of good faith. When trust is broken and these reasonable expectations are not met, moral outrage is often the response.

Yet trust is never enough. It is unrealistic to expect that a workplace can be organized entirely on the basis of trust; the law always remains as a complementary mechanism of control. Just as trust alone, however, is inadequate as an organizing principle, so is the law. If work relationships are to realize their greatest potential, what is needed is an appropriate balance of the two. Finding this balance requires us to keep discovering and rediscovering ways of nurturing trust—and leaders who operate from a faith-based perspective are in an extremely good position to do just that.

REFERENCES

Daft, R., and Lengel, R. H. *Fusion Leadership: Unlocking the Subtle Forces That Change People and Organizations.* San Francisco: Berrett-Koehler, 1998.

De Pree, M. *Leadership Jazz.* New York: Doubleday, 1992.

De Pree, M. *Leading Without Power: Finding Hope in Serving Community.* San Francisco: Jossey-Bass, 1997.

Fukuyama, F. *Trust: The Social Virtues and the Creation of Prosperity.* New York: Free Press, 1995.

Lipset, S. M. "Malaise and Resiliency in America." *Journal of Democracy,* 1995, 6,1–11.

Mouw, R. *Distorted Truths: What Every Christian Needs to Know About the Battle for the Mind.* San Francisco: Harper San Francisco, 1989.

Sako, M. *Prices, Quality and Trust: Inter-Firm Relations in Britain and Japan.* Cambridge, England: Cambridge University Press, 1992.

# 4

# CONFIDENCE UNDER PRESSURE

## HOW FAITH SUPPORTS RISK TAKING

*Winston E. Gooden*

Winston E. Gooden is associate dean in the School of Psychology at Fuller Theological Seminary, where he is also associate professor of clinical psychology. His current research interests include shame and its impact on intimacy and aggression, adult development, midlife crisis, and the development of African American men.

○

IN CONTINUING TO EXPLORE virtues that are highly relevant to leadership in the workplace, it is important to distinguish between faith and certain related attitudes that are sometimes equated with it. Integrity, trustworthiness, humility, and vision are important dimensions of (and separate complements to) faith. In general conversation, however, they are unlikely to be the first features or correlates of faith that spring to mind; instead, people are more likely to talk about self-confidence or the capacity to take risks. And, given the introspective cast of our society, talk of these qualities will often include psychological references.

In keeping with this volume's inquiry into transcendent forms of leadership, this chapter specifically focuses on connections and distinctions among confidence, risk taking, and faith. My thesis here is that the leader's faith provides a source of confidence that transcends what comes from training and experience. Faith helps leaders remain aware of their vulnerabilities without eroding their confidence, and it sustains them when they must pursue values and visions that put them and their organizations at risk.

Recent conceptions of leadership have shifted away from images of leaders as powerful figures, vested with great authority, who through force of personality take charge, direct others, and get things done. Although power and authority are still central to the understanding of leadership, the new paradigm of leadership focuses more on crafting a vision, empowering others, embodying core values, and service. For example, Bolman and Deal (1995) and De Pree (1997) articulate images of leadership as a spiritual process that includes and transcends the pragmatic motivations of profit and marketplace success, and Bolman and Deal specifically point out that the gifts leaders present to those with whom they work include authorship, love, empowerment, and significance. Moreover, these images of leadership require a more vulnerable role for the leader than is presented in more classic pictures of leadership. Indeed, De Pree (1997, p. 182), discussing the need for moral purpose in groups and organizations, says that leaders should treasure the gifts of followers and "abandon themselves to the strength of others." This image of a decidedly more open and vulnerable leader arises in part from rapid shifts in the environment in which organizations function. These changes have meant that leaders will now depend more and more on the knowledge, skill, and competence of others. Leadership will be much more diffuse, and there will be a need for people at all levels of the organization to exercise it.

Continuous learning is another hallmark of leadership for the next millennium (Senge, 1990). Kanter (1996) points out that organizations also function in a world with fewer and fewer fixed boundaries; leaders who succeed in this environment will be better at building bridges than at defending turf, less interested in protecting than in connecting with other companies or organizations for mutual benefit. Highly skilled, well-educated workers increasingly demand more autonomy in work, more satisfaction from work, and more meaningful engagement at work. Those leaders who understand and are sensitive to the need for meaning, and who value environments that help workers realize their potential, are likely to be more in tune with the new environment than are those who are insensitive to these trends.

Nevertheless, the changing environment for business and charitable organizations may not be the most important reason for the rise of the new leadership paradigm. More important may be a deep hunger, felt in society at large, for meaningful moral leadership on the part of individuals and institutions that care for the resources of our planet and, in our greedily competitive culture, show us a way out of destructive conflict. There is a spiritual hunger for leadership that will take the need for meaning and significance seriously and look beyond the efficient creation, satisfaction, and profitable exploitation of material hungers.

The literature on the new leadership paradigm seems to reflect a search for a transcendent type of leadership in which the ends that leaders and organizations serve go beyond profits and narrow measures of success. The pragmatic approach, which focuses on doing what works and getting things done, does not seem to satisfy the hungers provoked by fast-paced change, nor does it address the boundaryless environment or the intensified quest for meaning through work. The recent literature reflects the need for a source of vision and values that go deeper than the competence gained through education and the experience acquired during years on the job. Knowledge and experience are certainly important, but they need a center of value that transcends the pragmatic. The leader's faith or religious tradition is one source of principles, values, and a sense of moral purpose powerful enough to generate commitment and passion.

No leader singlehandedly creates the future, of course, but leaders together create the future that we will all inherit. Because the future that leaders create is not simply their own or that of their organizations— rather, they are creating the future of their industries, their communities, their countries, and the world as a whole—leaders' rootedness in vision and values is critically important. Our interdependence and our common future call for leadership that is multitextured, diverse, and vulnerable. Leadership also has to be grounded in principles and traditions that can promote a generative vision of the future in which all the earth will be blessed.

## Faith

Faith has been conceptualized as a natural process of making meaning, a process that rests on a person's evolving cognitive and relational capacities. In this process, cognitive development, relational capacities, and moral development all contribute to the way in which the content of experience is constructed to produce a meaningful sense of self in relation to an intelligible world (Fowler, 1995). In this model, then, faith is more than the content of the beliefs drawn from one's religious tradition; it includes but is not limited to religious beliefs and practices. Against this constructivist and developmental view of faith, a view of faith as natural to human functioning, stands the more traditional religious understanding that conceptualizes faith as a person's accepting response to God's self-disclosure and his or her commitment to a life of obedience and love.

The constructivist view has been criticized for making the religious content of faith relative (see, for example, Dykstra, 1986), but it helps clarify the link between our natural need for coherence and meaning and the vital place of faith in human functioning. From this perspective, life makes sense when we are engaged in a web of relationships and activities through which we experience meaning and significance. The people we become attached to, as well as the roles we choose and commit ourselves to in work, contribute to a coherent sense of self-identity. This firm sense of who we are, which we gain through commitments and emotional self-integration, helps promote our capacity to be faithful. Trust and commitment, key ingredients of faith, are important aspects of the process of forming an adult identity. Any unraveling of the attachments and commitments that bind us to a world of significance, and that hold our past and present in tension with our future, leaves us in despair.

Leaders need to understand how their commitment to leadership binds them to transcendent values and purposes as well as how their sense of meaning and integration is tied to this important role and to the way in which they play it. It is important for leaders to understand that work at its best nurtures a sense of identity. Work is valued not only for its tangible rewards but also for the intangible ways in which it sustains a sense of significance and meaning. Faith-based leadership needs to see engagement in work, and particularly the work of leadership, as providing nurture through creativity, service, and sacrifice.

When we invest ourselves in work and construe work as vocation, we do so with no firm or concrete evidence that our investment will yield the hoped-for return. We must jump in without certainty of where we will land, or of what shape we'll be in when we do. Faith is about staking everything on a future we can't determine or predict. Yet without this investment of ourselves, life remains absurd. When we start a new business, enter a new market, or develop a new product line, there is no firm assurance that the business will do well, that the new product will be accepted, or that we will make a return on our investment. We go forward with the belief that our planning and hard work will be repaid by acceptance in the market. Success, meaning, and fulfillment, in business as in personal life, require the exercise of faith.

The hunger for meaning and purpose can create idols out of success, power, and material achievement. Work and the material rewards it promises can be used to fill the place in our hearts where only God should live. The new paradigm of leadership seems sensitive to the need for a link between work and organizational vision, on the one hand, and transcendent values, on the other: values that can transform work and organizational vision from idolatrous preoccupations to genuine service in faith and love. We discover our deepest purpose when we respond to God and dedicate our work, indeed our whole lives, in trust and obedient service.

Fowler's constructivist approach to faith (1995) provides a helpful framework for understanding how people develop meaning and purpose as they weave commitments together in various areas of life. Yet Fowler's approach is not sufficient to explicate how Christian faith or any other specific tradition of faith affects the work of leadership. The specific content of a Christian faith accepted and lived is crucial to my own view of the place of faith in leadership.

In my understanding, Christian faith is a response of the total person—heart, mind, will, and body—to the initiative God has taken with respect to humanity, an initiative expressed in the suffering, death, and resurrection of Jesus Christ. This response involves an intentional acceptance of who God is and what God intends for our lives. People of faith commit themselves to living a new life patterned after God's loving expectations, as found in scripture and church teachings and as mediated through the presence of the Holy Spirit. Faith establishes a relationship of belief, trust, and commitment between ourselves and God, and it yields significance and coherence in our lives. (This conception of faith is close to the one offered in Chapter One by Robert Banks, although I find room for a constructivist element and suggest, in this chapter, a more overtly developmental dimension.)

Faith is transformative. As we pray, serve, study scripture, and worship, and as the Holy Spirit acts in our lives, we grow spiritually. As we pass each area of life through the prism of faith, seeking to understand the will of God, our trust and commitment are strengthened. In this way, faith is an active process of trusting God and shaping our lives to the ends that God ordains.

Our work life, when taken up in faith, becomes much more than our doing a job. When the work of leadership is taken into the life of faith, it becomes a vocation. Leaders seek to respond to the call of God through their particular responsibilities. Thus one leader may join with God in redemptive work; another, if she feels called to lead, and if she believes that her talents and capacities are gifts from God, will seek to fulfill the role of leadership in a way that is consistent with her own sense of God's expectations. The daily routine of responding to God's call will vary with each context and person. In religious organizations, this response will be most explicitly expected and carried out; in secular settings, it will be more implicit.

Leaders who intentionally allow their faith to shape how they lead will find some way of experiencing God as their senior partner. They will actively reflect on how their practice of leadership includes God's presence and partnership. For example, God's presence may influence the structures and procedures of the workplace, or it may influence the way in which ethical behavior is modeled, or it may find expression in efforts to shape an organizational culture that is just, tolerant, and supportive of workers' reaching their potential. Most important will be leaders' attempts to connect institutional vision with God's redemptive purposes. Leaders whose faith is more reflective or informed are more likely to be explicit in making such connections.

Faith, then, may shape leaders' understanding of their role, the way their roles are enacted, and the ends toward which leaders seeks to move their organizations. When it is included in the leadership equation, faith helps shape a spiritual identity in which a leader's sense of personal coherence and meaning rests on the tie between the execution of his or her role and the transcendent values to which he or she is committed. When there is great disjunction between a leader's values and the way leadership is being carried out, the leader will experience spiritual dissonance. (Chapters Seven and Thirteen recount two different approaches to connecting one's leadership role and one's values.) Those who work in the secular arena, who sense a need for leadership that is responsive to the spiritual yearning of the culture, and who are committed to responding to that need will blaze trails for which traditional models of leadership are not an adequate compass. The rich tradition of faith and sacred stories of faith can help to provide that compass, shape the ends that leaders choose to serve, and provide alternative frameworks for understanding the task of leadership as a spiritual process.

## Faith and Confidence

Faith is a unique source of confidence for those who lead from within a spiritual framework. Faith does not replace the usual sources of self-confidence but blends with them to provide a transcendent source of strength. Before we explore these ideas more fully, however, a clarification of the meaning, sources, and role of confidence in the work of leadership is warranted.

## Meaning of Confidence

The terms *confidence* and *faith* are often used interchangeably. I will use the term *confidence* to refer to the belief we have in ourselves (or in others) that we (or they) can and will accomplish a particular task. The Latin root of the word—*confidere,* a word formed from *con,* "with," and *fidere,* "to trust"—makes trust a part of what is meant by the term *confidence.* When we have confidence in another person, we rely on that person to deliver what he or she has promised. The term *self-confidence,* which is what we are focussing on here, refers to the trust that we have in our own capacity to succeed at certain tasks.

## Sources of Confidence

Experiences of acceptance and support in early life foster a sense of one-self as worthy and valuable. The validation of a child's efforts at walking, exploring, relating, and so forth, encourages a sense of self-efficacy. Praise and guidance provided in a nurturing environment enable children to trust their capacities and to trust those around them to provide safe boundaries for the exercise of emergent abilities.

Confidence is also a by-product of the level of competence that we have at completing certain tasks. The experience of success at given tasks boosts the degree of confidence that we possess. We are more likely to be confident when we feel valued and worthy, when we have the knowledge and skill to accomplish specific tasks, and when we have continual experiences of success at performing those tasks. Conversely, when we are deficient in knowledge or skill in a particular area, we are less confident about accomplishing things in that domain. The absence of confidence is displayed in self-doubt, lack of self-assertion, a nagging fear of failure, and feelings of low self-worth. Consistent patterns of failure, absence of support and encouragement in early life, and low levels of competence erode self-confidence and fuel self-doubt. Our level of confidence may also vary according to the context in which we have to perform. We may be quite confident in one domain but may not transfer that level of confidence to another domain, or our level of confidence may fluctuate according to particular experiences of success and failure.

Confidence energizes performance. In many areas of life, from athletics to academics, and in the marketplace as well as in the professions, low confidence means fewer attempts to achieve. Because the expectation of success drives performance, we will have little motivation to try when we anticipate failure. But high confidence leads to attempts to achieve even when the odds of success are against us. People who appear decisive, sure of themselves, and confident are often asked to lead. Those who doubt themselves or who seem uncertain or anxious are often overlooked when it comes to the choice of a leader. We tend to follow those we trust to accomplish a task. We place confidence in those who seem to be confident themselves.

Yet there are people who are drafted for leadership despite their lack of experience or special expertise in particular domains. These leaders may have grave doubts about their own capacity to lead a particular business or organization and may begin their tenure with a lack of confidence. Banks (1998), in exploring the widely held belief that a leader's position and personality always match, gives two very good examples of leaders whose personalities did not fit the positions they were asked to fill: the Danish philosopher Søren Kierkegaard, and Václav Havel, who became president of Czechoslovakia in 1989. Both, at times, were plagued by anxiety and self-doubt, yet in different ways they answered the call to provide extraordinary leadership.

Cattell and Birkett (1989) report that people who scored high on factor O of the 16PF, which measures how subjects feel about themselves, are rarely selected as leaders and are often not promoted. High scorers on factor O express self-doubt in addition to feelings of low self-worth and inadequacy. People low in confidence may be too preoccupied with their internal distress or too worried about acceptance or rejection to focus effectively on leadership tasks or to inspire others to face challenging or uncertain situations.

Unlike those who are overlooked for leadership roles, effective leaders have positive self-regard. Bennis and Nanus (1985), in their study of highly effective leaders, found that effective leaders tended to emphasize their strengths and minimize their weaknesses. This way of viewing oneself enhances confidence. These leaders were not self-centered or narcissistic; they were aware of their worth, respected themselves, and trusted their abilities. They knew what they were good at and found ways to compensate for their weaknesses. They actively invested in developing their skills and in making improvements where they were weak. The effective leaders were also able to turn down jobs that didn't match their capacities. Knowledge of their areas of strength and weakness, along with the wisdom to avoid commitments for which they weren't well prepared, enabled these leaders to avoid loss of confidence and the demoralization that would come with attempting and failing at tasks for which they were not prepared.

Further, instead of using failure as data to support feelings of incompetence, the effective leaders used failure constructively. They saw it as a

challenge but did not dwell on it or let it stop them. The perspective
they took was that all learning involves failure. They drew lessons from
failure and tried again. These leaders did not expect or fear failure; they
were optimistic about outcomes and confident in their capacity to achieve
success.

### Role of Confidence in Leadership

Leaders and those who study leadership agree that a seminal task of leadership is the shaping of a vision for the organization. Once the vision is
crafted, the next important job is to get followers to help make it a reality.
Confidence is crucial in getting others to believe in the leader's vision and
to commit themselves to making it a reality. The leader's confidence in his
or her ability to select the right vision, choose the right course, and stick
with it inspires followers to get behind the effort. The leader's determination, perseverance, decisiveness, stability, and strength generate confidence
and enthusiasm in followers.

The relationship between leaders and followers is not simply a rational
one in which followers estimate the ability of the leader and decide to
trust and follow. The relationship involves unconscious processes through
which followers identify with leaders and thus participate in the leader's
mystique and power. The leader's confidence is one of the signals that
followers read in the process of constructing an image of the leader as
trustworthy. Unlike self-centeredness and narcissism, which thrive on
admiration, deference, and even adulation from followers, confidence elicits trust, respect, and cooperation from others.

Confidence allows the leader to support the growth of team members
without fearing competition from them. It allows the leader to celebrate
the success of others without feeling diminished. The leader's confidence
is a great asset when unpopular decisions have to be made. The highly
confident leader elicits and respects the views of others but does not
need to have everyone agree with his or her opinions. The confident
leader can stand firm on matters of principle, despite disagreements or
unpopularity.

The uncertainty and risks that leaders face in moving organizations into
the future are a major reason why leadership requires people with high
confidence. Imagine Abraham leaving Ur with everything he had—his
family and his livestock—for an unknown destination. No doubt many
in his party were afraid, critical, and reluctant to leave without certain
knowledge of the obstacles in their path, the opposition they would face,
or the length of the journey. Abraham would not have had any firm data

with which to convince his people that leaving was a wise decision. We can assume that they went along because Abraham had a confidence that was rooted in God's promise. The leader's confidence in times of uncertainty becomes a foundation on which the confidence of followers can be built. When followers have to be persuaded that the opportunities for gain outweigh the risks of loss, their perceptions of the leader's confidence are vitally important. Self-doubt and indecisiveness in a leader are communicated directly to those who follow, and, like the common cold, they are contagious. Yet leaders have doubts and worries at times, especially in the complex reality of corporate and organizational life, where rapid change makes even the most confident people nervous. Leaders who surround themselves with good workers can be encouraged and uplifted by the confidence of their teams. The competence of workers and others on their teams will compensate for or carry leaders when they temporarily lose confidence, for confidence is also contagious. When leaders exude confidence, they energize the organization. An energized organization will view its obstacles as less overwhelming and its resources (including its ingenuity) as capable of meeting and beating the odds.

## Faith and Trust

Faith, like confidence, involves trust, but the object of trust is typically different. Whereas confidence is intrapersonal and reflects our belief in our own abilities, faith is interpersonal and reflects our trust in God. When we place confidence in God, we are trusting God. The meaning of the term *faith,* then, is not much different from the meaning of the term *confidence,* but the difference is significant: faith involves not only trust but also commitment.

Faith responds to God's invitation. In faith, we are grasped by divine love and invited into a loving relationship. The foundation of faith is this deeply felt personal partnership with God. It is nurtured through worship, prayer, study of scripture, and obedient service.

## Faith and Risk Taking

Faith and risk taking are also closely related. Abraham, for instance, is the father of faith because he believed God, took his family and possessions, and went toward a place promised but not seen. There were obvious risks involved in Abraham's leaving a life that was known and the security of a settled existence and moving toward the unknown, with no concrete, tangible evidence either that he would arrive at the promised destination or that the destination even existed. Risk taking, which is sometimes involved in the mobility that accompanies today's work patterns, is one part of the life of faith but is not synonymous with faith. Let us look more carefully at risk taking, its place in leadership, and its connection with faith and confidence.

Risk taking involves making decisions in a climate of uncertainty, where information is incomplete and the potential for gain is balanced by a potential for loss or harm. A decision not to act may expose us to losses brought about by rapid change in the environment, whereas a decision to take action may expose us to losses brought about by a failed strategy. Risk taking is motivated by the desire to take advantage of opportunities for realizing gains or to avoid the losses that may come from inaction.

In a study of the impact of personality factors on risk taking, Kowert and Hermann (1997) found distinct differences between people who were willing and those who were very reluctant to take risks. They found that thrill seekers—described as imaginative, open in their thinking, humorous, and mischievous—were more likely to take greater risks, especially when opportunities for gain were inherent in the situations that they needed to resolve. More risk-averse people were conscientious, agreeable, and altruistic. They typically avoided risk anyway but were even more cautious when facing a potential loss. People who took risks without considering the costs were less conscientious, less sensitive to threats, less inclined to judge situations, and more impulsive.

The central task of leadership is to imagine a future and move people toward it. Therefore, the leader is a risk taker by definition because he or she leads others in particular directions, with no proof of eventual success. It is in the nature of leadership to stake the organization's future on decisions that have to be made with insufficient and ambiguous information. As leaders move an organization from intentions to the realization of those intentions, and from a vision to the actualization of that vision, risk becomes a permanent element of the leadership landscape. The actions of leadership expose leaders and the organization to the risk of loss, no matter how well planned the program is or how careful the leader is in managing it. It is impossible to eliminate risk. But effective leaders rarely take risks for the thrill of it. They approach risk prudently. According to Kindler (1998), prudence and risk taking may appear to be contradictory, because prudence implies careful management and sound judgment, and yet only sound judgment allows decisions made in risky circumstances to be made responsibly.

Preference for and tolerance of risk varies from leader to leader, just as in the general population. A leader's taste for risk may leave the organization vulnerable if the leader underestimates uncertainty, overestimates the probability of attaining the desired outcomes, or makes impulsive decisions. The leader with a taste for risk may operate by the motto "Nothing ventured, nothing gained." By contrast, the leader who is highly motivated to avoid risk may overestimate uncertainty, avoid taking action because he or she is pessimistic, or underestimate the probability of attaining certain goals. This leader, who may operate by the motto "Better safe than sorry," likewise may leave the organization vulnerable. A prudent approach to risk taking involves careful analysis and planning. Decisions should take the reward-to-risk ratio into account, and attempts should be made to maximize gains, reduce the impact of losses, and lower uncertainty by gathering information. (See Chapter Eleven for a discussion of inclusive and exclusive forms of leadership, multiple perspectives, and the impact of the leader's own risk-taking preferences.)

Leadership at every institutional level involves risk taking; it is important for the organization to create a culture that supports risk taking, but some organizational cultures may punish it. Members of an organization should be helped to learn from their mistakes instead of being blamed for them. When organizations encourage innovation and reward risk taking, people will feel less vulnerable in making decisions that involve risk.

Much of the literature on risk taking and leadership focuses on how businesses manage risk to attain greater profits, but risk taking clearly is not limited to business or profit making. Political leaders, for example, weigh the risks involved in key decisions, and in times of conflict they are particularly concerned with decisions that may exacerbate tensions. Leaders in educational, civic, charitable, and religious organizations are also concerned with risk in many different ways. A key area of risk taking for faith-based leadership involves the attempt to align an organization's vision for the future with leaders' vision of the Kingdom of God. A leader's efforts to create a workplace climate that is hospitable to the spiritual life may expose him or her to various risks. Similarly, efforts to promote diversity, equality, and socially responsible organizational practices may prove costly and even disruptive in the short run. The gains realized from these efforts are not necessarily measured in financial terms. They are reflected in the ultimate quality of the organization's contributions to its stakeholders and to its community. Risk taking in these ways is clearly tied to leaders' faith, both because their faith traditions may be a key source of the vision and values that they seek to actualize and because the courage to persist in achieving those goals, despite risk and threats, may be based on these leaders' sense of participating in God's new creation.

Risk taking, like faith, involves committing oneself to certain goals and taking action to achieve them, with no assurance that they will be attained. But risk taking does not necessarily involve or imply trust in a divine agent who will bring about the realization of these goals. Prudent risk taking calculates the probability of the desired outcome, given the known context and forces likely to affect it. Religious faith does not abandon prudence, but in situations where probabilities cannot be calculated, its expectation of positive outcomes rests on trust in God to bring good things about.

## Faith and Reliance on God

Leaders are vulnerable to the normal range of human frailties, from physical illness and moral lapses to eventual death. No matter how well leaders manage themselves, they cannot hope to lead flawlessly. In small and large ways, their shadows will fall over the organizations they lead. Faith can help leaders construct an integrated picture of themselves that includes their flaws and vulnerabilities as well as their sense of competence. What faith makes possible is not denial of or compensation for a leader's weaknesses but rather their inclusion in self-awareness. Faith in this context does not negate the leader's efforts at self-improvement, but it does allow the leader to accept of his or her human limits without losing confidence in his or her capacity to lead.

The apostle Paul, in the twelfth chapter of his second letter to the Corinthians, serves as an example of this kind of self-acceptance. Defending himself against charges that he was unfit to lead, Paul acknowledged that he had been given a "thorn in the flesh"; he had asked that it be removed, but God denied his request, and instead it had been disclosed to Paul that God's strength is made perfect in weakness—that it was when Paul was weak that God's strength could best work through him. What was Paul to do in the face of the limitations brought about by his weakness? Let God's grace suffice!

Leaders who pray, open themselves before God, and examine their lives and their character cannot escape knowledge of their flaws. But this knowledge helps promote a reliance on God. The confidence born from the life of prayer rests as much on such leaders' belief in God's faithful partnership and presence as on the gifts with which God has endowed them. Confidence bolstered by faith is hedged about by gratitude and humility. These leaders know that if they seek to fulfill God's purposes through the way they lead and the ends they serve, they can rely on God's presence and partnership.

Faith is particularly important when decisions involve situations of extreme risk. When no one can predict outcomes, and when action seems as dangerous as inaction, a leader's faith helps galvanize the decision to act. For example, all the available analysis showed that the civil rights movement, under the leadership of Martin Luther King Jr., faced overwhelming odds. Racial discrimination in education, transportation, housing, and employment were legal in many areas. To attempt change meant working to challenge not only laws but also deeply ingrained practices and prejudices. King's opponents used jailings, beatings, bombings, and executions in trying to instill fear in him and his followers. Their message was that those who dared to march against or otherwise oppose racism and discrimination would be severely harmed or even killed; indeed, the church bombing in Birmingham, Alabama, that killed four little girls was a grim reminder of the extreme risk involved in pursuing direct action and civil disobedience in order to create change. King and other leaders were well aware of the risks to themselves, their families, and their followers. King attempted to inoculate other leaders and their followers against fear by training them in techniques of passive resistance. But the training, discipline, and preparation, although they were important, were not the only source of the courage that allowed King and the movement to battle and beat the odds. In his writings, speeches, and sermons, King made clear that his dream of equality for all the races was based squarely on his understanding of what God wanted for society (Washington, 1986). He drew on the image of Israel moving toward the Promised Land as he encouraged his followers to "walk together . . . and not get weary." Like the prophet Amos, King called for "justice to roll down like waters and righteousness like a mighty stream." King's deep faith that God was working His will through the movement for civil rights was what enabled him to risk and eventually give his life in the struggle for freedom and equality. This extreme level of risk and threat easily could have eroded the confidence of the civil rights leaders, and yet their confidence seems to have been extraordinary. It did not negate their awareness of their vulnerability—there was frequent talk of death, and King, in the "mountaintop" speech, was explicit about the imminent threat to his life—but the sense of a personal fellowship with God, as expressed in "Precious Lord," one of King's favorite songs, seemed to be a unique source of strength during times of distress and certain danger. The presence of the Lord as protector is cited frequently in scripture as the guarantor of courage and success, and King and other preachers in the movement drew on this tradition for confidence. The leaders of most organizations are not faced with this sort of radical situation, but they still can draw on the biblical tradition for models of reliance on the presence and power of God.

## Conclusion

A sense of God's grace, which transforms leaders' weaknesses into opportunities for God to work, allows leaders to place their confidence in God while using their gifts to do the work that they are called to do. A firm sense of God's partnership and presence makes it possible to take risks in achieving ends that are in keeping with the values of the kingdom of God. Leaders, in seeking to take organizations to places where they have not gone before, act by faith. When the sought-for destinations are seen through the lens of the traditions and values of the Christian faith, leaders can rely on the models of faith-based leadership expressed in scripture and in the history of the Christian movement. They can also rely on the presence and partnership of God and on their abiding trust in Him as they face their demanding and risky tasks.

REFERENCES

Banks, R. *Myths in Leadership*. Pasadena, Calif.: De Pree Leadership Center, 1998.
Bennis, W., and Nanus, B. *Leaders: The Strategies for Taking Charge*. New York: HarperCollins, 1985.
Bolman, L. G., and Deal, T. E. *Leading with Soul: An Uncommon Journey of Spirit*. San Francisco: Jossey-Bass, 1995.
Cattell, H., and Birkett, H. *The 16PF: Personality in Depth*. Champaign, Ill.: Institute for Personality and Ability Testing, 1989.
De Pree, M. *Leading Without Power: Finding Hope in Serving Community*. San Francisco: Jossey-Bass, 1997.
Dykstra, C. "What Is Faith? An Experiment in the Hypothetical Mode." In C. Dykstra and S. Park (eds.), *Faith Development and Fowler*. Birmingham, Ala.: Religious Education Press, 1986.
Fowler, J. W. *Stages of Faith: The Psychology of Human Development and the Quest for Meaning*. San Francisco: Harper San Francisco, 1995.
Kanter, R. M. "World Class Leaders: The Power of Partnering." In F. Hesselbein, M. Goldsmith, and R. Beckhard (eds.), *The Leader of the Future: New Visions, Strategies, and Practices for the Next Era*. San Francisco: Jossey-Bass, 1996.

Kindler, H. S. "The Art of Prudent Risk Taking." *Training and Development,* 1998, *52*(4), 32–35.

Kowert, P. H., and Hermann, M. G. "Who Takes Risks, Daring and Caution in Foreign Policy Making." *Journal of Conflict Resolution,* 1997, *41*(5), 611–637.

Senge, P. M. *The Fifth Discipline.* New York: Doubleday, 1990.

Washington, J. M. (ed.). *A Testament of Hope: The Essential Writings and Speeches of Martin Luther King, Jr.* San Francisco: Harper San Francisco, 1986.

5

# HUMILITY AND VISION
# IN THE LIFE OF THE
# EFFECTIVE LEADER

*Benjamin D. Williams*

Benjamin D. Williams is director of sales support services for Protocol Systems, a manufacturer of medical instrumentation in Portland, Oregon. He has extensive experience in Christian ministry and the marketplace and is actively engaged in leadership development within the Orthodox Church in America. He is coauthor (with Harold B. Anstall) of *Orthodox Worship: A Living Continuity with the Temple, the Synagogue, and the Early Church* and (with Michael T. McKibben) of *Oriented Leadership: Why All Christians Need It.*

———— o ————

The purpose of this chapter is to consider vision and humility as correlates of faith. Humility and vision are not concepts that operate in isolation. In terms of leadership, we must be concerned with how they are related to our faith and how they operate in our organizations. To that end, they are among the core aspects of faith-based leadership. We must ask, "What are faith and faith-based leadership, and what is the belief system or worldview that goes along with it?" We must also ask, "From a Christian perspective, what is the relationship of humility and vision to faith, and how do they all operate organizationally?"

## The Heart of Leadership

What is faith-based leadership? Obviously, at one level, it is a form of leadership that is informed by a leader's faith. Would the answer be any different for a Christian in a leadership position than for others, and would that leader's answer be different from the answers of his or her first-millennium counterparts?

Leadership is defined in a variety of ways in contemporary society—as authoritarian leadership, for example, or servant leadership, or team leadership, and so on. Be that as it may, these are mainly styles of leadership that are shaped and informed by the background, understanding, and experience of the practitioner. Whatever the style, Christian leadership is different because it has a different starting point. That starting point is a relationship with Jesus Christ and a vision of the Kingdom that He came to inaugurate. This is a vision of what really is, and these experiences take place through the work of the Holy Spirit. Therefore, such leadership is "perceiving and articulating the vision of the Kingdom of God, and effectively defining and communicating its incarnation, following Christ's example of service"(Williams and McKibben, 1994, p. 23).

This definition of leadership may surprise some because of its three areas of emphasis:

1. It is based on the premise of serving as Christ served.
2. It is vision-dependent and Kingdom-centered.
3. Its task is to incarnate that vision.

In the tradition and theology of Eastern Christianity, one of the pivotal theological concepts is that of image (*ikon* in Greek, *imago* in Latin). The biblical basis is in the creation narrative (Gen. 1:26), where we are told that God created humankind in the divine "image and likeness." In the patristic thinking of the first millennium of Christianity, this passage was understood not as a curious Old Testament turn of phrase but rather as a description of the calling and potential of humans to move from "image" to "likeness," from fallen to completed, from imperfect to perfect, in Jesus Christ.

Jesus Christ manifested a particular style of leadership, today commonly referred to as *servant leadership*. He did not come as a military hero or as a great political strategist or as an astute globetrotting businessman. He came as a humble servant, both of the Father and of those around Him; thus the style of leadership we are expected to imitate is servant leadership.

Jesus gave his followers a "new commandment": to love one another as He has loved them (John 13:34). The "new" element of this commandment is that the essence of God is Love. It is the revelation, scandalous to lovers of power and ridiculous to lovers of wisdom, that God manifests Himself as Love by dying in human flesh for the life of the world. As Hopko summarizes (1988, p. 88), "Human beings are created to imitate the loving humility of God Himself, the divine service revealed to the world in the person of Jesus, the Son of God in human flesh. The disciples of Jesus are called to imitate their Master and Lord in His self-emptying sacrifice of love upon the Cross."

Is it possible to lead without faith? No: in the sense that all people have faith, even if it is basic and generic faith, the answer must be no. As human beings, we intuitively know and understand that the universe operates by certain laws. The earth revolves through cycles of day and night, water flows downstream, and so forth. In other words, we learn at the human level that life is not characterized by chaos but rather by order. From this very basic understanding develops a primitive personal faith. As children we learn first to have faith in our parents, that they will be there for us, and from this develops a basic faith in other people. But what of Christian faith?

Fowler (1976, p. 11) makes the point that faith "is the relation of trust in and loyalty to the transcendent about which concepts or propositions, our beliefs, are fashioned." He goes on to make the case that in the understanding of the ancient church, faith was never spoken of in ways that could be translated by the modern meanings of belief or believing. The modern concept of belief is a rational one, the result of a weighing of evidence that leads to a decision. Belief puts "I believe in God" in the same category as "I believe in democracy," or "I believe that vitamin C cures the common cold." By contrast, Fowler (1976, p. 12) shows that in the understanding of the early church, faith or credo was not an intellectual proposition; rather, it was an existential one that "involve[d] an alignment of the heart or will, a commitment of loyalty and trust. . . . It mean[t], almost without equivocation, to set one's heart on. To set one's heart on someone or something requires that one has seen or sees the point of that to which one is loyal. Faith, therefore, involves vision. It is a mode of knowing, of acknowledgment. One commits oneself to that which is known or acknowledged, and lives loyally, with life and character being shaped by that commitment."

Faith is an existential reality that gives shape to our life. Faith-based leadership must be congruent: it must correspond with and manifest the process of believing and the content of our basic beliefs. Our lives are living images of the faith we hold; we live out what we believe. The Latin root of the word *religion* means "that which binds us together" as a people or community: it is what we commit ourselves to, and how we manifest it in our lives. This, of course, puts before us the difficult tension between actual and professed faith, which Jesus had in mind when he said, "You will know them by their fruit" (Matt. 7:16). We all struggle with this tension, and it should sensitize us to the importance of asceticism for the training, self-discipline, and self-restraint that must characterize our lives. It is the spiritual preparation and pursuit that enables us to achieve our potential. When we strive to discipline ourselves to be conformed to the likeness of Christ, we are truly religious. We are faithful. We are ready to consider vision and humility as correlates of our faith.

## The Source of Implementation

The term *vision* as it is used today was foreign to the patristic mind, but the concept of clarifying one's inner sight in order to perceive the desired goal was not. *Vision* is a term that has almost lost its value and meaning. For example, some of the most autocratic business organizations in the marketplace have "vision statements" that talk about teamwork and empowering the person, and the single most common experience with "vision" for the majority of people occurs in a business setting when a very expensive outside consultant disrupts the organization to craft a cute phrase that is labeled the "vision" of the organization, after which business continues as usual. Is it any wonder that most people feel uncomfortable when the subject is raised?

What, then, is vision for a faith-based leader? McKibben (1990, p. 157) argues that vision, at its most fundamental level, is "our source of direction and decisions" and that the Holy Trinity "is our Christian vision." This statement should tell us two things.

The first is something that we know intuitively: without a clear sense of purpose as we approach the task at hand, the outcome will probably be unsatisfactory. We take this for granted at the practical level: a house without a good foundation will crack and settle, and a trip without a clear destination will be aimless wandering. Why don't we recognize that this precept applies to the larger aspects of life—in fact, to the very course of our lives and the lives of our organizations? The reality is that Solomon's oft-quoted statement, "Where there is no vision the people perish" (Prov. 29:18), is an organizational statement. What this definition also tells us is that for the person of faith, vision works in a particular way and has a specific reference. For Christians, this reference

is God, and the purpose of vision is to achieve the incarnation of
the Kingdom. From this understanding develops a Christian working
definition of vision: "A clear mental image of the Kingdom of God that
pictures things as God would have them be and which guides implementation; the Holy Trinity as the source of our direction and decisions"
(Williams and McKibben, 1994, p. 94).

The second thing McKibben's definition (1990, p. 157) should tell us
is that our lives ought to be in harmony with God, and that vision guides
our implementation. It is no coincidence that vision, like leadership,
is Kingdom-centered, and the final element of Williams and McKibben's
definition (1994, p. 94) is the affirmation that God is our ultimate reference and should be the source of our direction and decisions. Vision is
part of our created nature and, as we have seen, faith involves vision
in that it requires seeing the point of that to which one is loyal. Just as
each of us, as a person, possesses vision, so also do our organizations,
which are made up of people who possess vision. Vision is the picture that
drives all action. It conveys an image of where we want to go and how
we want to get there.

Believe it or not, many people struggle with the concept of vision; they
deny that they possess vision or "have a vision." The issue, then, is to
get in touch with the vision that we possess as part of our created being
and to make it work. My favorite example of the role that vision plays
in our lives is that of the English athlete Roger Bannister, who on May 6,
1954, became the first person to run a mile in less than four minutes.
The year before this achievement, a major university had released a study
of human physiology, proving that it was physically impossible for a
human being to run a mile in less than four minutes. Not only was Bannister ignorant of this study, he also had a vision of himself breaking the
so-called four-minute barrier. Bannister's experience explains in part why
visualization has become so popular in psychology, and especially in the
teaching of sports: if people can be brought to envision themselves
performing an action in the correct way, they will actually perform it
correctly.

We all operate with pictures of our goals in mind. We see the desired
outcomes. We all daydream about the things we'd like to do. This is why
we are subject to the power of advertising. In fact, our most common
response when we finally understand a difficult concept is "I see!" Belasco
(1990) points out that vision is effort, but it inspires action and validates
decisions: the right vision inspires action and fosters success; the wrong
vision stifles action and promotes failure. As we have seen in Fowler's
definition (1976), it is no coincidence that faith includes vision as one of

its components: our being created "in the image" means that we have the power to envision things spiritually. The challenge for Christians is that we can't just latch onto any vision or whip up a new vision or repackage a vision in our own words, some vision that has made someone else or some other organization successful. Why? Because ours is a Christian vision that must be informed and shaped by the truths of the faith, and in harmony with the vision of the Kingdom of God. A key question, then, is how we acquire a vision that can become the source of our direction and decisions.

Our vision, like faith, must be consistent with its source: the Holy Trinity and the Kingdom of God. In the marketplace, the source of a vision is generally the ideas of one person or of a few key people. For Christians and their organizations, the vision of the Kingdom of God is the icon (model) for local visions, and it is from the vision of the Kingdom of God that Christians discern and develop personal and organizational visions. What is the vision of the Kingdom of God? That question is too big to deal with here, but we can ask what a Kingdom-oriented vision involves in the marketplace. We can begin by saying that we are able to discern the nature of the Kingdom because Jesus Christ inaugurated it. His incarnation and revelation are the foundations of our knowledge. Built on this foundation are tradition, scripture, theology, and so forth, which further define it. Our job is to define the local incarnation of the Kingdom in the time and place where we live and work.

How is this idea translated into practical reality for those of us in the marketplace? We can approach it through the life of Jesus. At the end of a thorough study of the New Testament, we don't have a picture in our minds of the Kingdom, any more than we have a mental picture of the Father or of the Holy Spirit. Apart from the miracles that He worked, what Jesus revealed and taught was truth—principles and values such as we find in the Sermon on the Mount. Much of the rest we have to take on faith. At a minimum, then, our personal and organizational vision (or purpose) must incorporate those principles. Among the best sources for a personal or organizational vision are the attributes of relationship as they exist among the persons of the Holy Trinity. These attributes include the following principles:

- The notion of being "first among equals"
- The idea of elements that are unique yet inseparable from other elements
- The idea of elements that are equal in value but different in function
- The idea of unity as a communion of love

St. John Cassian, among the earliest monastic saints, said, "The objective of our life is the Kingdom of God, but we should carefully ask what we should aim for," and St. Neilos the Ascetic counseled that "when people proceed from contemplation to action, this right understanding enables them to make great progress. The action is good because it has first been contemplated by clear-sighted eyes of spiritual knowledge" (Palmer, Sherrard, and Ware, 1979, pp. 95, 218). If this is true of the average believer, then what of the faith-based leader? The first responsibility is to define the local incarnation of the Kingdom for the organization. This must be the case both in the church and in the marketplace, for they are not in opposition; inasmuch as the Kingdom is the ultimate reality, our job is to define all that we do in terms of it.

How do we receive this Christian vision so that we can pursue its local incarnation? The beginning of Christian vision is God the Trinity, Who has created and sustains all that exists. Within the Godhead, the Father is the source or fountainhead of all things, and therefore the source of our heavenly vision; the Son is begotten of the Father, and the Holy Spirit proceeds from the Father.

We might describe the work of the Son as implementing the Trinity's divine plan for humankind through the Incarnation, and that of the Holy Spirit as being the source of our energy, joy, and life. Yet the reality is that sin dims and obscures our vision of the Kingdom and of the truth, and we are called to struggle to perceive and implement the Kingdom.

Sin causes us to be less than Godlike, and when we are implementing the vision, sin rears its ugly head. A common problem is "my plan" versus "your plan." In other words, it is "me" versus "you." This is sin at work, putting me and my rights above you and your rights—the opposite of unity and harmony in love. This disharmony appears in marriages and families, in churches and Christian organizations, in businesses and societies.

The process of defining and implementing a vision that is in harmony with the divine vision is not easy; it is a struggle. Nevertheless, it is a process that we must understand and be willing to enter into, one that we may even find ourselves getting excited about. We cannot go to the same sources for our vision and its implementation, as we would if we were secular humanists, for example. Are our visions intrinsically better than theirs simply because we label ours "Christian"? Hardly. Can a secular humanist's vision contain Christian elements? Yes, it can. Where, then, do the fundamental differences lie? They begin, as we have seen, in the source of vision and in how we achieve it. Our starting point is God the Holy Trinity; one God and three Persons. From this overarching beginning and ending point (alpha and omega) we can know who we are: people created in the image of God. This is the source of our identity. That identity provides the foundation of our vision, and it informs our vision, from which we draw the imagery, strength, motivation, and direction to do everything in our lives.

From this follows the work: the effort of getting in touch with and defining our personal or organizational purpose, ensuring that it is congruent with the vision of the Kingdom, and, finally, defining it for our own time and place. Here, we recognize that our Christian life is a lifelong process of discernment and implementation as we strive to carry out the will of God. The definition of our vision (or purpose) sets the context for our mission, which is the definition of how we are going to implement or achieve the vision. With this vision and mission, at the big-picture level, we move naturally on to more detailed tasks: defining our key goals and objectives and, ultimately, our day-to-day goals in living. The process is complete when we achieve the results of our actions, which are the fruit of the Spirit. The challenge is effective action. St. Mark the Ascetic was another of the Desert Fathers (the fourth- and fifth-century monastics who were found principally in northern Egypt). He counsels us here, "Think nothing and do nothing without a purpose directed to God. For a journey without direction is wasted effort" (Palmer, Sherrard, and Ware, 1979, p. 110). When we look to our vision for direction and motivation, the probability of our effectiveness increases.

What about organizational vision? The vision of an organization is the composite of the visions of the people who make up the organization. Optimally, these personal visions are synthesized into an organizational vision; more often than not, however, each person operates independently, with his or her own vision of the organization, and so there is no integrated organizational vision.

What may surface instead of a shared vision is what McKibben (1990, p. 101) calls "sortavision," defined as "a fragmented mental image that sporadically pictures things as we would like them to be; a cloudy picture that confuses thinking, causes endless arguments, avoids decisions and generates half-hearted action; a picture that resigns one to the way things are now." This is a frequent outcome when no effort has gone into defining an organizational vision: sometimes it's there, sometimes it's not, but the common theme is frustration. In the absence of a true organizational vision, a second possibility—the most common marketplace reality, unfortunately, found all too often in Christian organizations—is a vision that originates with the founder (or with organizational leaders) and is then imposed on followers, who essentially are allowed no input. There are three problems with this second dynamic. First, from an organizational perspective, the result of not achieving a shared vision is a suboptimal organization. Second, in terms of faith-based leadership, an imposed vision is un-Christian; it means settling for "sortavision," which is simply bad stewardship. Third, at the personal level, an imposed vision is sub-Christian because it is depersonalizing: we are all created in the image of God, and so we all have the responsibility of treating each person with whom we interact accordingly.

A shared organizational vision is the healthy synthesis and integration of personal visions. A shared vision leads to a high-performance organization, with high levels of productivity, motivation, loyalty, and commitment. Pragmatically and organizationally, we need to recognize that a human organization will be no better than its shared vision, and that it will succeed only to the extent that it has defined and developed a shared vision. This development may or may not take place overtly, through a process that results in an external vision statement. The point is that a shared vision must be achieved.

How do we achieve a shared organizational vision? We can do this only by building consensus. A shared vision can't be imposed by decree; our moral obligation is to achieve it in a person-affirming way. A consensus is not a "majority rules" position statement reached though a process of voting. It is not even a unanimously approved position. Rather, it is a position that can be supported by everyone. How is this possible? Through the work of the Spirit, in a process that affirms each person and allows everyone to participate and have input. Then, even those who may disagree with the decision can agree to support it. This is the method by which we fulfill our first responsibility: to facilitate the local definition of the vision of the Kingdom for a given organization in its time and place. In a public corporation of thirty thousand employees, however, is consensus possible, practically speaking? Consensus may not be possible, but it is possible to achieve consent, at least, or some combination of consensus and consent. Consider, for example, that all employees have to consent to certain givens (involving corporate profits, earnings to shareholders, market share, and so on), without which there would be no public corporation. It is neither appropriate nor possible to replace these givens with social propositions that would ultimately bring about the demise of the organization. There are boundaries, in other words, and not everything is up for grabs. The practical reality is expressed in terms of a simple inverse relationship: the larger the organization, the less consensus and the more consent; and the smaller the organization, the more consensus and the less consent.

Consensus can be achieved if leaders believe that its achievement is possible, and if they are willing to do the work of building consensus. And shared vision is not only work: it must also be *worked for.* I was once in lay leadership in a congregation that apparently had a high degree of shared vision. The mood of the congregation was positive and supportive, the atmosphere was open and cordial, people worked together, and there was growth. But there had never been a formal undertaking of any sort to define the organizational vision or to achieve a shared vision, and this, I was soon to learn, was a catastrophe waiting to happen. Why? Because all organizations go through difficult times: markets change and market share slips; contributions fall and financial pressures develop; capital campaigns create stress or leadership styles are incompatible. Whatever the particular issues that cause the problem, it will test the organizational vision. In this case, as problems developed and stress increased, the divisions began to appear. The reality was that there were three or four organizational visions at work, with enough commonality among them that they appeared to be the same until the problems began. When the divisions became apparent, the tension escalated, and so did the pain. At that point, it was too late for consensus; the organization was polarized. Within a few months, the congregation had lost half its members, and within a year it had happened again. Almost everyone looked back and said, "It seemed so wonderful. How could this have happened?"

We are all responsible for defining a personal vision. If we are leaders, then we must work with others to define a shared organizational vision and strive to achieve it. The visions we strive to implement must be informed by the divine vision. To the degree that we achieve this goal, our lives will be local incarnations of the divine will.

## Humility: The Mother of Virtues

There is growing recognition of the wisdom of the ancient Christian Church, and of a tradition that possesses a tremendous body of practical spirituality. In the spiritual tradition of the ancient church, humility was considered the most mysterious of the virtues—difficult to define and elusive of explanation. In this tradition, humility is a subject principally and most poignantly treated in the monastic literature, especially in the teachings of the Desert Fathers. The ascetic challenge is to overcome the vices and passions that control us and prevent us from conforming to the likeness of Christ.

The pivotal role of humility in the spiritual life derives from Jesus' teaching: "Truly I say to you, unless you turn and become like children, you will never enter the kingdom of Heaven. Whoever humbles himself like this child, he is the greatest in the kingdom of Heaven" (Matt. 18:2–4). All who exalt themselves will be humbled, and those who humble themselves will be exalted. He commands all to learn from His divine humility and meekness.

St. Dorotheos of Gaza, abbot of a sixth-century monastery, began his teaching on the subject of humility by saying, "One of the Fathers used to say: Before anything else we need humility; a being ready to listen whenever a word is spoken to us, and to say, 'I submit,' because through humility every device of the enemy, every kind of obstacle, is destroyed" and, a little later (explaining Christ's invitation, in Matt. 11:29, to "learn of me, for I am gentle and humble in heart"):

> There you have it in a nutshell: he has taught us the root and cause of all [evil] and also the remedy for it, leading to all good. He has shown us that pretensions to superiority (pride) cast us down and that it is impossible to obtain mercy except by the contrary, that is to say, by humility. . . . And I call that real humility which is not humble in word and outward appearance but is deeply planted in the heart for this is what He meant when He said that "I am meek and humble of heart" [Dorotheos of Gaza, 1977, p. 95].

How, then, is humility to be understood? These teachings understand it essentially as the safeguard of the soul. When we lose control, when we are swayed by the passions, then we are open to the power of temptation. As St. Dorotheos counsels, "Humility protects the soul from all passions and also from every temptation" (Dorotheos of Gaza, 1977, p. 99). Humility was understood as a remedy, an antidote, enabling progress in the spiritual life.

This perspective on humility is based on an understanding of the human condition that differs from our contemporary understanding of it. As fallen humans, all of us, even those who are believers, are understood to be weak and subject both to external spiritual forces and to the passions. The term *the passions* is common in the spiritual tradition of the ancient church, and perhaps the best contemporary English equivalents are *habits, fixations,* or *addictions*—the things in our lives that really control us. Thus the starting point is the view that we are spiritually weak and need to develop our spiritual capacity. This idea contrasts markedly with some of our self-assured contemporary views, which bypass the spiritual struggle and assume that by becoming believers we automatically develop spiritual competence. The ancient church, by contrast, understood that we begin as spiritual apprentices, that advancement requires work on our part (with specific spiritual direction), and that because body and soul are so inextricably linked, the work begins with the body.

In the teaching on humility, much of the emphasis is on the most severe vice that hinders spiritual growth—namely, pride, or pretensions to superiority. We are all aware of the saying "Pride goeth before the fall" (Prov. 16:18), and there is a solid foundation for it: pride blinds one to the truth. In fact, St. Dorotheos describes two types of pride: pride of self and pride of this world. Pride of self is the condition wherein we place great value on ourselves and consider others worth little or nothing. Pride of this world is the condition wherein we consider ourselves above others because we are richer or more handsome or have more possessions (in other words, we suffer from vanity).

Of great practical interest for us in modern times, and especially in the marketplace, is the thesis that St. Dorotheos puts forward: humility, as a virtue, stands between the two extremes of the vices: "Therefore, we say that virtue stands in the middle; and so courage stands in the middle between cowardice and fool-hardiness; humility in the middle between arrogance and obsequiousness. Modesty is a mean between bashfulness and boldness and so on with the other virtues" (Dorotheos of Gaza, 1977, p. 166). In other words, humility is the divine middle ground that can keep help us attain balance between self-loathing and self-centeredness. It is clear that a leader (or a follower, for that matter) who exhibits self-loathing and self-centeredness either has no faith or possesses a very shallow one.

The practical tension that leaders and all people in authority must deal with is the one between ability and pride. Being able—having the requisite skills, gifts, and talents—should be the basis of one's being placed in a position of authority and influence. Obvious though this idea may seem, the Peter Principle (Peter and Hull, 1969), whereby people rise to the level where they become incompetent, demonstrates that ability is not always the basis of advancement into a position of leadership and authority. Because advancement often leads to pride, however, shouldn't humility be a qualification as important as ability? It is interesting that Jesus' teaching about the need for being "humble like a child" is linked directly with a specific consequence: that anyone causing those more vulnerable to stumble would be better off dead (Matt. 18:6). If we put people who lack humility into positions of authority, who is responsible? Without humility, not only may people become prideful and abusive of others, but those who have put them into those positions will have done so at the peril of their own souls.

An analogous practical tension is felt at the other end of the humility continuum, where self-loathing is found. Humility is usually dismissed as a virtue that is undesirable in the marketplace because being humble is understood as being mealymouthed and soft or, worse yet, not having a positive self-image. In our society, image, and especially self-image, is everything. We rarely worry about being humble in the biblical sense of the word; rather, we emphasize the need for self-esteem, assertiveness, and a strong, positive self-image. The problem is simply that this emphasis on self-esteem is frequently not tempered with humility, and the outcome is often the types of pride that St. Dorotheos has described: self-centeredness and vanity.

Our challenge is to achieve a balance between the two extremes of self-centeredness and self-loathing. Of course a healthy and positive self-image is desirable; in fact, it is good. But where does it come from: from being the most powerful person around, or from being created in the image of God? What kinds of things make us feel good about ourselves: our accomplishments and possessions, or the cultivation of the virtues and progress in the spiritual life? We live in an age that is still busy casting off the draconian self-loathing of our puritanical ancestors, and too many people are still riddled with guilt and a poor self-image. More often than not, however, this is the result of hearing only that they can do nothing good apart from God, not that God loves them and that they are essentially good. Thus begins the fruitless cycle of pursuing fulfillment and personal satisfaction wherever they can be found.

When it comes to the workplace and the role of leadership in it, few people manifest the virtue of humility. In my life I count fewer than five people in all who have manifested humility, and only one of them was a businessperson. Most of us would agree that more humility in the marketplace in general, and in leadership in particular, would be a good thing. Its virtual absence from the business lexicon is a commentary on what informs our values.

Why are these understandings of humility, of vices and virtues, passions and self-discipline, so foreign to us? Because, like the Prodigal Son, we have forgotten our true home and gone wandering off to a foreign land, where we have squandered our inheritance. We are so influenced and shaped by our culture and its values that we have largely lost our understanding that the true basis of our personal worth is our having been created in the image of God. We have forgotten that our true home is the Kingdom of God, and we have settled merely for this world. We have forsaken the path of spiritual discipline and fulfillment, and we have settled merely for those values and means of personal fulfillment that our society proffers.

Is it any wonder that humility is misunderstood and therefore rejected? That may be the fact of the matter, but rejecting humility is not an option. The word *humility* comes from the Latin *humus:* soil or earth. Therefore, a humble, down-to-earth person has his or her feet on the ground. A humble person is centered, balanced, integrated, whole, and healthy—physically, emotionally, and spiritually. Humility is the soil out of which grow faith, hope, love, and all the other positive qualities of the spirit that are congruent with high-quality leadership.

## Conclusion

We have been considering vision and humility as correlates of faith. Clearly, faith is the central element. But we must begin to see humility as critical to our spiritual life and to faithful leadership and followership. We must recognize and affirm the divine image in every person, whether we are leading or following. Those in positions of leadership especially must heed the words of Abba Motius: "For this is humility, to see yourself to be the same as the rest" (Ward, 1975, p. 148). Distinctions in our organizations have to be based on actual abilities and skills, not on prideful beliefs about self-worth. Our motivation to be in positions of leadership should flow from our desire to serve as Christ served, not from the desire for power and control. Personal and organizational vision enables us to achieve a local incarnation of the vision of the Kingdom of God. Our desire to serve, motivated by love, is what enables us to implement and achieve that vision, and humility, the mother of virtues, is what keeps us centered so that we can do it all for God, and for all those created in God's image.

REFERENCES

Belasco, J. A. *Teaching the Elephant to Dance.* New York: Plume, 1990.

Dorotheos of Gaza. *Discourses and Sayings* (trans. E. P. Wheeler). Kalamazoo, Mich.: Cistercian Publications, 1977.

Fowler, J. A. *Stages of Faith.* San Francisco: Harper San Francisco, 1976.

Hopko, T. *Lenten Spring.* Crestwood, N.Y.: St. Vladimir's Seminary Press, 1988.

McKibben, M. T. *Orthodox Christian Meetings.* Columbus, Ohio: St. Ignatius of Antioch Press, 1990.

Palmer, G.E.H., Sherrard, P., and Ware, K. (eds.). *The Philokalia*. Vol. 1. London, 1979.

Peter, L. J., and Hull, R. *The Peter Principle*. New York: Morrow, 1969.

Ward, B. *The Sayings of the Desert Fathers*. Kalamazoo, Mich.: Cistercian Publications, 1975.

Williams, B. D., and McKibben, M. T. *Oriented Leadership*. Wayne, N.J.: Orthodox Christian Publication Center, 1994.

## ADDITIONAL READINGS

Chrysostom, J. *On Wealth and Poverty*. Crestwood, N.Y.: St. Vladimir's Seminary Press, 1984.

Climacus, J. *The Ladder of Divine Ascent* (trans. C. Luibheid and N. Russell). New York: Paulist Press, 1982.

Sheehan, G. *Running and Being: The Total Experience*. New York: Warner Books, 1978.

Tikhon of Zadonsk. *Journey to Heaven*. Jordanville, N.Y.: Holy Trinity Monastery, 1991.

Yannaras, C. *Elements of Faith*. Edinburgh, Scotland: T & T Clark, 1991.

## PART TWO

# KEY PRACTICES OF FAITH-BASED LEADERSHIP

6

# FINDING WISDOM AND PURPOSE
# IN CHAOTIC TIMES

*Isabel O. Lopez*

Isabel O. Lopez heads Lopez Leadership Services in Denver, Colorado, where she approaches leadership development with innovative methods. A former telecommunications executive, she writes on personal development and servant leadership.

_____o_____

MY AUNT *was dying. My grandmother, who no longer ventured out of the small New Mexico town where she lived, traveled with me to a city two hours away to see her. I was a young mother at the time, with little experience of losing someone I loved. At times like these, your whole world contracts; everything in the world is happening just in one time, one room, one place.*

*My aunt's daughter, my eldest cousin, was taking care of her mother's affairs. She would be taking her mother, my aunt, to California, where she would die and be buried.*

*The sun was shining. There was a slight chill in the air. My cousin was determining which of my aunt's effects she would keep—packing some, discarding others, and selling several items. It all seemed frantic. I had expected that at a time like this I would feel different, but I could not make sense of my feelings.*

*My grandmother, as was her way, had brought her lunch. She went to the table and sat down to eat. At that moment my cousin entered the room. She said, "You have to move away from the table. Someone is*

79

*coming to see if they would like to buy it." My grandmother serenely
moved to the rocking chair, spread her lunch out on her lap, and ate. No
one ever came to see the table. I was very angry—how could my grandmother have been shown such disrespect?—but I said nothing.*

That angry memory remained with me for years. Still, my anger was
not a clean one. It was confusing. It was partly about how my aunt
was being treated, partly about the overall frantic nature of the situation,
and partly about my own feelings of loss. At that time, though, I could
not have articulated any of these feelings.

Today I have a different memory, preserved for me by the fire of anger.
Today I remember my grandmother's utter serenity, even as she knew that
she would not see her eldest daughter again. Today I know that she had
found the place where passion and serenity are joined. Meeting the world
with wisdom, with laughter, and utterly secure in her center: that was my
grandmother. What an example for me on that day, on this day, and for
many days to come.

And what an example for working in today's chaotic world! Today
we are faced with situations over which we have no control, situations
that require the highest degree of elegance despite how others may
respond. Many of those writing on leadership today—Farson (1996),
Peters (1987), Wheatley (1992)—speak to this area, to making friends
with chaos; Wheatley, for example, points us to the acceptance of chaos
as an essential process by which natural systems, including organizations,
renew and revitalize themselves.

Chaos is a process that is entered into willingly when one decides
to make a career change; uncertainty and questions abound. Others may
make career changes unwillingly, because of downsizing; they also enter
into a time of uncertainty. In both cases, those who embrace the potential
for renewal are the ones who thrive. In the meantime, organizations are
going through their own process of chaos. Much healing is required in
order for an organization to grieve and be revitalized. My guiding question is, How can we be more like my grandmother in these times?

Given the difference between my world and the one in which my grandmother lived, I have tried, for my own understanding, to create an intellectual map of her life:

Life experiences ⟶ Knowing self ⟶

Faith ⟶ Wisdom ⟶

Purpose ⟶ Loving others ⟶

Serving others ⟶ Clarity in chaos ⟶ Passion and serenity

Life experiences provide opportunities for learning, and the knowing of self is the basic lesson that we learn. Faith allows us to honor the unknowable, and wisdom emerges both from knowing ourselves and from accepting the unknown. We then develop our life purpose, and our purpose leads us to truly loving others. Love leads to serving others, and from this base we then develop clarity in chaos, emerging as people who live life at the intersection of passion and serenity. This map, like any other kind of intellectual construct, falls far short of the truth of the woman about whom I am writing, for surely my grandmother had received "the fruit of the Spirit [which] is love, joy, peace, patience, kindness, generosity, faithfulness, gentleness, and self-control" (Gal. 5:22–23).

## Knowing Self

I am convinced that we must find our own center, and that once we have found it all the chaos becomes irrelevant. "To find our own center"—so easy to write, and so difficult to do. I also know that we can easily forget the truth of our center and fail to be true to it when we are tested. There is a Native American tradition based on the following saying: "Where I stand is the center of the universe." I think this saying is about knowing yourself . . . first.

*When I left my corporate life to try something different, a vice president came to me and asked, "Did you see the film* Tender Mercies, *starring Robert Duvall? Do you remember when the old man came up to him and asked, 'Didn't you use to be . . . ?' Robert Duvall said, 'That is who I am.' The old man then said, 'No, you're not.'" In the film, Robert Duvall was no longer the famous singer he had once been.*

*This vice president kept in touch with me. Several years later he said to me, "I want you to know that you are still you."*

I think he had been trying to warn me: he had seen too many people have no identity beyond the jobs they held.

The path to wisdom is not an easy one. Its difficulty lies in facing oneself. An old Chinese saying points the way: "He [she] who feels punctured must have once been a balloon." Becoming less of a "balloon" requires us to gain perspective on and understanding of what is truly important. It requires us to find our center and work from that place. In our life and work, the small can take on its own importance and seem large indeed. Our feelings of being punctured can be a gift to use in discerning what is important.

## Faith

*We never ate black beans when I was growing up. I learned from my Cuban mother-in-law to eat them, as well as how to cook them.*

*One year I took a package of black beans to my grandmother. I told her how to cook them: Clean the beans by picking out any broken ones, small rocks, and dirt. Wash. Cover with water. Cook until tender. Season with garlic, onion, olive oil, roasted green pepper, and salt.*

*My grandmother thanked me for the gift. When I returned later that year, in the fall, she had a gift for me: she had planted the black beans that I gave to her, and on this day she returned their harvest to me. To this day I do not know if she ever cooked any of them.*

My grandmother was a planter more than a formal gardener. She planted wildly and exuberantly, replacing her lawn with flowers, growing a pineapple in an arid land. Both planting and gardening are acts of faith. My grandmother knew what she could do: prepare the soil, seed, water, weed. Faith was her belief that the plants would grow.

As we uncover more and more of who we are at the center, we stretch into the area of faith. Faith is the place where we have confidence in what we do not fully know with our minds—that is, in the ineffable. For my grandmother that place, at the highest level, was God. Perhaps her life was an expression of the Dutch saying "Who does not keep faith with God will not keep it with man."

## Wisdom

If one were to create an equation for wisdom, it might be written thus:

$$KS + F = W$$

Knowing of self (*KS*) plus faith (*F*) equals wisdom (*W*).

The knowing of self of which I speak is the knowing of the heart. It is a different knowing than the knowing of the mind. The sheer power of our minds can oftentimes lead us astray. In the knowing of self, which is an ongoing quest, we find a sturdy place on which to stand. From the sturdiness of this place, the mystery of God seems less threatening, even though it always remains mysterious. Faith is that ineffable mystery. Wisdom marries the seemingly contradictory words *sturdiness* and *mystery*. From between these two anchors emerges understanding.

The word *sturdiness* reminds me of the earth. It reminds me of the firmness of a foundation. It reminds me of safety. The word *mystery* calls to mind images of clouds, some soft and fluffy, some long and narrow, some dark and powerful. In looking at the clouds, one can imagine something larger, and yet one can also imagine familiar images reflected in their shapes. When I fly, I remind myself to look at the clouds. They look as if I could walk on them, though I know this is impossible. Yet between the earth and the clouds there is much that we understand. In this is our wisdom.

## Finding Purpose

*We lived next door to my grandmother in her small New Mexico town. Normally for our Christmas we baked biscochitos and empanadas, our traditional sweets. One year, inspired by the holiday issue of McCall's magazine, I asked her if we could bake ten new types of cookies for our holiday.*

*My grandmother agreed, and we set out to bake the new delights. Snickerdoodles—I could almost taste them, although I had no idea what they were like. We took out the tins in which my grandmother kept her baking ingredients. We took out the bowls, the spoons, the measuring cups, and the cookie sheets. We read the recipes, we measured, we mixed, we formed, we dropped, we baked.*

*All day long, one of my younger brothers kept trying to sneak a cookie, but of course I refused to let him have one. These were for Christmas, not for him. Nevertheless, he persisted. Late in the afternoon, he succeeded in stealing a handful of cookies and ran away. Although I tried, I could not catch him; by now I was tired from a day of nonstop baking.*

*My brother quickly reappeared, a look of great dismay on his face. We had made every batch of our cookies with salt.*

For those of you who have never done such a thing, snickerdoodles made with salt are not only inedible but also hard as rocks. We couldn't put holes in them from which to suspend a wire or a string, and so we couldn't even hang them on the Christmas tree. My grandmother's first reaction was to laugh. As we began to throw the cookies away, she said to me in Spanish, "Had he been allowed to have a cookie earlier, we might have discovered our error more quickly"—a gentle lesson in what was important. We ended up with no cookies that year.

This story is a touchstone for me. It reminds me, in my work as a consultant, to be intentional about my purpose. In baking those cookies, I forgot where I was going even as I stayed busy—busy mixing, cutting, shaping, baking, transferring, cooling, and especially keeping my brother away. Busyness can blind us to what is important; wisdom can help us keep our purpose in sight. When we lose our perspective, we may try to exert control over what is less important.

The uncovering of purpose is not a small undertaking. Our purpose is often hidden by our activity, our human needs, our fears, the demands on our time, our lack of reflection, and our desire to avoid examining our lives and beliefs. Our minds guide our activity, but using only our minds can lead us into self-absorption and justification of wrong decisions and choices. Only when our minds are guided by our hearts and spirits do we question the rightness of our activities.

Activity can fool us, just as it fooled me in the baking of the cookies. Had I been wise enough to connect my activities to my purpose, I might have been helped in that situation. This lesson was one I also appreciated in my life as a corporate executive, where I sought to be clear about the focus of our activities and to make sure that we were all pointed in the same direction. More than anything else, a focus on purpose allows for reduction of conflict, as well as for laughter in the midst of activity, because those are the outcomes of allowing room for others to participate in our purpose.

Our individual human needs can also stand in the way of our uncovering our purpose. We may trade our purpose away in exchange for others' approval, for the status that comes with a particular position, or for the power that comes with wealth. This is not to say that approval, position, or wealth are wrong, but only that, unless we act with intention, we may gain approval, position, and wealth only at the expense of meaning. For example, at a conference I recently attended, a speaker reminded me of the path to wisdom. He spoke of having everything—titles, positions, companies, wealth—and yet he knew something was missing. He began to search, and he found the purpose of his life: serving others. He glowed as he spoke. Paul's letter to the Philippians points in the same direction: "Let each of you look not to your own interests but to the interests of others. Let the same mind be in you that was in Christ Jesus" (Phil. 2:4–5).

The demands on our time can also stand in the way of our uncovering our purpose. When we are exhausted, it is difficult for us to consider our purpose. Paradoxically, however, when our lives have a deep meaning, our time and our emotional energy seem to multiply. When we are clear about our purpose, it is easier for us to say no when we must, to respond authentically, and to remain true to ourselves. In an odd way, clarity of purpose protects us from the energy-draining minor issues of life. The important things emerge more clearly, and their emergence allows us to use our time more wisely. We gain perspective.

Sometimes fear can become an obstacle, working on us in strange ways. From my corporate days I remember how often managers would insist on "dry run" presentations, to make sure that they would not be embarrassed, and how often strategies were developed around personalities rather than around issues. Both phenomena are reflective of fear.

I tend to think of fear as having two faces: one alerts us and warns us, and the other is a trickster. The trickster face of fear makes us focus on the negative. It both heightens and adds inappropriately to our fears.

*In a class I was taking on the sociology of work, we were discussing the work that was particularly important to us. People offered examples of creating new systems, implementing new processes, and the like. Then a woman spoke. She was an emergency room nurse, and her story was about saving someone's life.*

*Once I was asked to give a presentation at a university campus forty-five minutes from my home. A university campus can be an intimidating place, and it is easy to get lost. I prefer to meet the day in a gentle manner, and so I decided to spend the night in the city where I would be speaking.*

*The evening before, I explored the campus. I found the parking area and the building where we would be meeting. I was now ready to meet the day unhurriedly.*

*In the morning, I put on my makeup (lipstick, and dots of lipstick that I rub into my cheeks for blush) and had my breakfast. I made my way to the campus and gave my presentation. At the end, I was asked the following question: "I'm curious about the red dots on your cheeks. Are they something ethnic?"*

*I had forgotten to rub the color into my cheeks. I laughed and explained my makeup regimen, but I was also glad the session was not being videotaped.*

Some events involve life-or-death situations; most do not. If we can discern the two faces of fear, we may be able to avoid elevating ordinary work-related stress or ordinary embarrassment to the level of true importance.

To use wisdom in a chaotic environment, we must become genuinely reflective. We may be afraid that people will think we are not busy enough if we are reflecting, and yet only through reflection do we find our purpose and the core of who we are. Reflection enables us to become our own teachers, and we never finish—never finish taking our own class, reading our own book, finding our own heart, and liberating our own spirit. Reflection forces us to face our own lives and beliefs. In less chaotic times, we can live others' lives and wear others' beliefs, and chances are that we will not be discovered. But in times of chaos, secondhand lives and beliefs will not serve us well. In times of chaos, our lives and beliefs must be true.

I often find people trying new techniques in their workplaces—techniques for improving productivity, lifting morale, or communicating more effectively. These techniques do not take root in chaotic times, because they have no basis in belief. As we experiment with dispersing the decision-making function, for example, we sometimes want people to think that they are involved rather than actually being involved, and so we look for another technique, another best-seller to manage by, and then we wonder why nothing works. Perhaps the gift of reflection is that we, too, as my grandmother did, can find the place that is true for us, the place where passion and serenity meet, both personally and professionally. Indeed, all the most passionate people I have known also had the strongest sense of purpose. Their passion and purposes may have been in different areas, but I have been struck by the similarities: the twinkle in their eyes, the power of their beliefs, their easy laughter, the perspective they seemed to possess. Their passion has not been destructive or addictive but liberating. For me, my grandmother offered the first example of a sense of purpose and its attendant passion; maybe a strong sense of purpose is the key to our being centered in what is true for us, and perhaps that is what allows us to create meaning in our lives.

## Loving Others

When we find our purpose, we find the direction for our lives. If we get this far, we begin to understand love.

There is a difficulty with the word *love* in the English language. It is used to describe many kinds of emotion. Some of these uses of the word *love* seem inauthentic, some embarrassing. The love I speak of is the feeling that we are not alone. This feeling fills our hearts. We see it, we feel it, we are overwhelmed by it, and we are warmed by it. We are called to this kind of love. How often we fall short of the love described in 1 Corinthians 13; how often we forget Jesus' commandment to love one another (John 13:34–35).

*I recently attended a church retreat at a rustic camp in the Colorado mountains with the members of two congregations. The scenery was stunning, a faraway lightning storm was rumbling, the air was fresh, the sun was warm. As we gathered for dinner, I noticed an elderly man being pulled along by a younger man who had an odd gait. I watched them making their way to dinner and was overcome with the thought that they were angels. This thought became stronger as the weekend progressed.*

*The old man was blind; the young man, his son, was mentally ill. During the first evening's hymn sing, I saw the older man wipe a tear from his eye when the group sang the familiar hymn "How Great Thou Art." All weekend the young man dragged his father along the unfamiliar terrain, a little too rapidly perhaps. In the city, people might have taken them for homeless men. There might have been feelings of distaste, or (one hopes) of compassion. Here, they elicited feelings of love.*

I'm sure there are many angels in our lives. The love they both radiate and elicit brings out the very best in us—at home, at work, at play. Just notice those who are angels, and you need do nothing; you can just ride the wave of love. Perhaps our being enveloped in this love also radiates out to others, who can then ride the waves of our love.

## Serving Others

Love first—then serve. It is possible to serve first and then love, but a different dynamic is then created. When we serve first, we may be motivated, consciously or unconsciously, by approval, guilt, social ambition, or recognition. We serve for a reward of some kind. We may even bring harm to someone if he or she is ungrateful for our service. Serving first and loving later does have its benefits, however: we can learn more about ourselves and about areas that may be of true importance to us; or, if others love us as we serve them, we may learn to love ourselves, and then we may learn love.

But when we love first, serving others simply means serving others—nothing more, nothing less. Yet there is a reward. It is the reward of the Spirit: "Give and it will be given to you. A good measure, pressed down, shaken together, running over, will be put into your lap; for the measure you give will be the measure you get back" (Luke 6:38).

## Clarity in Chaos

Chaos is a natural phenomenon. We see plants sprout, grow, bloom, and die. Each cycle is succeeded by a new one. In the natural world, this is all that chaos is—new cycles, new rhythms.

As we grow to know ourselves better, we can become aware of our own new cycles and rhythms. Our own center remains strong, and we are less disturbed by changes taking place. Sometimes we can even anticipate the next cycle and meet it with a minimum of discomfort. As Wheatley and Kellner-Rogers say (1996, pp. 89–90), "Life moves, exploring and extending its space of possibilities. In constant motion, all creation discovers original newness. These motions of life have direction. Life moves toward wholeness. It seeks coherence. This is a journey of paradox that pursues a clear direction." Surely they are speaking, poetically, of clarity in chaos.

*A Methodist bishop from South America, in the United States as a visiting seminary professor, had been hospitalized with cancer. The bishop's wife was about to arrive from South America, and I was asked to go to the hospital and translate for her.*

*When I got to the hospital, she had already arrived and had been taken to store her luggage. The bishop smiled when he saw me. We introduced ourselves, and he asked me if I would take a walk down the hall with him. We arranged the devices to which he was connected and began to walk.*

*"My Lord is full of surprises," the bishop said. "I had planned to go home and retire by the sea. But as a minister, one must be ready always for two things: to die, and to give a sermon with no prior warning." And he laughed.*

The bishop knew about clarity in chaos. I grew to love both him and his wife.

## Passion and Serenity

This is the place where my grandmother lived, at the intersection of passion and serenity. She seemed not to be bothered by any of the situations that bothered me, and bothered me a lot. At one time, wishing to be as accepting as my grandmother was, I imagined that she had been born that way. Now I think she got to that place of passion and serenity as a result of her life experiences.

She was born and lived her early life in a tiny hamlet. She had ten children and lost four of them. One daughter died of an illness as a young adult, another died of unknown causes, and a son died when he went to war. Then her eldest daughter died. She was widowed in her early forties. I am sure there were other trials, although these seem like more than enough for anyone.

And yet Luisa Ortiz, my grandmother, met each day with a prayer and a smile. She sang her way through the day. She marveled at all that we brought her—a pretty rock, a salt shaker, an empty milk carton with a growing seedling, a loaf of bread, a horned toad. The item did not matter; the perfect acceptance of the gift did.

Some may say that I see my grandmother with less than objective eyes. Perhaps this is true. Objectivity is too cold a way to see a woman who gave me an understanding of how life is to be lived, too cold a way to see a woman who loved me with great gentleness, too cold a way to see a woman who, when I was a child complaining about my eldest cousin's behavior, told me, "She lost her father when she was very young. *Pero tú, no hay otro hombre como tu papá*"—but you, there is no other man like your father.

And so I see my grandmother with my heart. I am but one of her many grandchildren. Others may have different specific memories and may use their memories in different ways. I know their love for her to be true, like her love for each of us.

She had requested Psalm 4:8 for her headstone: "I will both lie down and sleep in peace; for you alone, O Lord, make me lie down in safety." She was of those who "still yield fruit in old age; . . . [who are] full of sap and very green" (Ps. 92:14).

## Building Bridges

When I think about my grandmother, I think first about love and then about wisdom. To use all that I have learned from her, I had to create my own bridges. These bridges connect her world to mine. One bridge connects my history—rural, Hispanic, a member of an extended family—to my life as an urban wife and mother. Another bridge connects these personal historical features to my identity as a corporate executive. Today the bridge extends to my life as an entrepreneur and to my continuing spiritual development. The story about the Christmas cookies is an example of how these bridges work: something I learned at home served me well as I grew into an adult and into a professional life. The things I learned about—uncovering meaning, developing purpose, and pointing toward the place where passion and serenity meet—are guiding principles that extend to the world of work and to the living of each day.

This is not to say that there have not been many failures along the way, but only that it has been necessary for me to take the wholeness of who I am into my work with others. The understanding of who we are, at deeper and deeper levels, is our real work. Then and only then can we become real and therefore authentic with others. Being real, being authentic, being whole, is on the other side of the bridge.

I find myself wondering what bridge is missing when a corporate executive is ruthless with her work group and yet loves to grow herbs. I wonder what bridge is missing for the person who sees other people as the enemy and yet has the deepest love and compassion for animals. I wonder what bridge is missing for the person who is abusive at home and yet is a pillar of the community. I wonder what bridge is missing for the executive who sees downsizing purely as a profit-making strategy and misses its effect on people and on the organization. I wonder what bridge is missing for the work group that withholds work information and yet shares all the gossip. It may be that I was given a head start on the building of such bridges—after all, I knew my grandmother. In any case, the development of wisdom requires us to create bridges. Sometimes questions help in this process:

Why does this situation bother me?

What do I know about myself in these circumstances?

Am I seeing the larger picture?

What is it in my life or history that leads me to this response?

Is my decision wise?

Have I taken the time to reflect?

Am I at peace?

Each of these questions leads to others, which in turn help in the creation of a bridge. With these bridges in place, employees can be treated as gently as herbs, people can be treated with love and compassion, and families can be seen as deserving the same respect and care as those in our public lives.

I am not suggesting that this is easy work—indeed, sometimes it is very difficult—but only that it is intentional work. A bridge collapses and must be rebuilt, or maybe the wrong bridge was built to begin with and we have to start over, or we may even fall off a bridge. But when we are standing on a bridge, we have a larger view. We can see both where we came from and where we are going. This bridge-building work is ours and ours alone. To judge where others are in their bridge-building process is not ours to do; we have enough bridge-building work of our own. In building bridges, we begin the journey to wholeness.

During this time we are testing, and we are being tested. With each failure we learn. Sometimes the lessons come fast and heavy, and everything can seem to be in chaos. Our initial reaction may be to try to regain control—even a control that we never had. At work, for example, we may issue a flurry of memos, inaugurate new policies, convene innumerable strategy sessions. With friends, our talk may focus on the troubles we've seen. At home we may collapse in a state of near-catatonia in front of the television, or we may enter upon a frenzy of activity.

But it really is easier to know what we actually control, and I now know that, in reality, I control very little; mostly it is only myself that I control. Even today, though, I insist on maintaining a belief that I exercise complete control over where my furniture is placed. This belief may be shattered at some point. If that time ever comes, I hope I can meet this shattering with bemusement rather than terror, anger, or tears.

For me, this writing has been an act of bridge building. How, I asked myself, could I possibly explain my grandmother and the relevance of her teaching to the world of today? She did not even like to answer the telephone. How could I possibly explain my own understandings? And isn't it somewhat arrogant, after all, to think that my understandings are any greater or more important than those of many others? The power that came from my sharing this story was the bridge I needed in order to cross over to this writing. Maybe by sharing this story, I have made a small contribution to healing—my own and perhaps yours as well—so that the bridge, in some way, also connects us.

The work required of us is work of the Spirit. It is the work of healing and being healed. When we speak of creating balance in our lives, perhaps that balance is created only when the largest part of our lives is the performance of this spiritual work and every other part is smaller. This perspective, generally speaking, is a nonlinear one. In a linear perspective, the elements of a life—work, family, and all the other pieces—are measured according to simple chronology. But even with a linear perspective, in most cases, we are found wanting; no wonder, then, that we resist learning! It seems so large, so impossible. If we can remain hopeful, however, the work is worthwhile. In my experience, we really don't have a choice anyway: the work of the Spirit gently, and sometimes not so gently, demands that we engage in it, and so we learn to build our bridges.

## Conclusion

Once we are on the other side, even though there are always new bridges to build and cross, things become a little more peaceful. Our self-absorption is minimized—everything is not all about *us*, not everything is directed at *us*. Situations are less personal. Once we understand this, chaos simply becomes a sign of new life emerging, of new songs to be learned. The gift in this lesson is the gift of clarity, which lets us focus on the important things.

*When my son was diagnosed as being mentally ill, I wept. How was it possible for one person to have so many tears?*

*In time I understood him to be, like my grandmother, a spirit teacher. She taught me through example; my son teaches me through experience.*

*Today great joys come from small things: his smile, the red rose bloom-ing, my own grandchildren's laughter, my daughter's silliness, the gift of another day. It seems so clear—the joy of this moment.*

REFERENCES

Farson, R. *Management of the Absurd: Paradoxes in Leadership.* New York: Simon & Schuster, 1996.
Peters, T. *Thriving on Chaos: Handbook for a Management Revolution.* New York: Knopf, 1987.
Wheatley, M. *Leadership and the New Science: Learning About Organization from an Orderly Universe.* San Francisco: Berrett-Koehler, 1992.
Wheatley, M., and Kellner-Rogers, M. *A Simpler Way.* San Francisco: Berrett-Koehler, 1996.


ADDITIONAL READINGS

Costa, D. *Working Wisdom: The Ultimate Value in the New Economy.* Toronto: Stoddart, 1995.
Sofield, L., and Kuhn, D. H. *The Collaborative Leader: Listening to the Wisdom of God's People.* Notre Dame, Ind.: Ave Maria Press, 1995.

7

# SHARING POWER AS
# AN EXPRESSION OF FAITH

*Janet O. Hagberg*

Janet O. Hagberg is codirector of the Silent Witness National Initiative, which has as its goal the elimination of domestic violence–related murders by the year 2010. She is a public speaker and the author or coauthor of five books, including *The Critical Journey: Stages in the Life of Faith* (with Robert A. Guelich), *The Inventurers: Excursions in Life and Career Renewal* (with Richard Leider), and *Real Power: Stages of Personal Power in Organizations*.

o

I WANT TO TELL YOU about an experience with faith and power that transformed the way I think about power and leadership. It is a personal story, and I hope that if I tell it from my heart, it will resonate with your journey as well, whether your journey includes your family, your neighborhood, your church, or your country.

## Putting Passion to Work

By 1997, I had invested seven years of my life in a project whose goal was healing this country of domestic violence. It all began for me in the summer of 1990, when five women were murdered in a three-week period in my city, in acts of domestic violence. One had been stabbed sixteen times in the chest and stomach. Another was killed on a busy sidewalk on her way to work, a few hours after she had obtained a protection order from a judge. A third was shot by her physician husband while she was holding the hand of her ten-year-old son.

Since 1994, Jane Zeller and I had been codirectors of the Silent Witness National Initiative. We had worked almost nonstop, recruiting thousands of people in a collaborative grassroots effort to orchestrate several events in Washington, D.C., events that included a conference and the March to End the Silence. We hoped to enlist support in all fifty states to construct and then transport 1,500 red, life-size wooden figures representing all the women who had been murdered in one year in our country in acts of domestic violence. We wanted to honor the women's lives and call for a healing of domestic violence. We called these figures Silent Witnesses.

For us, this work of healing was not a job; it was a calling. Our faith was intimately connected with this initiative, and we believed we were helping to bring hope and light to the issue as God had directed us. We were in contact with individuals, in more than thirty organizations across the country, who were working diligently on this effort. Hundreds of people were praying for our initiative, and many angels were going ahead of us. It was intense and exciting.

Each state's effort involved a different configuration of people and organizations, from the Junior League and the National Council of Jewish Women to coalitions on domestic violence, prison staffs, YWCAs, nursing groups, and men's groups. Networking was the sole means of recruitment, and we were excited about how participants in many states were reaching out and helping people in other states. It was heartwarming to see so much good will and creativity at work.

## Learning to Share Power

After several states had joined our initiative, disagreements arose about notifying the families of the victims that we were making figures of their loved ones. People in some states wanted to notify the families in one way, and others wanted to do it in just the opposite way. Instead of choosing one way ourselves that everyone else would have to follow, we decided to let each state decide for itself. For most states, this was an energizing decision.

Then we stumbled onto the best way for us to work with this national network: halfway into the recruitment effort, we started having steering committee meetings around the country, for anyone who wanted to attend. The purpose of the meetings was to involve more people in the planning and to have our members meet and network with each other.

(This process became the catalyst for the formation of a strong core of leaders, a core that emerged over time to bring us to Washington.) The themes of these meetings were hope, healing, and mutual help.

The outcomes were amazing. At two of the meetings, states that had finished making their figures volunteered to give figures to other states, to help them get going. The energy and goodwill that emerged were heart-warming. A few women said they had never been in meetings in which people were so willing to help each other. We were increasingly convinced that sharing decisions and resources was an energizing experience for our participants.

We had just two guidelines: the life-size figures representing murdered women needed to be similar in pattern, color, and size across the country, with each woman's story written on the chest plate of her representative figure; and each state had to make the commitment to bring the figures to Washington for the March to End the Silence, but how each state worked, the people who were recruited, and the means that were used to get the work done was totally up to the particular state.

In Arizona, women in their seventies and eighties bought saws and made the figures. In New Hampshire, two sisters worked together to cut out the figures; one of the sisters had been battered, and as she worked she had a realization: "My God, this could have been my sister cutting out *my* figure!" New York made 220 figures; Texas, 160. A high school home economics class and shop class made and painted the Nebraska figures.

In the first year, we recruited sixteen states and had more than 500 figures. By the end of two years, we had recruited twenty-eight states and had 800 figures. In three years, we had recruited forty-five states and had 1,350 figures.

Several months before the Washington march, a small group of powerful leaders in other domestic violence organizations planned a conference call with me. I assumed that this call would be a way for us to share information with them and get their endorsement for the Washington events. Instead, the call turned out to be a confrontation, and several of the leaders spelled out the issues on which they disagreed with us. The call ended on a sour note, and we were convinced that we would not get these leaders' support.

When they sent a follow-up letter, we learned that their grievances struck at the core of what we stood for: our goals, our process, and our methods of healing. Because they represented national organizations with state affiliates, all of whom might potentially frustrate our efforts, this confrontation affected me deeply. Here we were, working hard to recruit people in all the states, raise enough money to support several events, and carry the light of hope to the country. We thought we were living out our spiritual calling to bring healing and light to this dark subject. We had found several projects across the country that had already helped eliminate, reduce, or heal domestic violence, and we were eager to share their experiences with other states. We knew that healing was possible, but now our goals, our means, and our projects were being called into question.

Then we got a call from a friend in the movement, who told us that we needed to mend fences with these leaders. This information stunned us: before the phone confrontation, we hadn't had any reason to think that these leaders were even aware of our existence. But we didn't want to alienate anyone, and so we agreed to meet with two of the leaders in Washington a few weeks later, to see what we could do.

That meeting took place, and afterward both Jane and I thought it had been a good one, with each side listening to the other and airing its differences. We left thinking that we had a working relationship with these leaders, and we were relieved, even though we were still a little shaken by the need for this meeting in the first place.

As a result of listening at that meeting, however, we started to understand what was happening. Many people had been working in this field for twenty years, with no one listening to them or thanking them. They had been on the front lines, seeing the violence every day and saving women's lives. Money was tight, and burnout was high. Many were themselves survivors of domestic violence and were doing this work as an outcome of their own experience. And now that the Crime Bill had been passed, and publicity surrounding the murder of Nicole Brown Simpson had brought domestic violence to the country's attention, more money and more attention than ever before were being directed at this issue.

We had been thinking that everyone in the movement was moving toward the same goals, but we found out that this was not the case, and we learned that we were perceived as naive newcomers to the movement. We had not spent twenty years in the trenches, and we were bringing new, inexperienced people into the movement, in addition to projects that these leaders were skeptical of. For example, the money we were raising for the Silent Witness National Initiative was money that some thought should be going instead to shelters for battered women. And now, with so many states on board and a march planned, we were at the table with the other organizations, and we hadn't even realized it. Apparently, and suddenly, we were a force to be reckoned with.

I am not accustomed to public confrontations and strong opposition, and, frankly, I was intimidated and afraid. Moreover, I was already tired and frustrated, and I felt that I had enough work to do on the Washington events, and we still had to raise a lot of money in the six months we had left. The stress was more than I wanted, and I thought seriously about quitting. I was doing this out of passion, and I couldn't believe it was so difficult.

The next month, when a funder and friend turned sour on the initiative, I began to wonder if any of our plans were going to work out. My journal from those days illustrates my mood at the time: "I came the closest I ever have been to quitting this project last Thursday. I can't believe all that is closing in on us and I am pretty low. I wonder what it is for, what it is all about, and why I am doing this work at all." Within the next few days, we got a large and unexpected check from an individual donor. It was a sign that we had not been forgotten, a sign of life and hope and angels out there remembering and supporting us.

I needed hope then, lots of it. And, thank God, Jane and I had each other. In the darkest moments, we still could always find one little thing to laugh about. Our support for each other got us through many of the toughest times. Another thing that helped me during those days was to put the conflict into a larger perspective by reflecting on the dynamics of power that I thought were at work.

## Stages of Personal Power

To see if I could gain any insight, I went back to my own book, *Real Power* (Hagberg, 1994). That book discusses six stages of power as they present themselves in individuals and in organizations. I attempted to think through the six stages and apply them to the current conflict.

### Stage 1: Powerlessness

This is the stage at which people feel trapped, angry, and unable to make things happen for themselves. They feel that things just keep piling up, and there is nothing they can do. They are, in a word, victims. They become dependent on others, and as a result they have low self-esteem. They are not actually trapped or helpless, but believing makes it so.

### Stage 2: Power by Association

At this stage, people are apprentices to power. They are learning from others and trying to figure out how to do things right so that they can function effectively in their lives. They need models, mentors, teachers, or coaches who can help them acquire knowledge, learn more about themselves, and gain the skills and confidence they need in order to grow.

## Stage 3: Power by Symbols or Achievement

At this stage, the dynamic stage, people feel that they have attained success. Stage 3 is represented by all the goals that most people strive for in order to feel successful and good about themselves and their lives. To achieve these goals, they work hard, meet challenges, become assertive, and are willing to act. They strive for as much control as possible in life and in work.

## Stage 4: Power by Reflection

When people move from stage 3 to stage 4, they move from external to internal power. They experience the crisis of integrity, which means being honest with themselves and finding out who they really are deep inside. They must let go of being in control. They must let their egos diminish. At this stage, people are exploring who they are, what they want, and why it all matters. Power is no longer finite; now it is infinite. The more they give away, the more there is to give. As they proceed through this stage, their sense of power emerges from the ability to touch others' lives by modeling integrity and sound judgment.

## Stage 5: Power by Purpose

This is the stage at which people appreciate their strengths and weaknesses and find out their simple and spiritual purpose in life. One's vision of life reaches beyond one's own realm, and energy shifts to empowering others instead of oneself. It may be hard to understand the motives of people at this stage, for they are really not self-serving; people at this stage see power as something that allows them to serve others.

## Stage 6: Power by Wisdom

This is the stage where people operate from a daily regimen of wisdom. They are simple yet very complex, personally powerful yet apparently powerless. They fear nothing, and as a result they can act on principles that require deep courage. They are on the fringe and easily misunderstood, and yet they are highly respected by others. They are calm and peaceful inside, even when they are active or stressed.

## Applying the Six Stages

In reflecting on these stages, I got insights into what might be happening to the National Initiative in terms of power. The leaders of the other organizations had toiled thanklessly for many long years on issues related to domestic violence—building shelters and working on legislation, education, and prevention. For years, I think, the movement operated at the early stages of power—stages 1 and 2—with little clout, little money, and little gratitude. Its activists were survivors, and sometimes they felt like victims themselves. For the most part, they felt powerless.

By the time Jane and I arrived on the scene, there was already significant legislation, and there was more money. Many of the veteran activists were suddenly thrust into the center of the action, at stage 3. With money came power. The women in the movement had moved very quickly from relative powerlessness to power by symbols or achievement.

Jane and I had emerged quickly, too, and were outsiders to the original movement, pulling new groups into an initiative whose goals and process were not in total agreement with the existing movement. And because we had not sought enough counsel from the national leaders, the perception was that we had not paid our dues. Because of our focus on a national march and conference, we had moved through the stages of power quickly, and we didn't realize that we, too, were operating at stage 3 and had become, in a word, competitive.

Once I realized this, at our meeting with the leaders in Washington, I became aware of a darkness within me that almost made me quit the initiative. This darkness was fear. It was much stronger than I realized at first, and it was persistent. It was more than just a glitch in the process, a block in the road. Some stronger dynamic, a spiritual and psychological dynamic, was involved—one that I had to deal with, or else I would miss the whole meaning of this work in my life. God was at the middle of this crossroads, and I realized that I was, in some way, in training.

In terms of power, Jane and I were faced with three options: we could submit to all the demands of the leaders and let the Silent Witness figures become just a nice art exhibit; we could compete with them on their own terms; or we could develop a new set of ground rules, calling for a new way to operate within the movement and, in the process, facing our fears. The first option would lead us back to stage 1 (powerlessness) or stage 2 (power by association). The second would keep us squarely at stage 3 (power by achievement). The third would move us into stage 4 (power by reflection).

I realized that we would have to decide, in the next few months, how to approach this crisis if it was not to destroy us. I had two important jobs to do. One was to share leadership of a national initiative and to plan for several events in Washington. The other, my real work—my faith work—was to face the darkness within in order to heal myself, and to face the darkness, looming all around us, in the movement against domestic violence.

## The Heart of the Issue

Let me put this inner work into perspective by going back again to 1990, when the Silent Witnesses were created. I was one of seven originators of the Silent Witness project. When the project began, we made figures for the twenty-six women who had been murdered in Minnesota that year, and we made one more figure that we called the uncounted woman, for all those women whose deaths had not been officially counted as domestic violence. We wrote each woman's story on her figure's chest plate so that it would be heard. Five months later, we took the Silent Witness exhibit to our state capitol.

On the morning of the day we were to march to the capitol, I awoke early with such a severe pain in my side that I couldn't move. My husband took me to the emergency room, and the trouble was narrowed down to one of two things: a gall bladder problem, or a muscle spasm. By eleven o'clock I was sufficiently recovered to get to the march on time, but I was weak and shaken. I was annoyed; I had wanted to be at the march early.

Five hundred women escorted the figures to the capitol. As we carried them up the steps and into the rotunda, we felt that we were carrying their stories, and as we set them up in the rotunda, hugging them in order to fit them to their stands, we felt we were giving them the love they deserved. They became real to us, their spirits touching ours. We came to know them as Carmen, Linda, Rita, Barbara, Kim.

A month later, speaking about domestic violence at a meeting, I felt a similar but less severe pain in my side. It was enough to suggest a connection between the pains and my work on domestic violence. But what was the connection?

With the help of friends, my massage therapist, a spiritual director, a psychotherapist, and lots of prayer, I figured out that this was my body's way of trying to protect me from danger—the danger of breaking one of my family's rules about speaking out on our family's issues. My father had been an alcoholic, and then he experienced a religious conversion, but he never addressed the problems that his alcoholism had been covering up, and so we lived with a religious dry drunk, verbally and emotionally abusive although not physically violent. My mom was loving but also afraid, and she felt powerless (this being the 1950s) to get help. I had never connected my family to my work, and now I realized that my work in the arena of domestic violence was very much a part of my own healing process. Then I had a dream that cemented my decision to do the work with the Silent Witnesses. I was locked inside a burning boxcar, going around in a figure eight, the symbol for infinity. On the outside of the boxcar was a plaque with my mother's name on it. I knew I had to do this healing work, for myself and my family but also for all the women whose lives had been lost.

It became my passion, my calling, not just a volunteer activity or a job. Over the next few years, I brought my work on domestic violence to my sessions in spiritual direction and supervision, and I also committed myself to half a day of prayer every week, to stay grounded and discern what my calling would ask of me. I gradually cut back on most of my other community activities and much of my paid employment, to devote more time to the Silent Witness National Initiative.

## Facing the Darkness

Now, several years later, here I was facing my core fear, the fear of being abused, this time not by my family but by my work in the movement. This time my calling felt bigger: I was being called not only to stand up to this but also to be part of the healing. Yet how, and with what courage? Where would I turn, and for what?

This was one of the most difficult moments in my career, and it was pivotal. I was making more than a strategic decision. My life was changing. I knew God would take me where I needed to be, and I asked God to give me the courage and strength to face the fear, to not back away from the darkness but find the light there. I quake a little even as I write this, because the fear was palpable. At times I was afraid to answer the phone, and I was anxious when I got the mail for fear of what it would contain. I was facing the threat that my seven years of work would be destroyed.

One of the most comforting things in the middle of this turmoil was that I received the gift of deep, comforting prayer experiences unlike any I had had before. Everyone experiences God differently. I gradually came to hear an inner voice that I believe is God's way of guiding me. In addition to speaking to me in that voice, God soothed my soul in deep and imaginative ways and gave me promises of angels and hope, asking me to be a light bearer in the world. God strengthened my courage and my willingness to be faithful and assured me that this was holy ground and sacred work. That helped me put it all in perspective and prepared me for what was to come.

I was led to two writers and a few strong memories, all of which fortified me for the months to come. I will share briefly what I learned from these sources, for they have become integral to the way in which I now see the world of power and leadership.

The first writer was Henri Nouwen, who wrote an article (Nouwen, 1995) in which he talks about the disciplines that keep us moving from dividing power to uniting power, from destructive power to healing power, and from paralyzing power to enabling power. From Nouwen I learned three important things.

The first thing I learned from Nouwen was to focus on the poor in the world. I think what Nouwen means by "the poor" is anyone who is waiting for us to care and reach out; for me, the poor are the women who were murdered, and whose stories will now be lost forever. I kept reading their stories, listening to their family members, and remembering every day that I was doing this work not just for myself but for all of them. Remember the women, I said to myself.

The second thing I learned from Nouwen is to trust that we will have financial, emotional, and physical support when we need it, and to the degree that we need it. How do we find that support? Nouwen says (1995, p. 174), "If we dare to take a few crazy risks because God asks us to do so, many doors, which we didn't even know existed, will be open to us." This idea was more difficult for me to accept. I had to keep reminding myself of all the people, all across the country, who were behind us and working hard to make the march happen.

The third thing I learned from Nouwen was the hardest one for me to grasp. Nouwen talks (1995, p. 174) of being surprised not by suffering but by joy: "Be surprised by the immense healing power that keeps bursting forth like a spring of fresh water from the depth of our pain." I knew that this was certainly a possibility, but it was a stretch at first, although it proved to be the most rewarding idea of all. Miracles were everywhere.

The second writer to whom I was led was Joyce Hollyday, whose gift to me was one line: "Joy is the infallible sign of the presence of God. Where there is no joy, God is absent" (Hollyday, 1997, p. 95) Therefore, if I was to experience God in the midst of all this stress, fear, and conflict, I had to change my perspective. Instead of seeing myself as the object of a personal attack, I tried to see an opportunity to embrace my pain and find light and joy in the middle of the darkness.

Two memories also helped motivate me. One was of a trip I had made to see the home and convent of Teresa of Avila. As I stood in the cell where she had lived for twenty-seven years, I heard her say to me, "My dear, power and courage and love. One without the others is nothing." I knew she was right—and she ought to know, because she, who was part Jewish, had lived and made her reforms of the Catholic Church during the time of the Spanish Inquisition. She is an outstanding spiritual mentor for me because of her courage and her rich life of prayer.

The second memory was of Margaret Mead's words: "Never doubt that a small group of thoughtful committed citizens can change the world; indeed, it's the only thing that ever has" (cited in Warner, 1992, p. 5).

Feeling fortified and renewed, I started formulating some guiding principles about how we could best work in this movement. I decided that we needed to model the behavior we were promoting, and to act consistently on our life-giving principles: to face fear, to heal, to remember the women, to laugh, to look for the light, to keep moving forward. But I still had to figure out how to hold on to these principles day by day and in the middle of the chaos. I wrote in my journal, "The issues are multiple and mostly mine. First, it's OK to be weak sometimes; second, I don't have to do all this work by myself. And I can look to the people who've gone before me for help and hope."

At the time, to deal with my fear and anger, I started practicing the technique outlined by Stosny (1995). Whenever I felt anger, I stopped and really experienced it, and then I looked at the feelings hidden underneath. From those feelings I chose whichever were the worst ones, ranking them in order from bad to worse. They turned out to be feelings of being disregarded, unimportant, accused, guilty, mistreated, devalued, rejected, powerless, and unlovable. Then I would let myself experience the awful feeling for a few seconds; I've found, for example, that when my anger is with a loved one, the underlying feeling is always about being unlovable. I would then heal that feeling by having compassion for myself. I affirmed my lovability by asking, "Is there anything that this other person could do or say that would make me absolutely unlovable as a person or a child of God?" If the answer was no, I affirmed myself as lovable and knew that I had been healed. I could then move on to having compassion for the other person, asking, "How might this person be feeling, that he or she would act this way toward me?" Usually the answer was that the other person was feeling the same way I was. When I could see that, I was usually able to solve the problem more effectively with compassion than with anger.

## The Test: Moving Ahead with Healing

At this point, I felt better than I had felt in several months. The healing process had taken four months but I was stronger than I had ever thought I could be in the circumstances. I felt that I was starting to heal deep inside, to become whole.

Jane and I decided to write to the leaders in the movement against domestic violence, to thank them for their hard work on behalf of battered women everywhere and invite them to go to Washington with us and be publicly recognized for their work. We invited them to be on our national advisory board, and we also invited some of them to speak at the conference that we had planned for the day after the march. We also encouraged their state organizations to be active with our Silent Witness National Initiative.

As a result of our conversations with them, we made several other changes in our plans. We broadened the content of the conference, reached out to more diverse populations, and commissioned a drama on the history of the movement, to be presented at the conference. I was pleased with our efforts, and because several of the leaders responded to our invitation to be recognized at the march, I thought that we had made progress, and that I was learning to share power, be collaborative with our opposition, and face my own fear.

I had more to learn. Three months before the march, we had our last steering committee meeting. Nearly twenty people from ten states attended. This was the meeting where we shared ideas for getting the Silent Witnesses to Washington, and we learned from our members what they wanted from each of the Washington events. About thirty minutes into the meeting, we were confronted by a participant whom we had never met. She told us we were approaching our initiative in entirely the wrong way. I listened for several minutes and then tried to find out what she wanted us to do instead, but my efforts were futile.

During a break I again attempted to listen to this participant, hear her concerns, and then discuss our position, but to no avail. She thought we should just give up the core of our initiative. Later in the day, through an intermediary, she stated firmly that if we did not pull back from a specific healing-treatment program that we were advocating as successful, she would get others to join her in a public protest against us in Washington.

I excused myself from the discussion for a minute, to go to the restroom, and when I was alone I asked God to make clear to me whether the healing route we had chosen was the one we should stick with; there was too much on the line to risk making a big mistake. God replied simply, "We're here to heal."

I went back and said to the intermediary, "We would very much like to work with other groups on domestic violence issues. We invite them to join us. But we believe that this program is so integral to our initiative, and to the healing of the domestic violence issue, that we can't back away from it. If that means they protest, I guess they'll have to protest."

We offered to look at an approach that our opponents might want us to include in our conference. The intermediary agreed to relay the message, and the matter was left there. I was still worried that a confrontation in Washington would cast a pall on the events, and that a great deal of energy would go toward deflecting this woman's threats.

## Sharing Power Versus Responding to Intimidation

You may be wondering how this incident illustrates the sharing of power and faith. Here is how it appeared to me.

God was calling us to adhere to some basic principles of healing in the face of adversity. Discernment is necessary in the exercise of power. This means knowing when "sharing power" really means caving in to pressure and not taking risks—in other words, being codependent and unable to speak for oneself. There is a difference between sharing power and being threatened into relinquishing power.

We had shared power successfully with our members in other states, and we felt that we had done our best to listen to the national leaders who disagreed with us. Still, people can easily deceive themselves, and I asked myself several times if that was what I was doing. Each time I checked it out with God, I heard the words "Move forward with the healing models," and I realized that the other side of sharing power is knowing when to accept the vision that you are being asked to carry forward.

We were not there to fight or overpower our small group of critics but to work on another vision for the movement, building on all the good work of the twenty years that had preceded us. We were being asked to set forth a hope-filled, healing vision for the movement, and we would do that by sharing power and collaborating with those who could also share it, claiming our own power for our vision, naming our principles, and empowering others who needed hope.

It turned out that one of our best learning experiences came from that difficult meeting of the steering committee. As we had offered to do, we opened a space at our conference for an approach that was advocated by the woman who had confronted us. At the same time, however, we did not back down on our healing principles, and we decided not to do anything that had the character of retaliation or revenge. That decision was difficult because we felt hurt by our critics' actions, but we used our compassion-based model and once again tried to understand their feelings. It was harder this time, with threats looming, but we decided to move forward with our plans for Washington and make hope the central message of the events. Every week, we found angels all over the country who were working hard, honoring the women, telling us we were making a difference, and assuring us that they were going to Washington.

Out of this experience emerged our official Silent Witness guide to conflict, which we now try to practice routinely. It consists of five simple steps:

1. Listen, and take notes if necessary.
2. Treat everyone with respect.
3. Negotiate on the things you can reasonably change.
4. Know what your basic principles are, and never violate them.
5. Engage in no revenge or retaliation.

## One Final Act of Faith

Because this whole process forged in me a deeper faith and a newfound way to work with conflict, I thought I had learned the lessons I needed to learn from this experience. But not yet.

The march was scheduled for October 18. In late September, three weeks before the march, we still did not know for sure whether representatives from all the states were going, or how many Silent Witnesses there would be. We had half the money we needed to stage the events (with several proposals still out), and we had less than half the registrations we needed to fund the conference. I was nervous, to say the least, but I knew that this was my inner darkness looming up, to try one last time to squelch my faith.

On September 24, God told me to start the celebration, that everything had already been taken care of, and the party was to begin. I realized that my real work all along had been to believe that everything I needed had already been provided, as Nouwen (1995) suggests. But here I was, faced with the decision of either cutting the conference's speaker roster by half or moving forward on faith.

I decided to move on faith. I sent an e-mail message all across the country, saying that we could all start celebrating, that everything was in order and we were looking forward to seeing everyone. It was my biggest act of faith in the whole seven years.

With amazing grace, God showed me that everything was indeed in place. We got the money we needed. The conference was filled. All fifty states were represented, and 1,500 Silent Witnesses appeared. We carried them down the Mall to the U.S. Capitol, accompanied by the solemn cadence of bagpipes. Twenty state attorneys general came to support our efforts, Senator Paul Wellstone was our master of ceremonies, the recording artist Collin Raye sang, and Silent Witness leaders from fifteen states committed themselves to being the first leaders to create strategic plans for having no domestic murders at all by the year 2010.

I cannot tell you that all is well, and that healing and light are flowing through this movement as a result of our actions, but several conversations since the march have suggested to us that we are taking small healing steps. Only time will tell the whole story.

What I can tell you is that ten of the twelve leaders we invited to be recognized at the march did come and did participate. One of the national organizations helped sponsor our reception. The woman who threatened to protest, and another woman who threatened us later, also both came to the march. Two leaders joined our national advisory board. Three spoke at our events. Several of their member organizations participated at the state level. There was no protest against us.

And I've changed. The result of living with all this conflict has been strength, compassion, and humility as a leader of the future in this initiative. We model the behavior of the God we know. This God, for me, is loving, faithful, challenging, supportive, and humorous. I learned many things from God in all of this. As for our ongoing efforts, those of us in Silent Witness are still collaborating and healing, both within ourselves and with the rest of the movement. We're committed to the long haul. In my opinion, that's what faith and leadership are all about.

REFERENCES

Hagberg, J. *Real Power: Stages of Personal Power in Organizations* (rev. ed). Salem, Wisc.: Sheffield, 1994.

Hollyday, J. *Then Shall Your Light Rise: Spiritual Formation and Social Witness.* Nashville, Tenn.: Upper Room Books, 1997.

Nouwen, H. "Power, Powerlessness, and Power." In J. Mogabgab (ed.), *Communion, Community, Commonweal*. Nashville, Tenn.: Upper Room Books, 1995.

Stosny, S. *Treating Attachment Abuse: A Compassionate Approach*. New York: Springer, 1995.

Warner, C. *The Last Word: A Treasury of Women's Quotes*. Upper Saddle River, N.J.: Prentice Hall, 1992.

ADDITIONAL READING

De Pree, M. *Leading Without Power: Finding Hope in Serving Community*. San Francisco: Jossey-Bass, 1997.

# 8

# MENTORING THE NEXT GENERATION OF FAITHFUL LEADERS

*Karol D. Emmerich*

Karol D. Emmerich is president of the Emmerich Foundation and
consults on issues of philanthropy, governance, and strategic planning.
She is a former vice president of the Dayton Hudson Corporation, in
Minneapolis.

———— o ————

MENTORING HAS BEEN a major focus of articles and books written on
leadership development over the past twenty years. Next to actual hands-
on experience in leadership, a relationship with an older, experienced
leader is the most powerful force in the development of a younger leader.

## Mentoring Versus Other Types of Leadership Development

Is mentoring different from other types of help and guidance (such as
supervision or coaching) that may be offered to a developing leader? If so,
what are the differences?

The job of a supervisor is to manage work flow and evaluate performance. The job of a coach (or of a supervisor acting in that role) is to help
a person develop task-related skills and accomplish specific growth needs
or objectives through hands-on teaching, motivation and feedback. A
mentor, by contrast, serves as a wise and trusted counselor and guide.

According to Clawson (1985, p. 35), the mentoring function may include "teaching, modeling, directing, evaluating, providing feedback, protecting, introducing, challenging, sponsoring, assigning, counseling, listening, caring, respecting, responding and encouraging." Mentoring is generally longer term, more proactive, and more personal than other types of leadership development. It's usually more comprehensive, often addressing physical, emotional, spiritual, and relational aspects of a mentee's life in addition to the professional and vocational aspects. The Woodlands Group (1980, p. 918) describes the characteristics of a mentor as follows: "Mentors possess genuine generosity, compassion and concern and . . . are more apt to be concerned with the needs of the protégé than with the needs of the organization. . . . Caring is the core of this relationship."

## Who Makes the Best Mentee?

Mentoring often involves a tremendous investment of time and energy. My personal preference is to work primarily with Christian "difference makers" because what I invest in them will be used for purposes of the Kingdom. Believer-to-believer mentoring is the strongest, deepest mentoring relationship possible, for it taps the core of who we are. The presence of the Holy Spirit in the relationship is an exciting and powerful dynamic; you never know what amazing things God will do next. Mentors often look for the following qualities in their protégés:

○ Self-motivation
○ Capacity for mutual respect
○ Teachability
○ Desire to reach potential
○ Mutual affinity

## Is There One Right Model for Mentoring?

The classic mentoring relationship is that of mentor and protégé, but other common models have the mentor serving as a partner or as one member of an individual's personal "board of directors." Which type of relationship works best? The answer often depends on the relative ages and levels of experience of the people involved, and the relationship may evolve over time as the mentee grows.

A rapidly emerging model, especially among women, is that of the mentor as peer. Dahle (1998) gives several reasons why this model has emerged: peers often have the best solutions to problems because they are currently facing the same ones, women aren't always welcome in the "old boys' club" of mentoring, and there aren't enough senior-level women to mentor all the younger women.

## Who Makes the Best Mentor?

Masterplanning Group International (1990) suggests that the mentor be a person with the following characteristics:

- Capacity for and interest in teaching
- Capacity for objectivity
- Honesty and ability to speak the truth in love
- Ability to provide constructive feedback
- Capacity to be open and transparent
- Ability to live out his or her teachings
- Belief in the protégé
- Desire to help the protégé develop spiritual and leadership potential

### Bosses as Mentors

Sometimes bosses are effective as mentors, but more often they are not. Effective mentoring usually requires a personal relationship, with good chemistry and caring between the two people involved, and most successful mentors are self-appointed rather than assigned by their organizations. Usually mentoring occurs outside the normal boss-subordinate relationship.

One difficulty when the boss is also the mentor is the formal power differential between the two parties. There may also be a perception of favoritism, which may give rise to ill will among other staff members. Given the inherent intensity and constant scrutiny in the daily work environment, conflicts in the mentoring relationship may have ramifications for on-the-job performance.

### Opposite-Sex Mentors

Because a mentoring relationship can become so personal, many advise against mentoring people of the other gender. The vast majority of my mentors have been men, however, and my development would have been (and would continue to be) severely stunted without their godly counsel. Although I myself have served in the role of coach to almost equal numbers of men and women, the majority of my mentoring has been with women, because of a combination of chemistry, my personal interest in their ministry, and their desire for a mentoring relationship.

## One Mentor or Many?

A wise person will usually seek the counsel of many other wise people, and the more people who care about you and take an interest in you, the better. A mentee's life also has many aspects: professional and vocational, physical, emotional, spiritual, relational. I'm primarily a vocation-and task-focused mentor because that's my strength and my interest. I probe other areas, to determine which ones may have an impact on the vocation or task, and to see which of them may need to be addressed, but I'm not well equipped to deal with them in depth. Because I'm concerned about the whole person, not just aspects of the person with which I can help, I encourage my mentees to have other, complementary mentors who can assist them, as necessary, in other areas where they seek to develop.

## Being Helpful Without Being a Mentor

Does someone have to be a mentor in order to be helpful? Of course not. When I work with people, for example, my typical role is that of an adviser. I listen to their goals and give suggestions, generally spending just an hour or two with them because that's all they need from me in order to take the next step. In other cases, I serve as a coach and am more actively engaged over a longer period because that's what is needed. And sometimes, but not very often, what's needed is a long-term mentoring relationship.

Given the nature of mentoring, most mentors can take on only a few of these relationships, and so the person seeking development may never have a mentor per se. Nevertheless, he or she can gain almost as much by seeking counsel from a diversity of wise people. Most of these people will be flattered and will be happy to pass on advice about a specific issue.

## Faith-Based Mentoring

Is there a difference between the faith-based mentor who is genuinely Christian and the one who is simply a good person? Does faith play a distinctive role in how each one plays the role of mentor? Are there distinctive features of mentoring from a position of faith? I believe that there are, although they may not always be obvious to the outside observer. These distinctive features are found in the following areas:

○ The mentor's motivation, intensity, tenacity, and priorities

○ The mentor's goals

○ The wisdom of the counsel provided by the mentor

○ The initiating force behind the mentoring relationship

○ The presence of God (as the Holy Spirit) as an integral part of the mentoring relationship

○ The mentor's accountability to God

## Motivation

The primary motivation and role of the faith-based mentor should be to serve as an obedient steward of God's resources—in this case, the person whom God has brought across the mentor's path—furthering God's Kingdom by helping the mentee become more effective in his or her ministry or vocation, through greater competence or spiritual growth. By contrast, mentors who are simply good people are usually motivated by a natural affinity with their mentees, enjoying their company and caring about them and their success. They may also be motivated by a sense of personal satisfaction and by the significance they gain from being mentors.

The faith-based mentor may have similar feelings toward a mentee, but such feelings are not necessary to a successful mentoring relationship. For example, I'm able to mentor people with whom I might not normally have an immediate affinity, because I believe God has called them to their work and has called me to assist them. What's important is that I care for them, in the sense of agape: I want what's best for them, and I love them because God loves and cares for them. It means I'm committed to their growth and development. This kind of relationship is a matter of the will and, as such, may be more enduring than a relationship based solely on personal chemistry. The faith-based mentor is also more likely to be proactive in his or her mentoring—making it a higher priority, taking more time, and mentoring more people—than might be the case if he or she were not a believer, for this kind of mentor recognizes that God may be leading him or her toward purposes that may be intuitively sensed but not fully comprehended.

## Goals

I'm concerned about the "What's in it for me?" attitude of many mentors and mentees. For example, a mentee may be tempted to limit the search for a mentor, approaching only powerful insiders whose counsel can have immediate payoffs for his or her career. Similarly, the goal of a corporate mentor may be to enhance his or her own career by finding superstar protégés, for "a good protégé is a good worker and good workers advance their bosses' careers" (Zey, 1987, pp. 3–4), helping their mentors build their empires, gathering intelligence from within the organization, and providing an inner circle of loyal confidants. I believe that wise mentees will put aside self-seeking and instead look for mentors who have godly perspective and wisdom, people who will help them become all God designed them to be in order to serve Him well. Similarly, I believe that Christian mentors must also put aside self-seeking and help mentees become what God designed them to be, not what their mentors want them to be or what their mentors think they can become.

## Wisdom

Counsel from someone who is simply a good person may be very helpful, but faith-based counsel has the added reinforcement and benefits of prayer, scripture, and insights from the Holy Spirit. God gives faith-based mentors perspective and the heart for eternal growth. This means that faith-based mentors should be much wiser, more competent, more insightful, and more discerning than they would be if they were acting only on their own power and offering only the world's wisdom.

How does this work in practice? Say that someone calls me (as many people do), asking for my advice on a vocational or ministry-related issue. Often, at the outset of the conversation, I have no idea how I can be of assistance because this person's background is so different from mine. The first thing I do is pray for help, for I know that I may soon be in over my head. God knows those who call and what they need far better than I ever will, and so my responsibility is to be open to divine leadership. It is amazing that by the time our discussion has ended, the Holy Spirit will have brought to mind ideas, files, and contacts that are just what the person needs in order to take the next step. One woman I've mentored says that as we've worked together, the Holy Spirit has taken her to things that were beyond her imagination but that were also the desires of her heart. In other words, God's plans for her life have turned out to be bigger than either she or I could have imagined on our own.

## Initiating Force

I believe that God is the initiator of the faith-based mentoring relationship. Behind the scenes, the Holy Spirit is finding ways to link people. Ever since I left my corporate job, rather than seeking people out, as a mentor typically does, I've waited for God to bring people to me. I've been amazed by the diversity of "difference makers" from across the country that God has brought to me—people I could never have found on my own, and whom I would never have sought out because of the differences in our interests and backgrounds. But I'm completely confident that these are people with whom God wants me to work. The story of how they've found me always fills me with delight and awe at how God works. It's as if God is saying, "I'm using this person. She needs something from you. Give her what you can so that she can take the next step." I've discovered the wide range of issues on God's agenda by meeting painters, and lawyers, and widows who never learned to drive or balance their own checkbooks. These people have given me a chance, as I've met their needs, to see God use His strength through my weakness.

## Presence of God

When I serve as a mentor, I am keenly aware that God is an integral, ever-present part of the relationship. What are the implications? For one thing, I know that God cares about our efforts and will bless them. I also know that we can always rely on Him for assistance and guidance. We're not in this work alone!

## Accountability

As a Christian, I know that I'm accountable to God for my interactions with the person who comes to me, and that this is a serious undertaking. I'm careful not to give advice frivolously, and I always try to pray for wisdom before I meet with someone. Again, I believe that our task is to serve as faithful stewards of God's resources (mentees, in my case) so that, as in the parable, when God checks up on us, He will find that we have served well and that His resources have increased—that mentees, in this case, will have been made more productive for God's Kingdom.

## Fred's Influence

My experience with Fred is an example of what faith-based mentoring looks like. I met Fred in 1989 in Atlanta, where he was putting on a conference for Christians who were between the ages of thirty and forty-five and who were on the professional fast track. The conference setting was a place for them to come together and explore ways of living out their faith and making it relevant to the marketplace. The conference addressed such questions as whether it is possible for a person to take faith to the marketplace, and whether there are real people who think, lead, and win while also following Christ and keeping a commitment to making a difference.

My husband and I immediately felt a great affinity with Fred. We were impressed with his work and with his heart, and the three of us soon became great friends. Fred also became a mentor to us, coming alongside (as he has done with so many others) to help us grow in our faith. He exposed us to a wide range of learning opportunities and connected us with peers who were on the same journey. He helped us find our giftedness, our spiritual DNA—the unique way in which God had designed us to serve. He also suggested opportunities for us to learn how to be more effective givers to Christian ministry, another of his passions. He involved us in his projects, and he offered opportunities for me to speak at conferences. He prayed for us and cared about our family. His goal for us was that we should become more intentional in our service to God, that we should really trust God with all our time, talent, and treasure and fulfill the purpose for which we were uniquely created.

For me, Fred is a model of what an intelligent, businesslike Christian can do in ministry. He showed me that I could be who God designed me to be and still serve Him, and that I didn't have to conform to a stereotype, which to me would have meant being soft-spoken, gentle, nonassertive, constantly beaming, and acting holy—not the way anyone would have described me!

Fred and his boss, and others with whom they put us in contact, played an important role in my having the courage and vision to leave the corporate world in 1993. I had been the top financial officer of a major U.S. corporation, and one of the highest-ranking women in corporate America. I was well paid, well known, and highly respected. But God was calling me to something different.

My dreams included coming alongside Christian "difference makers," to help them grow and develop in order to become all that God had designed them to be, and to help them realize their difference-making dreams. I planned to do this by providing necessary help, which might include encouragement, brainstorming, networking, advocacy, financial resources, perspective, advice, coaching, and mentoring. I wanted to work with people rather than organizations because what is invested in people goes with them wherever they go and lasts for eternity, whereas an organization is only as strong as its current leaders.

My dreams also included turning some property adjacent to our home into a garden, retreat, and conference center where seeds could be planted in seekers; where believers could be encouraged to get off the bench and into action in God's Kingdom; where "difference makers" could gain mentoring, coaching, and perspective and be recharged; and where weary believers could be nursed back to spiritual health. I saw myself as a catalyst and facilitator, not as someone running a large organization. I wanted to work on issues related to voluntarism, philanthropy, governance, partnerships, women, work, and faith, and I wanted to work primarily where my unique skills and background were needed, and where more energy would be created than spent.

I was concerned that my walking away from my corporate job would mean loss of my platform, loss of respect, and loss of the financial resources with which these dreams might be realized. But that was God's problem; all that was needed from me was obedience. What God did was to give me a different kind of platform, greater respect, and greater financial resources than ever before with which to carry out a ministry beyond my imagination.

Fred is a man of very deep faith, but I think even he has been struck by what God has done. What began as a mentoring relationship has evolved into a partnership. Fred and I now work together on a number of initiatives related to Christian stewardship, and I even serve on his board of directors. We value each other's counsel and perspective, and we communicate almost daily by e-mail, bound by our commitment to serve the God who has called us to be "difference makers."

## Lu's Influence

I was put in touch with Lu by a mutual acquaintance. Lu was in her middle fifties, had a background in sales, and for many years had been a fund-raiser on behalf of various Christian organizations. Often when she met with women donors, especially widows with substantial financial resources, she heard story after story of how they had been dismissed or abused by fund-raisers and executive directors. Many of these women expressed to Lu the desire to have someone they could trust teach them about giving; others did not understand that they could give more in the present without putting their futures at risk. Lu's dream was to find a safe environment where they could be educated, inspired, and encouraged in giving their time, their talents, and their financial resources to God's work.

When Lu and I first began to talk, she was beginning to plan her first symposium as a volunteer. I was impressed with her vision, her commitment, her energy, her passion for her target audience, and her ability to energize and involve other people in her work. It was clear that God was in what she was doing. I talked with her about her dreams and gave advice, in addition to funding and participating in the first symposium. She was looking for someone who could complement the gaps in her background (for example, in governance, strategic planning, and finance), and I became a partner-style mentor to her.

It soon became apparent that if Lu was to realize her dreams, she'd have to leave the safety of a regular paycheck and begin a freelance ministry. We talked the decision through, and I provided some seed money. What began as an informal network of volunteers, with myself as a part-time adviser and mentor, has evolved into an organization in which I play the formal role of chair. Much of my assistance to Lu has been in the area of governance. I've worked with her to write a mission statement, and I've taught her how to choose and work with a board of directors. I have a hands-on but supervisory role in all aspects of the ministry.

This has been one of my most rewarding mentoring relationships, but it is not one I ever would have chosen on my own. For one thing, I'm used to working with very assertive, savvy, professional women, and many of the women whom this organization serves are older and used to depending on their husbands for anything related to finances. For another, my comfort zone is among highly analytical business professionals, whereas Lu is a warm, gregarious, highly relational grandmother who loves people unconditionally. But God made it very clear to me that He was going to use Lu in a powerful way, and He wanted me to be part of her realizing her God-given dreams.

As Lu and I work together, we see how our strengths and experiences are complementary. With our different gifts, but with our passion for the same kind of service, God is using and teaching both of us. Our partnership is bound by a common obedience and by the knowledge that we're involved in something eternal. We continue to laugh at how God has brought us, this odd couple, together, but we're continually reminded that this is God's work, not ours.

## Clarke's Experience

I met Clarke when I was serving as a board member of a public policy organization. When the position of executive director opened up, Clarke was the leading candidate. He'd worked for the organization for almost a decade and had served as its chief legal counsel, but both he and the board were concerned about his limited experience of management and fund-raising.

My mentoring opportunities began immediately. I encouraged Clarke to see a management psychologist, to help him determine whether he would be able to succeed at the job and to make sure that his transition from lawyer to executive director would be consistent with his personal and professional goals and with what he thought God wanted for him and his family. The psychologist felt that Clarke would do a great job but noted that it would be very helpful if I were to actively mentor him for a while.

My primary role with Clarke has been to advise him on issues of management and governance. Sometimes all that's needed is encouragement that he's on the right track. Once I'd taken him as far as I could in certain areas, I encouraged and enabled him to take a mini-MBA course for managers of nonprofits. It provided him with new skills, contacts, and greater confidence in his functioning as a manager. Clarke has also made good use of other board members as mentors in areas where they can be of assistance. I also support Clarke by serving as a member of the board. It's often hard work and not very glamorous, but I believe that God has His hand on Clarke in this important work, which affects millions of lives. How could I face God and say I didn't try as hard as I could to play my part?

## Conclusion

I have had the privilege of serving in many leadership roles in addition to serving as a mentor, coach, and adviser to many people who sought my input while examining what they should do next with their lives or how they could become all that God had created them to be. Nevertheless, given the limitations of the mentoring relationship, it is likely that far more people will be affected by supervisors and leaders than will ever have the benefit of direct mentoring.

REFERENCES

Clawson, J. "Is Mentoring Necessary?" *Training and Development Journal*, 1985, p. 35.

Dahle, C. "Women's Ways of Mentoring." *Fast Company,* Sept. 1998.

Masterplanning Group International. *Mentoring.* Laguna Niguel, Calif.: Masterplanning Group International, 1990.

Woodlands Group. "Management Development Roles: Coach, Sponsor and Mentor." *Personnel Journal,* 1980, p. 918.

Zey, M. "The Mentor Connection." *Macmillan Executive Summary Program,* 1987, 3(10), 3–4.

ADDITIONAL READINGS

Bell, C. R. *Managers as Mentors: Building Partnerships for Learning.* San Francisco: Berrett-Koehler, 1996.

Kram, K. E. *Mentoring at Work: Developmental Relationships in Organizational Life.* Lanham, Mass.: Boston University Press, 1997.

## PART THREE

# VITAL ISSUES FOR FAITH AND LEADERSHIP

# 9

# DEALING WITH VULNERABILITY

*Shirley J. Roels*

Shirley J. Roels, dean of academic administration at Calvin College, Grand Rapids, Michigan, writes on business issues from a faith-based perspective. She is the author of *Organization Man, Organization Woman: Calling, Leadership, and Culture,* coauthor (with Richard C. Chewning and John W. Eby) of *Business Through the Eyes of Faith,* and co-editor (with Max L. Stackhouse, Dennis P. McCann, and Preston N. Williams) of *On Moral Business: Classical and Contemporary Resources for Ethics in Economic Life.*

○

THE CEO OF A PROMINENT company regularly regarded as one of the hundred best places to work in the United States is interviewed about his leadership. About the same time he's being quoted in a new book about leaders of the future (Senge, 1996), his board of directors fires him. The board concludes that he isn't the right CEO at this point in the firm's history. Didn't the board members trust him? Didn't they see what he saw? Didn't they hear what he heard?

Leadership in corporations, churches, schools, charitable organizations, the arts, and government seems to change frequently. The turnover in some sectors is almost as bad as the movement of baseball managers at season's end. But it hasn't always been this way. Society used to value the long-term leader, the college president who stayed for over a decade, the senior pastor with thirty years' experience, the corporate president who had been with the company for twenty years. Long-term leaders' sense of organizational history, their calm continuity, and their knowledge of the stakeholders were all deemed valuable.

Times have changed, and now turnover in leadership is almost expected. Faculty members don't think their presidents will stay more than four or five years, and statistics on the average length of a college presidency confirm their perceptions. Some churches become restless when their pastors don't begin to look for another "call" after five years. Some have even begun term appointments for pastors, with definitive dates for evaluation, and reappointment only if both church and pastor agree. Many corporate leaders and school superintendents, sensing that they have worn out their welcome, move on every few years.

Such changes occur in part because leaders are vulnerable. They sense that their followers' capacity to trust them, and their own capacity to lead their organizations in particular directions, are short-lived desert flowers: their leadership blooms when it receives the rain of trust and confidence, but the blossom quickly fades in the arid air of harsh decisions, and instead of staying in place until conditions are right for another blooming of their leadership, leaders prefer to be transplanted.

## Why Are Leaders So Vulnerable?

There are several reasons why leaders are so vulnerable in these times. Their environment is changing at the same time that society's expectations of leaders are also shifting.

The internal environments of organizations are more complex than in the past. Effective leadership now depends on whether a leader is well matched with the particular stage in an organization's life cycle (Schein, 1996). For example, an infant industry may need a go-getter and entrepreneur, whereas the stalwart, established company may need an operations expert or a low-key CEO.

The greater complexity of the workforce adds to the challenge for leaders. For example, the expectations of people at work have become more sophisticated as levels of educational attainment have risen. Followers have varied preferences about leaders, as well as a broad range of opinions about whether they are willing to support a given leader. Because sources of motivation are unique and hybrid for every individual in the workforce, no stable set of motivators can be assumed by any leader or successfully invoked in dealing with any given segment of the workforce. Moreover, because we live in an age of hyperdifferentiation, this may be a time when our identities are less defined by physical place than by our experiences and our psychological interiors (Schreiter, 1997). As a result, if individual encounters and interpretations define us, then perhaps every person in the workplace is expecting particular leaders to find the unique key to his or her motivation, perhaps a key that will inspire no one else in the same way. If leaders cannot understand the complex mix of motivations in an individual follower, then they will be criticized for their inability to lead, and this situation may make them vulnerable to complaints, sabotage, and inertia.

Particularly in mature economies, such as that of the United States, knowledge- and information-based organizations may hold emerging hazards for leaders. Such entities are intersections between knowledge specialists and particular organizational dynamics, and knowledge specialists' career identities are often tied to organizations or networks that focus on the further development of a field and on concern for its practitioners. For example, many skilled assembly workers are quite loyal to the United Auto Workers, many doctors have allegiances to the American Medical Association, and certified public accountants have a commitment to uphold the standards of the American Institute of Certified Public Accountants. Whether an organization is building cars, providing healthcare, or performing financial analysis, it needs knowledge- and skill-based specialists, but it needs their allegiance as well as their expertise. Loyalty to the guild, whether that means a union, a licensing entity, a professional association, or an idea-exchange club, competes with organizational loyalty. As a mature economy increasingly relies on quality and depth of knowledge, such guilds may gain more power.

Yet organizations are sets of particularities and must relate to particular stakeholder groups—namely, customers and clients, donors, suppliers, stockholders, and communities of influence. As society's appetite for greater workforce expertise increases, many knowledge-based employees become mobile, particularly in a strong economy. Leaders may then have more difficulty negotiating the balance between employees' allegiance to their particular organizations and their allegiance to the more powerful professional guilds. As a society, moreover, we seem to be upping the ante when loyalty to particular organizations is concerned. For more than a decade, organizations have been talking about developing a focused mission, customer sensitivity, cross training, and commitment over time to core values, and the probability may be rising for collisions between organizations, with their particularities, and globally capable specialists with knowledge and skills for hire. As knowledge industries develop, capable leaders often find themselves caught in the tug-of-war between their particular organizations and the professional guilds.

The information age has also made the task of the leader more complex. Computer-accessible information has smashed the mold for formal organizational communication systems. Historically, management theorists have described communication flows as clearly upward or downward, through a clear chain of command (Daft, 1988); today's preferred metaphor is of the organization as a network. Now that e-mail allows everyone to be interconnected, the old single thread of command has been woven into a spider's web. In a web of this kind, it is difficult for any leader to diagnose appropriate paths of connection and communication: paths change, veer off, add new loops, and cycle back, and the issue of who tells what to whom and why is a more complex one for a leader to fathom.

Given these changes in the internal environments of most organizations, is it any wonder that leadership theorists (for example, Bornstein and Smith, 1996) argue that for many in the workforce it is not a requirement but a choice to follow leaders? In effect, leadership cannot occur unless followers give the freedom and right to lead to those placed in leadership positions. If followers don't do so, paths that diverge from leaders' preferred directions will be numerous. Internally, followers can choose to thwart progress; they may also choose to jump ship entirely when their viewpoints vary from those who are setting the direction. Is it any wonder, then, that leadership theorists also argue that effective leaders are those with spiritual, referent, and coaching capacities?

Few analysts today would suggest that leaders who operate as command-and-control captains of industry can still be effective in the context of a shifting internal environment, but the external context is also more hazardous to organizational leaders. Adding to the complexity are the increasing interconnectedness of the world's economies and organizations' ability to interact instantaneously with people and other organizations all around the world. Leaders can now know more and control more at the global level, but remaining unknowns can rear their heads quickly and deliver a venomous bite. In the late 1990s, for example, could a college or university president in the United States have predicted that his or her institution's contingent of students from Asia would soon feel the effects of deteriorating Asian economies and find it difficult if not impossible to pay their tuition? Could this president have understood how those who were controlling the movements of global capital were exacerbating the spread of problems from one Asian country to another and, as a result, bringing stress to bear on the university's operating budget? This is only one example of the hazards that leaders regularly encounter in the external environment, hazards that may be impossible to predict.

There are many more: political and economic instability in influential countries (such as Russia), terrorist capacity all over the world, the behavior of global oil providers, the potential for religious wars, and even the potential effects on the physical environment of shrinking polar ice caps. All these factors in the external environment may seem remote from the decisions made in particular organizations, and yet any leader who was leading during the oil embargoes of the 1970s knows the implications of the unpredictable for planning, living, and behavior. Now, however, the effects of unpredictable unknowns at the global level are more rapid, undermining leaders' ability to develop plans with any assurance that they can be fulfilled.

One more environmental factor makes leaders more vulnerable to criticism than they have been in the past: the blurring of the boundary between internal and external influences. Organizations are becoming more and more like virtual entities, more fragile groupings that come together and break apart with greater ease. During the past two decades, the pace of organizational mergers and dissolutions has picked up. Organizations have continued to expand through acquisition, but they have also split up, spinning off new public and private entities in the process. The continuing movement of consolidation in the banking industry, for example, is changing that industry's face significantly. Regional banks that were formerly competitors have joined forces; at the same time, however, senior executives who were left in the backwash of these mergers have gone on to create new, personalized banks—organizations that may themselves be candidates for acquisition in a few years. In the process, bankers' loyalties have also shifted.

Traditional organizational boundaries, based on time zones and geographical areas, are more permeable today because of new technologies for computing and communication. As a result, the lines that organizations draw are self-defined boundaries of difference, not boundaries of space and time (Schreiter, 1997). The leaders of a regional symphony, for example, create its identity as such because its board of directors, executive officer, and conductor choose a regional identity; its identity is no longer a function of its geographical location when the Internet can carry its music all over the world. When boundary lines become choices, they may easily become another arena for strong differences of opinion.

And so leaders are vulnerable. More complex mysteries pervade the internal motivations and networks of an organization. A broader range of external variables affects organizational plans and upsets predictability. Boundary setters are needed to make necessary but difficult decisions for individuals who prize their freedom and for organizations less bound by time and space. Leaders are vulnerable because in this complex environment they must make choices—indeed, clear responsibility for making choices is what distinguishes leaders from followers—yet making choices always leaves one vulnerable with respect to roads not taken and the hazards of the ones chosen.

In addition to being vulnerable because they are decision makers, leaders cannot control all perceptions of the decisions they have made. The proliferative local and national media instantaneously dissect leaders' decisions, often without full information or understanding, and leaders cannot always release all the information relevant to a decision, particularly when their choices involve judgments about other people. For example, it is neither possible nor appropriate for a vice president of production to declare publicly that the operations manager of a local plant has resigned under duress because of his consistently poor performance; to do so would be to dishonor the humanity of the person being released, and it might also violate the confidentiality required by law. And yet media leaders may protest this development if the manager was heavily committed to and involved in forming business partnerships between employees and local schools. The local newspaper's snapshot of this manager may be quite different from the picture painted inside the organization, and the external snapshot might provoke public questioning to which the organization's leader could not easily respond. The media have a broader communications license than organizational leaders do because leaders must bring a different balance to public communication and the protection of personnel.

The media also affect our perceptions of leaders because the media can disseminate information so quickly, sometimes shaping reality before the reality itself is settled and can be confirmed. The rapidity of technologically based information flows has a significant effect on the impressions that we form of leaders, and a leader who cares deeply about coordination between a stated organizational mission and the organization's actions may be caricatured—by a sound bite, for example—as a control freak who wants to centralize power. This negative impression, once formed, may plant doubts in the minds of formerly loyal followers. Here again, leaders are vulnerable: thoughtful interpretation of their decisions may be replaced by any number of competing public perceptions, which can easily be delivered to followers.

Leaders may also be vulnerable because we don't always want to recognize their finitude. Our expectations of organizational leaders are very high. We prefer to believe that they don't need sleep, family life, friends, or the beach on a summer afternoon. Their cars shouldn't break down, nor should their furnaces or their teeth. We hope that they can work when they have the flu, and that they won't suffer the normal lapses in memory that afflict the rest of us. Leaders are also expected to work with the sometimes contradictory and always immediate demands of follow-ers. Moreover, we do not always want to accept that there are limits to leaders' expertise and wisdom, perhaps partly because leadership theory and models of leadership have created the expectation that leaders will know how to act if they have been properly educated in leadership. We want leaders with infinite skills, leaders who are technically proficient but also facile at strategic thinking, public speaking, and community relations. We want leaders with perfect knowledge, leaders whose views of the future are omniscient and whose judgments are profound. Our leaders should have infinite time; they should always take a lively part in our interactions, discussions, and events while also attending to external donors and strategic plans. We want leaders with perfect timing, leaders who deal with urgent and long-range matters in the proper sequence. We want leaders who have infinite empathy but are still willing to set bound-aries. We want quick, decisive action on the part of our leaders, but we still want to be consulted before they act. We want our leaders to be our peers, but we also want them to stand apart so there's no favoritism. In effect, we want our leaders to be infinite gods instead of finite humans. And what leader can measure up? Expectations like these, so divorced from human limitations, make leaders vulnerable.

## Faith for the Vulnerable

In the preceding analysis, my intention has not been to seek pity for those who lead. Many argue that the power, status, and financial remuneration typically accompanying a leadership post are more than sufficient compensation for the challenges. Nevertheless, if leaders are important to the well-being of organizations (and thus also important as leaven in the broader society), then they must function well. To do so, they must have answers to three basic questions with which all leaders wrestle:

1. Who can be trusted by a leader?
2. What does a leader see?
3. How does a leader hear?

In high-pressure, often confusing, always challenging contexts, what resources can biblical faith provide to leaders, and how can it contribute to leaders' ability to answer these three questions? Because the expression of faith is so varied in the public sphere, there are numerous approaches to the topic of faith in leadership. One avenue is to consider what biblical faith has contributed to leaders in the past, for their stories are complete ones, not works in progress, and they model for us what is possible over the course of a lifetime.

The author of the letter to the Hebrews (probably an intellectual Jewish Christian) describes many such heroes of faith, particularly in Hebrews, chap. 11. He considers early Jewish leaders, who in their day made a difference in terms of the economy, civic life, the family circle, and the cultural milieu. This author, who wrote during early New Testament times, reflects on those leaders in order to encourage his contemporaries who were also engaged in spiritual contest. He considers whom these earlier leaders trusted, what they saw, and how they heard.

## Faith as Personal Trust

"Without faith it is impossible to please God, for whoever would approach him must believe that he exists and that he rewards those who seek him" (Heb. 11:6). Leaders need to trust. In a turbulent environment, it is difficult to imagine how leaders can survive without sources of confidence and hope for the future (as discussed in Chapter Four). Leaders need others on whom they can rely, others whose characters, strengths, and truths can assuage doubts about leaders' purposes, values, roles, and decisions.

Trust can be vested in followers, to some extent, and yet it seems difficult to imagine leaders vesting all their trust in followers. Given followers' contradictory expectations, the fluid environments in which most leaders lead, and the doubts with which leaders struggle, trust in followers must be partial at best. Sometimes followers won't reciprocate with corresponding trust, and it is also true, to some extent, that leaders, for the sake of the organization, should not share their doubts with followers. As Bornstein and Smith note (1996, p. 286), "Leaders who are clearly struggling with personal or professional doubt will ultimately lose credibility with their followers and constituents." No leader can or should rely on followers to resolve doubts about his or her own value as a person and his or her capacity to lead. Given their vulnerability in their organizations, leaders must look elsewhere for sources of trust.

Perhaps the most reasonable people in whom to confide are peers who have similar responsibilities. They can help a leader sort through issues and scenarios, or they can reaffirm that a leader has done the best that was possible in certain circumstances. Even the leader's peers have limitations, however. Their perceptions of the challenges are limited because they don't walk every day in the shoes of the other leader; they cannot know his or her environment, the other people involved, and the organizational dynamics as intimately as the leader does. Peers can be helpful, but their helpfulness is limited. They, too, are human.

The only one whom leaders can trust and whose understanding is unlimited is God, a living being with complete knowledge, infinite time, and unlimited power to understand and work with leaders in their particular situations. Trust in God may help a leader walk out of step with followers when that is required; the descriptions of Noah and Abraham in Hebrews, chap. 11, indicate that they did just that. Noah survived the ridicule of the surrounding culture while he built an out-of-place ark. Abraham's decision to leave Ur was probably puzzling to his kin who remained behind. Similarly, trust in God may mean that a contemporary leader must walk with a different gait in weighing the mission of his or her enterprise, deciding on the customers and clients to be served, assessing the design of products and services, or reviewing employee policies.

Yet the leader's capacity to trust God depends on the nature of his or her belief in God and on the degree to which he or she has cultivated this relationship. Trusting God must be much more than belief in the deist "watchmaker" who no longer touches and tunes the mechanisms of the world. Leaders who trust God are involved in a daily connection to a living divine presence, a presence that can protect, undergird, and preserve, a God who through His Holy Spirit can "keep your going out and your coming in from this time on forevermore" (Ps. 121:8). This is a trust that can sustain leaders even when forces—corporate, social, economic or political—thwart organizational effectiveness, justice, and coherence.

Trusting God also requires the leader to learn to live with mystery. The leader, at the nexus of God's sovereignty and the effects of human decisions, cannot determine in any given instance the extent to which an outcome is the result of divine guidance or of the latitude allowed for human freedom. A leader cannot know whether it is truly God's will when a search committee eliminates a qualified, aspiring subordinate from consideration. A leader cannot know the balance of God's will and human error when an organizational strategy for expansion is derailed. Because leaders, as humans, lack perfect knowledge about the nexus of God's sovereignty and human responsibility, there is often pain associated with the outcomes of decisions. Yet personal trust in the God of the Scriptures requires leaders to replace that pain with the confidence of knowing that "all things work together for good for those who love God, who are called according to his purpose" (Rom. 8:28). For leaders, then, trusting God is learning to live with unknowns in a time of decision, but acknowledging that God ultimately controls the outcomes wherever human decisions intersect with divine purposes.

## Faith as a Reality Map

"By faith we understand that the worlds were prepared by the word of God, so that what is seen was made from things that are not visible" (Heb. 11:3). Both perception and reality define the world of organizations, and the two do not always match. Among other factors, the lens of personal experience and the filter of organizational rumors will shape perceptions. Thus our understanding may inaccurately reflect an actual decision or circumstance from which we are one or two steps removed. One goal for leaders must be to bring perceptions and reality together because both are crucial to the organizational directions that are chosen.

Biblical faith provides a basic reality map against which to test perceptions because biblical faith is based on the God of the Scriptures, who is separate from but connected to humanity. In this way, biblical faith provides for a creation in which truth can be pursued. The reality map that faith creates is not the result of humanistic or pantheistic projections about spirituality; instead, it describes a universe designed by a creator who exists apart from the creatures.

When leaders believe that faith provides a basic reality map, they can have the assurance that the past is real, and therefore that some explanations of it are more truthful than others. Faith provides a map that rejects the relative and competing realities that postmodernists tend to promulgate. The world and the behavior of its inhabitants have not simply been constructed in different ways by different people, with one construct of reality as valid as another. Instead, biblical faith posits a reality constructed by God.

Admittedly, people's particular experiences, training, and education color their perceptions. If truthful reality has existed in the past, however, then one goal of leadership can be to move followers to see through a lens that provides a sharper, clearer picture. For example, if leaders accept that responsibility, then they can ask followers to more clearly understand and share the truth of their organization's history as it really exists. They can rightly say that some observations and perceptions of events are more closely aligned with reality than others. Not only can leaders assert that organizations are able to come closer to ascertaining truth through a thorough review of the evidence, they can also believe that such truth, when uncovered, provides a basis for sound decisions.

Believing that truth exists and can be discovered has profound implications for organizational life. For example, the possibility of truth affects the resolution of clients' complaints, of claims of racial or sexual harassment, of disputed payables to a supplier, or of responsibility for a missing machinery safeguard. If truth exists, then competing claims about a manager's performance can be evaluated, and disagreements about an organization's financial health can be put to rest. Only if leaders truly believe that reality exists apart from perception can they look for true, right, and just foundations for their organizations. Faith provides the assurance that truth can be a real component of the organizational landscape. Truth is more than human creation and perception; it intimately involves the designs of a divine being.

Faith also helps a leader discern the reality map of the present and work with its contours. Hebrews, chap. 11, describes Joseph, Moses, Rahab, and others as engaging directly with the cultures in which they found themselves, despite their alien status. They were not pilgrims but resident aliens who invested themselves deeply in their societies. Joseph, while achieving a prominent role in the Egyptian economy, sensed his kinship as lying elsewhere but, through foresight and planning for the famines ahead, still made an investment in changing Egyptian economic strategy. Moses remained loyal to his Israelite heritage, although he was raised in association with Pharaoh's household, and he directly challenged Pharaoh and his public policies concerning Israeli slaves. Rahab, who determined that the alien culture was the one in which she had been raised, allied herself instead with foreign spies and became, in the process, a stranger to those who thought they knew her best. In each case, the discernment of the division between strangers and compatriots was not based simply on socialization. Each of these leaders' faith in Yahweh served as the basic compass for their present-day reality maps; faith was their guide as they determined with whom and in what ways they should forge allegiances and alliances.

Similarly, for the contemporary leader, faith can be a compass alongside the map of the present. Faith provides insight into the nature of human beings, their search for meaning in life, their idols, their aspirations, their motivations, and their commitments. Faith and its insights may help us understand why Jim is devoted to the memory of Elvis or why Amber presses so hard for promotion or why George's energy has been lackluster ever since his divorce. Because biblical faith offers unique perspectives on human purpose, evil, sin, grace, repentance, joy, hope, and a host of other themes, it reveals basic features of the present map of reality, features that leaders need in discerning the choices that they should make.

Maslow's well-known hierarchy of needs (1962) places self-actualization at the top, and his hierarchy is often used in organizations to argue that self-actualization is the highest, most important need to be satisfied in the workplace. Yet biblical faith frames the chief needs and purposes of human beings differently. The chief end of humans is to "glorify God and enjoy him for ever" (*Westminster Catechism*, [1928] 1956, question 1). The highest need of humans, according to biblical faith, is not self-actualization but rather fulfillment of the divine purposes for us in relationship to God, other creatures, and the whole of creation. When leaders operate from this perspective, they can fight the tragic drive for career-related self-actualization, both in themselves and in others, as a skewed construction of human existence. They can then work to position career development within a more healthy organizational perspective, balancing it with a host of other roles and responsibilities, both paid and unpaid. Thus faith provides a distinct contemporary reality map for understanding the human condition, the nature of meaning, and people at work.

Further, faith provides a trustworthy map by which to gauge the future. It offers perspective as leaders invest in work even when future outcomes are unclear: "By faith Abraham obeyed when he was called to set out for a place that he was to receive as an inheritance; and set out, not knowing where he was going" (Heb. 11:8). Abraham must have wondered about the future when he made his home in a foreign country, living in tents, and yet he obeyed God because "he looked forward to the city that has foundations, whose architect and builder is God" (Heb. 11:10). He and the other heroes of faith continued their obedient journey because faith provided for final fulfillment of God's purposes, inscrutable though they may have been at certain points in time. These heroes of faith had confidence in a particular reality map for the future, the one God has designed.

Contemporary leaders strategize. They create contingency plans for less known but threatening environmental factors. They worry about their limited knowledge, and they doubt the choices they must sometimes make. Yet faith affords a view of the future that allows leaders to rest in God, knowing that final outcomes do not depend on them alone.

Leaders who know that the future is in God's hands can take more risks than those who believe that future outcomes depend only on human decisions. Such leaders walk bravely into the future, even with its unknowns. No matter how substantial the involvement of faith-based leaders may be in the here and now, they know that the promises of God will be realized at the end of time. Christ's resurrection ensures that partial accomplishments will then be completed, uncontrollable evils brought to justice, and human errors corrected. Christ's victory ensures ultimate redemption for the creation. When events seem out of control, when evil penetrates an organization's best efforts to thwart it, and when seemingly good leadership decisions turn sour, Christian leaders can be comforted by the already secured reality map of the future.

Leaders are key contributors to the core visions and values of organizations, making meaning for their fellow human beings and choices that shape today and tomorrow. Vision, values, meaning, and choice are built on assumptions about the nature of reality. Leaders cannot create visions, values, and meaning for themselves and others without a solid reality map of the past, present, and future. Biblical faith and the assurances of Christ's resurrection provide such a map.

## Faith as Vocational Direction

"And what more shall I say? For time would fail me to tell of Gideon, Barak, Samson, Jephthah, of David and Samuel and the prophets—who through faith conquered kingdoms, administered justice, obtained promises, shut the mouths of lions, quenched raging fire, escaped the edge of the sword, won strength out of weakness" (Heb. 11:32–34a). When leaders accept the gift of relationship with a personal God and use their faith as a foundation for reality, how does faith affect their hearing about who they should be? Personal trust in God and an understanding of reality via Scripture are not enough. There is more that biblical faith can and should provide: a sense of calling and listening.

The word *vocation* is based on the Latin words *vocatio*, "summons," and *vocare*, "to call." The leader's hearing that summons, that call, involves his or her daily conversation with the one who calls, the one who tells us who we should be and who we should become each day. But it is difficult for leaders to focus their hearing on God: amid the cacophony in any organization, being deaf to God is easy. A leader's day may start early and end late, and concerns for family, church, and community must be woven through the particular demands of the leader's organizational role. Many a leader has forgone private devotional time in the interests of serving others. And yet, given the heightened but indiscriminate world of sound in which contemporary organizations are bathed, attention to the still small voice of God is even more important. Listening to that voice helps leaders affirm who God is and thus center themselves. If De Pree (1989, p. 136) is right in suggesting that "leadership is much more an art, a belief, a condition of the heart, than a set of things to do," then time with God is important in helping faith-based leaders be before they do.

The result of personal listening will be a call that is individualized for every person. Because God has a purpose for each one and desires to establish a special relationship with each one, every conversation, story line, and setting will be unique. Every call will be specific to a person, a moment, and a place in history. The calls to the heroes of faith whose stories are told in Hebrews are all particular. Abel's call was to sacrifice. Enoch's call was to walk with God. Noah's call was to build a different environment for both human and animal life. Abraham's call was to relocate. Sarah's call was to give birth in old age. Contemporary leaders can and should also hear the unique calling of God. Daily speaking provides the opportunity for leaders to ask, "What, Lord, is my call in this day? What do you require of me?" Daily listening provides the opportunity to hear answers.

Tension between the long term and the short run often frustrates good leaders who are eager to move beyond the immediate and particular and achieve the bigger goals that they have in mind. Yet if each day is the gift of a good God, then each day is to be lived for its own sake. The result of good hearing is that aspirations for the long run can be balanced with the needs of each day. Perhaps this truth can be a source of strength for leaders, given the unpredictable turbulence in which they and their organizations sometimes swim.

Another important aspect of having a God who calls is listening in all arenas of life. Vocation is bigger than the sphere of paid employment. It involves fulfilling both paid and unpaid roles, as well as balancing among them at different stages and phases, and even on different days of our lives. Martin Luther called these roles "stations" and argued that all who are called by God have a variety of stations that they occupy—as church participants, family members, community citizens, and paid workers (Hardy, 1990, pp. 46–47). All these roles are part of vocation, and the balance among them must be found through listening to the caller. To those who aspire to organizational leadership the caller may suggest that they wait until their children are older, or until they have assisted in getting their local congregations back on track, or until their skills and knowledge are more fully developed. To those who already are organizational leaders the caller may suggest plowing ahead, resting, stepping down, rebalancing leadership initiatives, or redirecting energies. The important thing to remember is that God's call covers our whole lives; it is not limited to the paid careers in which leaders are so heavily invested (Roels, 1997).

There is one more important feature of calling: the heroes of faith listened carefully to the caller and received unique callings, but they did not hear God's call in isolation. They heard and acted on their callings in social circumstances, with the involvement of their families and their communities of faith. Similarly, organizational leaders should never assume that vocation, although it is individual, is individualistic, or that the needs and decisions of others have nothing to do with one's calling. God did not create organizational leaders to function as highly independent individualists who believe that they answer only to God and listen to no one else. Such thinking is a recipe for authoritarian command and control, or for disastrous fantasies. Rather, one's calling, as described in Hebrews, chap. 11, involves one's place in the community of long-departed Christian saints, one's place among one's contemporaries, and one's place in the cloud of witnesses ahead. Organizational leaders must be careful not only to listen each day to the calling of God but also to remember that the nature and meaning of that calling materializes only in relationship with the people whom God places on their paths.

In a world of varied options, the continuous vocational decisions of leaders are complex. When there are multiple options and unknown effects, a faithful path is less easily discerned. Daily listening to God, hearing God's call as singular and the same in all spheres of one's life, and honoring others as having an essential role in one's discerning and undertaking that calling are all important for one's sense of vocation. Leaders who listen and who have this perspective on vocation can be the aliens of Hebrews, chap. 11, who cared about their immediate circumstances but located their citizenship elsewhere.

The biblical message about vocation can assist organizational leaders in strengthening their leadership. When daily vocation, properly understood, looms large in leaders' minds, they can cultivate the engaged detachment that allows them to thrive despite their vulnerability. They can then listen to what truly matters for today as well as for tomorrow. They can receive quiet guidance in balancing their daily time allocations, and they can draw strength and wisdom from others who contribute to their vocation.

## Conclusion

Leaders cannot simply choose to exercise faith because doing so is a pragmatic way of strengthening their leadership potential. This kind of pragmatism is a trap into which organizational leaders can easily fall, but faith does not enter our lives in this way. Instead, God, knowing the bankruptcy of human motivations, has chosen to embrace his creatures through Christ. Leaders must respond to this offer, but they must also acknowledge that they are not the authors of their faith. God is the author. Therefore, leaders cannot create any leadership benefits that God-given faith provides.

Yet leaders who accept God's offer of faith through Christ have the firmest foundation for effective leadership and the best protective shield for their risky positions. In an era of changing internal organizational dynamics, of a less certain global environment, of blurred lines of organizational purpose and direction, and of conflicting expectations, those who lead are expected to operate like gods, but they can't. They are human, not divine, and Christian faith requires leaders to be just that: human.

Faith is leaders' most critical resource for dealing with their humanity. It provides the divine person in whom leaders can have ultimate trust, a map of reality that matches the truth that God has created, and a calling that allows leaders to make choices beyond the tyranny of urgent, noise-filled demands. More than sixty years ago, Oswald Chambers ([1935] 1992), a Scottish pastor, teacher and chaplain, wrote:

> Certainty is the mark of the commonsense life—gracious uncertainty is the mark of the spiritual life. To be certain of God means that we are uncertain in all our ways, not knowing what tomorrow may bring. . . . We are uncertain of the next step, but we are certain of God. As soon as we abandon ourselves to God and do the task he has placed closest to us, He begins to fill our lives with surprises. . . . We are not uncertain of God, just uncertain of what He is going to do next. . . . Leave everything to Him and it will be gloriously and graciously uncertain how He will come in—but you can be certain that He will come [April 29 meditation].

Being certain that God will come in is the hope that leaders most need to sustain them on their path, and faith provides the path of "gracious uncertainty" that Christian leaders should travel.

REFERENCES

Bornstein, S. M., and Smith, A. F. "The Puzzles of Leadership." In F. Hesselbein, M. Goldsmith, and R. Beckhard (eds.), *The Leader of the Future.* San Francisco: Jossey-Bass, 1996.

Chambers, O. *My Utmost for His Highest: An Updated Edition in Today's Language,* ed. James Reimann. Grand Rapids, Mich.: Discovery House, 1992. (Originally published 1935.)

Daft, R. L. *Management.* Chicago: Dryden, 1988.

De Pree, M. *Leadership Is an Art*. New York: Doubleday, 1989.

Hardy, L. *The Fabric of This World*. Grand Rapids, Mich.: Eerdmans, 1990.

Maslow, A. H. *Toward a Psychology of Being*. New York: Van Nostrand Reinhold, 1962.

Roels, S. *Organization Man, Organization Woman: Calling, Leadership and Culture*. Nashville, Tenn.: Abingdon, 1997.

Schein, E. "Leadership and Organizational Culture." In F. Hesselbein, M. Goldsmith, and R. Beckhard (eds.), *The Leader of the Future*. San Francisco: Jossey-Bass, 1996.

Schreiter, R. *The New Catholicity: Theology Between the Global and the Local*. Maryknoll, N.Y.: Orbis, 1997.

Senge, P. "Leading, Learning Organizations: The Bold, the Powerful, and the Invisible." In F. Hesselbein, M. Goldsmith, R. Beckhard (eds.), *The Leader of the Future*. San Francisco: Jossey-Bass, 1996.

*Westminster Shorter Catechism*. Edinburgh, Scotland: Banner of Truth Trust, 1956. (Originally published 1928.)

# 10

# SHARING PERSONAL FAITH AT WORK

*William E. Diehl*

William E. Diehl is president of Riverbend Resource Center, a management consulting firm in Allentown, Pennsylvania. Formerly national manager of sales for Bethlehem Steel Company, he is the author of seven books on faith and its role in daily life, including *The Monday Connection: On Being an Authentic Christian in a Weekday World* and *In Search of Faithfulness: Lessons from the Christian Community*.

———— o ————

"I DON'T CARE what you say, discussing your faith in your workplace is like throwing a lighted match into a pool of gasoline!" the man thundered. "My faith is expressed by what I do, not by what I say!"

The classroom was still. No one disagreed. All eyes were on me. Here was an outstanding member of our business community, taking great issue with my suggestion that believers bear witness to their faith both by what they do and by what they say in the workplace.

I had been leading a Sunday-morning adult discussion group at our town's Episcopal church; my assigned topic was "Christianity in the Workplace." When I asked for examples of a Christian's behavior in the workplace, many participants had mentioned honesty, loyalty, high moral standards, compassion, dedication to one's job, friendliness, and other qualities. Then I asked a few more questions.

"These are all very fine traits," I said, "but can we say they are exclusively Christian? Don't non-Christians do these things as well? Are good deeds the only way we express our faith in the workplace?" I suggested that we also express our faith by talking about it, by telling others about it.

"That will turn people off," one participant had said.

"Perhaps it depends on how we do it," I replied. I mentioned that one of my favorite religious authors, Elton Trueblood, has often said that people who declare they can witness to their faith purely by their deeds are insufferably self-righteous—no one is that good, and so there are times when faith must be expressed in words.

And that's when the prominent businessman exploded.

He was indeed a person of great virtue. As a leader in his business and in our community, he was known for his great integrity, his kindness, and his generosity. He was also an active lay leader in his congregation, in his diocese, and in the national Episcopal denomination. I could understand why he felt sure that his good works outside the church flowed from his faith commitments inside the church. He was obviously angered by the suggestion that in not talking about his faith, he might not be doing enough.

If this noted leader took such a strong position against expressing faith in the workplace, then it is quite likely that no one working for him dared to challenge his view, nor was he likely to permit an on-site prayer group or Bible study group among his employees, on their own time, before starting work in the morning. As we shall see in this chapter, leadership, both in the workplace and in the church, is largely responsible for creating the fear of expressing one's faith on the job.

Why was this leader reluctant to speak about his faith in the workplace? Religion is a very personal matter; therefore, sociologists often tell us, many people want to be private about their faith. Those who flaunt their religiosity are often seen as self-righteous or hypocritical.

It was many years ago that Bellah, Madsen, Sullivan, Swindler, and Tipton (1996) originally revealed the extent of the privatization of religion, and Sample (1990, p. 114) states that middle-class religion has a "highly developed individual self-consciousness"; in particular, the religion of prosperous businesspeople is "intensely personal." Barna (1991) reports on an extensive survey that he did on religion in America. One of Barna's survey items was "'You have a responsibility to explain your religious beliefs to others who may believe differently,' Do you agree . . . or disagree with the statement?" Of the 1,005 respondents, 28 percent agreed strongly, 25 percent agreed somewhat, 20 percent disagreed somewhat, and 25 percent disagreed strongly. When the responses were broken down according to denominational affiliation, however, 43 percent of the evangelical Christian respondents agreed strongly, as did 20 percent of the Catholics and 19 percent of the mainline Protestants (Barna, 1991, p. 223). Admittedly, this survey item did not mention the workplace, but it suggests to me more of the privatization commonly found among "mainliners."

Is the privatization of religion biblical? Hardly. Jesus was constantly reaching out, in deed and in word, to those he encountered. There were times when he went away by himself to pray in private, but most of his ministry was public.

Matthew tells us that Jesus's last words to his disciples were "Go therefore and make disciples of all nations, baptizing them in the name of the Father and of the Son and of the Holy Spirit and teaching them to obey everything I have commanded you" (Matt. 28:19–20). Luke offers a similar theme: "You will receive power when the Holy Spirit comes upon you; and you will be my witnesses in Jerusalem, and in all Judea and Samaria, and to the ends of the earth" (Acts 1:8). The early members of the church most certainly told others about their faith.

These words from the Bible have been repeated many times from pulpits of churches to which my wife, Judith, and I have belonged. My pastors have preached on our calling to bring the Gospel to others, both in words and in deeds, in our daily lives.

Yet as a young salesman for Bethlehem Steel Company, I did no verbal "witnessing" in my place of work. I didn't know how. I knew from experience and from the stories of friends that the in-your-face evangelism of certain Christian groups had a negative effect on most people. I knew how *not* to witness to my faith in word, but I had no idea how to do it effectively, and my church provided absolutely no help. Occasionally I talked to business associates about my church, its pastor, and its programs, but I never said anything about my spiritual journey.

During my thirty-four years at Bethlehem Steel, none of my immediate bosses or senior managers ever hinted, by their own actions, that expressing one's faith in the workplace was acceptable. And so, over the years, I came to accept a position close to the one espoused by the irate local business leader: in-your-face evangelism (the only kind I knew) in the workplace was something like throwing a lighted match into a pool of gasoline.

A first conclusion, based on personal experience, is that this silence is explained less by the possibility of feeling ashamed about being labeled a Christian than by a conviction, supported by business leaders I knew, that personal faith is a very private thing, not to be expressed openly to others.

I have never hesitated to invite friends to visit or join our church, but I have been uptight about sharing my experience of Jesus with them. Also, unfortunately, in those early years of my career, my church never equipped me for anything except teaching children and youth in Sunday school.

As Judith and I moved around the country and joined various churches, the church leaders never concerned themselves with teaching church members how to express their faith in daily life—with one brief exception, when my denomination came out with an adult course called "Word and Witness." Our congregation was part of the pilot study, and what immediately became evident was that the church leaders who had created the course did not know how to witness to faith in the workplace. Reviews from all the other pilot congregations mentioned the same weakness. Finally, after two revisions, the course was revised in a way that made sense to the laity. Unfortunately, however, when our denomination merged with another, the course was dropped, and all appeals to maintain it fell on deaf ears; the national leaders who produced materials for adult study did not find the course worthwhile.

But there are other ways of expressing faith in the workplace; as already mentioned, there is the possibility of a small, on-site group that engages in Bible study, prayer, and discussion on its members' own time. In my business career, I tried this approach several times, with mixed results.

The first time, perhaps twenty-five years ago, I invited eight other people from my company, people who I knew were churchgoing Lutherans, to get together one evening a week at a local church to discuss our faith. This weekly meeting turned into a friendly discussion group that dealt only with how things were going in each of our congregations. We shied away from discussing the fundamentals of our faith or how our faith applied to our work. We never grew into a group for prayer, Bible study, or spiritual growth, primarily because none of us knew how to develop and lead such a group. Again, my local church had never trained me for such leadership. In fact, in those days, small groups were not encouraged at all, for fear that they would compete with the larger congregation.

I made a second effort about ten years later, when I asked my former pastor if he would meet for lunch with a few of our members who worked at Bethlehem Steel. He willingly accepted, and seven of us gathered once a month in a corner of our workplace's cafeteria. Our conversations dealt mostly with ethical situations, and the pastor helped us see the biblical and theological implications of the issues. These were good sessions, and they gave us an opportunity to tell curious friends what we were doing. Nevertheless, because most of us frequently traveled on business, attendance was poor. When summer came, a time when we would be taking vacations, we agreed to adjourn for two months. In September, I waited for just one person to ask about resuming these meetings, but no one did. I assumed that the group was not helpful to the others, and I dropped it. (Our present pastor has visited several large local companies where many of our members work. He began by getting in touch with top managers and asking to have lunch with some of his parishioners. In all cases, he was welcomed. He and his parishioners met mostly in cafeterias, but one company, the largest employer in the area, provided him a private dining room. In these lunch meetings and conversations, the pastor listened to ethical problems, helped with biblical connections, and led prayer. Nevertheless, as had been my own experience at Bethlehem Steel, travel and scheduling problems made consistent attendance impossible, and all these meetings were dropped by mutual agreement; topics for discussion seemed to have been exhausted. At no time, however, did corporate management interfere.)

In the ensuing years, I learned how to organize and lead small groups. After I had some success doing so in our congregation, my thoughts returned to trying a small group in my workplace, again on the members' own time. I was then the assistant to a national sales manager who was a Jew, the only one in our entire management structure. As I thought about organizing a small Christian support group in our department, I wondered how he would take it. Would he be offended? Would the rest of the company see the group as a reaction to my working for a Jewish manager? He was too nice a man to risk offending, and so I never went ahead, but I determined that if I succeeded him, I would organize a Christian support group in our office.

A second conclusion I have reached is that care needs to be taken not to offend people of other faiths.

A few years later, I became the national sales manager. After several months in the job, I began to draft an invitation to everyone in the department to join me in a voluntary fifteen-minute prayer session at 7:45 A.M. I stressed the voluntary nature of the proposition, but the more I thought about it, the more I wondered if a prayer session organized by the boss could truly be voluntary. After all, I was the one who recommended people for raises and did their performance evaluations. They naturally wanted to please me. Some would have the courage not to accept my invitation, but would they all? Would I, in effect, be manipulating some people to join a prayer group, not for their own spiritual needs, but just to please me?

I dropped the idea.

A third conclusion I have reached is that whatever expression of faith there may be in the workplace, it must not be seen as manipulation on the part of the leader.

Are these experiences typical of all Christians in the workplace? Apparently not. In some parts of the Christian Church in America, people have been given some leadership training in witnessing, particularly in the evangelical churches. The fear of looking foolish is minimized when one is instructed on what to say, even if one's words are rejected by the listener; at least the speaker has the assurance that he or she has given the right message. As for rejection, evangelicals remind themselves that Jesus was rejected by many during his lifetime. They seldom see themselves as being manipulative. Bringing people to Christ is the paramount goal.

Thus my experiences over much of my career had led me to conclude that expressing one's faith in the workplace was, if not like throwing a match into gasoline, at least like trying to mix oil and water. It just didn't work.

But that was then. This is now.

## Expressing Faith: A Survey

We hear from many sources about a growing longing for deeper spirituality in daily life. To test the reality of this trend, I decided to put the question to the members of my own congregation.

In May 1998 I prepared a survey that included twenty-one questions. It asked about various forms (other than good deeds) of expressing faith in the workplace. Using our congregational directory, which identifies all members by name, address, phone number, and occupation, I sent the survey to slightly fewer than four hundred members of the Lutheran Church of the Holy Spirit in Emmaus, Pennsylvania, who had paid jobs of one sort or another. Another forty surveys were mailed to non-Lutheran friends, including evangelicals, in various parts of the country. An accompanying letter explained the purpose of the survey. I indicated that people could sign their names or not, as they wished. I enclosed a self-addressed stamped envelope with the survey sheet and asked that the survey be returned by a specific date, about three weeks later.

In a matter of days the surveys started pouring in. By the deadline, I had received nearly two hundred replies. Most had come from the members of my own congregation, but a very high percentage of the non-Lutheran group also responded.

The demographic spread of the replies was broad: 51.2 percent of the respondents were men, and 48.8 percent were women. With respect to age, 71 percent of the respondents were in the prime working years (thirty-five to fifty-five years old), 21 percent were over fifty-five, and 8 percent were under thirty-five.

There was also good representation by types of employers: 36 percent worked for public corporations, 23 percent for private corporations, 18 percent for public schools, 8 percent in government (local, state, and national), 3 percent in social service agencies, 3 percent in higher education, and the balance in other fields. In selecting the people to be surveyed, I had avoided those (such as traveling salesmen) who did not have definite workplaces or who worked alone. With respect to size of employer, the respondents were almost evenly divided among those who worked for organizations with fewer than 50 employees, those with fifty to five hundred employees, and those with more than five hundred employees.

In some ways, our congregation is not typical of mainline Protestantism. For years we have worked hard at affirming, equipping, and supporting our members for ministry in daily life. We help our people see that the Sunday experience of worship can and should connect with the weekday experience of work. As in many congregations, however, a minority of our members is very active, a minority is very inactive, and a majority is only somewhat active. Because many respondents signed the survey sheets, I would say, on the basis of my knowledge about this congregation, that the number of returned surveys reflects the same proportions of active, inactive, and somewhat active members. The non-Lutheran respondents, a smaller group, are all very active church members, whom I have known over the years. Therefore, it seems reasonable to conclude that among the respondents there is a strong minority with a clear vision of the connection between faith and daily work.

Not everyone responded to every question. The tabulations for any particular question were made on the basis of how many responded to it. Ample space was provided for comments.

For me, a key question in the survey was "Have you ever discussed your faith with another person in your workplace?" Of those who responded, 85 percent said yes, and 15 percent said no. I would not have been surprised to learn that the 15 to 20 percent minority of the congregation who practiced ministry in daily life had talked at work about their faith to some extent, but the figure of 85 percent did surprise me. The next question was "If so, what was the content of your discussion?" The majority of the 85 percent indicated that they had talked about their pastors and various activities at their churches; very few had discussed their personal faith. Those who had discussed their personal faith reported having discussed some of the following topics:

> "How faith has helped me deal with fear or uncertainty."

> "I share with them my inspiration and support through my books and writing."

> "Personal beliefs about baptism, communion, etc."

> "The power of prayer for teenagers" (this response came from a public school teacher).

> "Ethics, spirituality, psychology of religion."

> "Personal meaning of faith."

> "Positive effect that prayer, belief and religion played in spiritual healing" (this response came from a man whose wife had been fighting cancer for more than four years).

> "Purpose and meaning of prayer."

> "My faith, religion in general, hot topics such as abortion."

> "There are a few men who don't believe, and I try to tell them that there is a God and cite examples and try to set an example."

The word *beliefs* was used by a number of other respondents, but what the content of their beliefs was is not clear. Of the 85 percent who said they had talked about their faith in the workplace, however, only four respondents had used the word *God,* and one had used *Jesus Christ;* not once did the terms *gospel* or *good news* appear. Was there a concern about being too explicit?

The survey then went on to other, less likely forms of expression in the workplace. To the question "Is there a Bible study group in your workplace that meets during the employees' free time?" the response of 93 percent was no; the 7 percent who said yes were all, with one exception, public school teachers. Nevertheless, only half the school teachers, or not quite 3 percent, belonged to such a group. To a follow-up question, 36 percent of all respondents said they "would join such a group if it started," 56 percent said they would not, and 8 percent said the decision would depend on certain conditions (such as who led it, for example). Those who said they would join a Bible study group were then asked "Why?" Some of the answers were as follows:

> "You become stronger in your faith when you join with others of like mind."

"It would, at the least, provide a basis for support for each of us within our profession. It would add a growth dimension not built around 'talking shop.'"

"My Bible knowledge is very limited. This would be a way to bring co-workers together."

"For support and encouragement of others with similar ethics."

"It could be a way to keep the job in proper perspective."

"To develop closer relationships with fellow workers and share the word of God."

The majority who said they would not join a Bible study group gave various reasons: "I have only 30 minutes for lunch," "My free time is very precious," "I know my company would never permit it"; only a very small number said, "My faith is a very personal matter."

A very similar pattern of responses came in response to the questions "Is there a prayer group in your workplace that meets during the employees' free time?" and "Is there a religious-based discussion group in your workplace that meets regularly to discuss issues of faith?" Again, it was public school teachers who said yes, especially to the question about a discussion group. It was interesting to note that the 31 people who worked in the public school system and participated in the survey were evenly divided on whether such activities as Bible study, prayer groups, and religious discussion groups should be allowed. The issue of separation of church and state was frequently cited by those who said no, but the "yes" responses expressed the feeling that such groups, with members meeting on their own time, would be helpful in an occupational setting where the expression of faith was forbidden. One man wrote, "My workplace is viewed as my ministry, and I need support, guidance, and to share my joys and concerns with other Christians." This teacher met with other Christian teachers at 6:30 A.M. twice a month.

It is interesting to note that although many people feel religion does not belong in the workplace, about one-third of those surveyed expressed interest in having Bible study, prayer, or discussion in their free time. But who would provide leadership? The survey explored the matter of leadership by asking, "If your manager or supervisor personally invited you to join a Bible, prayer, or discussion group, would you accept?" In addition to the raw responses, this question drew many qualifiers and suspicions; 59 percent of the respondents said no, with many concerned that the supervisor might want to push "her type of Christianity" on others. They were concerned, in short, about manipulation. Of the 36 percent who said they would accept this invitation, there were also some who added such comments as "It depends on who the manager is" and "Yes, but not from just any manager." There were also 13 percent who said, "Perhaps." It is clear that people do not want to be pressured in the workplace when it comes to their faith.

As for expressing one's faith in the workplace through symbols, 69 percent of the respondents felt it would be "appropriate for a supervisor or manager to keep a Bible in plain view on his/her desk." Among the 31 percent who said no were a few who commented that a Bible displayed on a supervisor's desk might be offensive to a non-Christian subordinate.

The question "Do you feel it is appropriate or inappropriate for a worker to wear a religious pin or necklace?" revealed that 83 percent of the respondents felt it was appropriate and 17 percent felt it was inappropriate.

Throughout the survey, there was a minority of 10 to 15 percent who seemed to feel that there should be absolutely no expression of faith in the workplace. These people said that their faith was a very personal and therefore private matter. There was also a minority of about 10 percent who apparently wanted to bring their faith into the workplace as much as possible. For example, the survey asked a high-risk question—"If a co-worker shared a personal problem with you, would you suggest immediately praying together about it?"—to which 11 percent said they would make such a suggestion (some qualified their responses by adding that they would make this suggestion if the praying could be done in a private place).

More traditional times and places for prayer drew stronger positive responses. For example, 58 percent of the respondents said yes to the question "If you were convening a group of co-workers for an important dinner or meeting, would you offer an opening prayer that would be inclusive of all faiths?"; many added comments like "Dinner—yes; meeting—no."

There is a very strong feeling that Christians should respect the religious expressions of others: an overwhelming 96 percent of the respondents said no to the question "Do you find it offensive if co-workers of another faith bring some of their religious practices into the workplace— for example, a Jew wearing a yarmulke or a Muslim praying in his/her workplace?" I find it interesting that whereas about 10 to 15 percent of those surveyed felt there should be absolutely no expression of the Christian faith in the workplace, most of those surveyed apparently had no objection to non-Christians having some expression of their faith in the workplace. My conclusion is that people who feel that their own faith is a very private matter do not object if others, including other Christians, express their faith in more publicly.

To summarize this survey, I believe that it shows a shift from attitudes that were prevalent twenty or thirty years ago. Whereas the Episcopal businessman and I lived a dualistic life, in which Sunday's experience in church was not connected with Monday's experience at work (apart from Sunday's shaping of the values we carried into the workplace on Monday), many churches today are advocating a ministry in daily life for all believers. In our congregation, the special attention given to ministry in daily life showed up in the way many people talked about their faith in the workplace, even if the content of their expressions of faith is not deeply spiritual. Our congregation and all other churches must do more to help people express their faith in a more spiritual manner.

As already reported, more than one-third of those who responded to this recent survey expressed interest in at least trying a Bible study, prayer, or discussion group in their workplaces on their own time, but a problem remains: there is no leadership. The survey also revealed that public school teachers constituted the only occupational group that was participating in such groups; these people have had small-group experience in their professional work, and so it is no great step for them to create and lead a religion-centered group on their own time. Congregations need to encourage the development of small groups in the workplace and train some members to be organizers and leaders. What better way to be in mission?

As we become a more diverse nation, we are learning how to live with diversity. As we learn to accept the religious practices of others, we can expect them to accept our practices. We do not want to offend people of different faiths, but we also do not surrender our own expressions.

But there is one large exception: the great change that has taken place in the public school system over the past twenty-five to thirty years. Fear of expressing faith has greatly increased because of the constitutional separation of church and state. When I was a youngster, each school day began with a reading from the book of Psalms, the recital of the Lord's Prayer, a salute to the flag, and the singing of "America the Beautiful." There were a few Jewish kids in my classes, but there were no other non-Christians, to my knowledge, and in those days I assumed that the Lord's Prayer was also offered in Jewish homes and synagogues.

Today the situation is dramatically different. Teachers are not permitted to say or do anything that could be construed as promoting a particular religion, although the interpretation of the policy seems to vary somewhat among schools and school districts, and individual teachers interpret it differently as well. For example, in response to the questions about joining a Bible study, prayer, or discussion in the workplace on one's own time, about one-third of the respondents said they would not join one, and one teacher offered the following explanation: "In a public school this will never happen"—even though some school teachers are indeed meeting for Bible study and prayer on their own time.

A similar divide came over the issue of a supervisor's keeping a Bible on his or her desk. Some teachers said it was a clear violation of the constitutional separation of church and state, whereas others said it was acceptable (one teacher called it a "reference book"). The question about whether it was appropriate for a worker to wear a religious pin or necklace also brought divided responses from teachers, with the majority feeling that it was inappropriate. One feisty teacher wrote "I wear a cross on my necklace, although I was told I shouldn't in a public school." One gets the feeling that because the constitutional separation of church and state bans religious expressions in these teachers' workplaces, a number of the teachers have reacted by finding ways to get around the rules.

It seems to me that congregations should be more aware of the workplace problems faced by public school teachers. Why couldn't pastors or other congregational leaders offer weekly breakfast meetings exclusively for their public school teachers at some local restaurant as teachers are on their way to school? The content of such meetings would be determined by the needs of the teachers. These meetings could include prayer or Bible study. Once the breakfasts were established, leadership might shift to the teachers themselves. In any event, there are numerous ways for congregations to support their public school teachers.

## Evangelicals

The survey I conducted reflects the views and experiences of a mainline denomination, but are there any differences in more evangelical groups? After all, there are many organizations for evangelicals in business: the Christian Businessmen's Association, the Fellowship of Companies for Christ, the International Christian Chamber of Commerce, Professionals and Employees for Christ—only a short list of the organizations that link faith and life overtly in the world of business. How and to what extent might evangelicals differ from the people I surveyed?

Nash (1994) conducted a study of more than eighty-five successful evangelical CEOs and executives. When it came to personal witnessing in the workplace, she discovered that

> participants tend to disguise their Christianity to varying degrees, especially depending upon the context. Several who are very active in the evangelical community said they were not even known by their own employees to be evangelical. Many interviewees try to keep their witness low key by creating passive opportunities to express their faith. Some keep Bibles on their desks or have religious pictures in their private offices but said they would speak about their faith only if asked. . . . On the one hand, their Christian duty clearly calls them to bear witness and, as leaders, they have the social status to make that witness a powerful statement. On the other hand, if they direct such witness at their employees they may be unfairly exploiting their power. . . . Several interviewees acknowledged that they would find it extremely uncomfortable if they were confronted with a statement of faith by a boss who was a fervent Zen Buddhist [Nash, 1994, p. 254].

## Employers

Employers today are well aware of the quest for spirituality among many people of faith. In fact, some business consultants want to incorporate the notion of spirituality (generic rather than Christian) into the culture of corporate life. Indeed, even some apparently secular business speakers and books have a quasi-religious character (see Chapter Twelve).

According to Ronald F. Thiemann, dean of the Harvard Divinity School, "The workplace is a middle ground, between specific religious beliefs held by employees and an older view that everything in the workplace must be purely secular" (cited in Ettorre, 1996). Neither the business community nor the government has established firm lines for religious behavior, but a recent article in the *Los Angeles Times* (Fuller, 1998) offered an unofficial list of the rules, as compiled by an attorney. Here are some examples:

> It is acceptable to keep a copy of the Bible or the Koran on one's desk.
>
> One may ask a co-worker if he or she has "found Jesus Christ," but one may not stuff religious tracts into a co-worker's in-box, desk drawer, or work files.
>
> It is acceptable for employees of a particular religion to meet weekly in an empty conference room for a lunchtime prayer

session, but a supervisor cannot schedule an important meeting that "just happens" to be preceded by a Christian prayer session.

It is acceptable to wear a yarmulke, crucifix, or Star of David to work, but one may not chant in such a way as to distract other workers.

It is acceptable to talk around the water cooler about religion, but planned corporate religious retreats are taboo.

It is acceptable for a supervisor to invite employees to a son's bar mitzvah, but a supervisor may not question an employee about his or her lack of church attendance last Sunday.

The extent to which employers are beginning to buy into this list of do's and don'ts is unknown, but the mere fact that such a list is being seriously proposed represents a significant shift from the long-established business ethos.

## Harassment

Harassment can occur when employees indulge in too much expression of their faith in the workplace, at the expense of others, or when normal expression of faith is always dismissed by others. My own most memorable experience with religious harassment came when I was an assistant district manager of sales, many years before any kind of workplace harassment was considered an issue. In today's world, the behavior I am about to report would be seen as inappropriate.

One of my responsibilities as assistant district manager of sales was to oversee the work of our sales support people, about thirty of whom had Alan as their direct supervisor. Alan had a glass-enclosed office in the large room where the support people also worked. He had recently joined a religious group with a strong evangelical mission and had become a born-again Christian. Alan did not openly proselytize among his workers, but he did feel that he had a mission to help them with their problems. Therefore, whenever he learned of a problem among one of his employees, he invited that person into his office and, in full view of the other workers, read appropriate Bible verses for him or her. He also frequently prayed with the people he was trying to help.

When some of the employees complained to me about Alan's "pushy" ways, I asked him to come to my office. I genuinely applauded the new faith he had found but reported that it was having a negative effect on his workers. He responded by saying that Jesus, too, was rejected, and he put me on the spot by asking how I, as a Christian, was expressing my faith in our office.

Because Alan's conferences with his people did not happen more than two or three times a month, and because the productivity of his unit remained high, I did not threaten to take action against him. But I did tell him that if his activity affected the performance of his unit in any way, we would have to take steps to discontinue it. I also assembled all his employees and told them I had talked to Alan. I encouraged them to turn down Alan's invitations if they wanted to, and I assured them that I would carefully watch to make certain that he did not engage in reprisals against them.

Alan was not a vindictive person. He gracefully accepted his employees' refusals. A few of them did continue meet with him, however, for reasons that I do not know; he may have been a help to them. I have told the story of Alan at many conferences, and invariably there are others in the audience who tell their own stories about aggressive evangelizing in the workplace.

The list of do's and don'ts cited earlier does not draw many sharp lines of separation. For example, posting a flyer on the company bulletin board to advertise a church bake sale is felt to be acceptable. But I wonder: Suppose the church is clearly identified as the boss's church? Suppose the proceeds are to go for supporting a missionary in Africa? I was surprised to note that asking a co-worker if he or she had "found Jesus Christ" was felt to be acceptable. Perhaps it is, but what happens if the co-worker says no? Encouraging co-workers to consider converting to one's own religion is also felt to be acceptable, but, again, what are the follow-up questions? When do they cross the line into harassment?

It would be a mistake to assume that all faithful evangelicals harass others in the workplace. For a number of years, I served on the board of directors of a family-owned steel-fabricating company in the mid-South. The owner, a devout evangelical, opened board meetings and dinners with Christian prayers. The company's quarterly newsletter always carried an article in which the owner praised God and Jesus and thanked them for his success. The company was generous in financial donations to Christian causes, and yet I never had the feeling that employees were pressured to follow the owner's lead. People were hired, rewarded, and promoted on the basis of their contributions to the organization, not their expressions of faith. I once asked the owner if he ever had Jews as employees. "Oh, yes," he replied, very casually. "I rate them on performance, just like anyone else."

There is another kind of harassment in the workplace, the kind in which employers do not respect the religious practices of their employees. For example, Jehovah's Witnesses should not be required to take a loyalty oath that contradicts their beliefs, nor should Sikhs be required to cut their long hair to meet corporate dress codes, nor should Christians be required to work during the only hours when their worship services are offered. In recent years, employers' practices and laws against discrimination in employment have minimized this type of harassment. But there are more subtle forms of harassment, in which co-workers make fun of a person of deep faith. Perhaps the person is referred to as a "goody-goody" because he or she wears a religious pin or necklace or keeps a Bible or the Koran on his or her desk. In a group, the telling of jokes suddenly stops when the person of faith approaches. In the course of a normal conversation at work, a person of faith begins to talk about a retreat or an unusually good religious event that he or she has attended, and co-workers turn the speaker off by quickly directing the conversation to another topic. It doesn't take much of this kind of treatment for the person with a faith commitment to realize that he or she does not have the respect that is granted to other co-workers.

## Conclusion

Is there fear of expressing faith in the workplace today? Yes, to some extent, but there is much less than there was twenty or thirty years ago. The public schools are the workplaces where this fear is highest, but in other workplaces there is still a vestige of the type of individualism that made religious talk at work taboo.

The situation has been changing as some of the Christian churches in this country have encouraged their members to carry their faith into all parts of their lives, even their workplaces. Along with this change has come greater sensitivity on the part of employers to the need for religious expression to be allowed in the workplace as long as it does not interfere with productivity.

This cultural shift has created a new problem: although some employees are interested in participating in small on-site groups (for prayer, or for Bible study) on their own time, there is a dearth of trained leaders. Churches that train laypersons for small-group work usually target their own members as participants, and they think only of church property or their members' homes as meeting places. Church leaders of the mainline denominations continue to overlook the need to train their members on how to witness effectively in the workplace.

There is a healthy fear that expressions of faith in the workplace may be used by some to pressure or manipulate co-workers, but the fear of offending people of other faiths has decreased. Because we live in a multicultural society, there is greater understanding that all groups have the right to their own religious convictions.

There is still uncertainty about what constitutes appropriate or even legal expression of faith in the workplace. Our society is working out its own distinct means of establishing boundaries in a healthy manner; with the search for boundaries will come greater protection against religious harassment.

This chapter and the survey it reports have dealt with Christian witness in the workplace through words and symbols, but many of the survey respondents pointed to the hypocrisy of talking about one's faith but not living the faith through action. Words and symbols ring hollow if a Christian's actions do not accord with the will of Jesus. Christian witness through words does not replace the need for witness through deeds. There are times and places for either and for both. That's the way Jesus lived, and that's the way we should also live.

REFERENCES

Barna, G. *What Americans Believe*. Glendale, Calif.: Regal, 1991.

Bellah, R. N., Madsen, R., Sullivan, W. M., Swindler, A., and Tipton, S. M. *Habits of the Heart* (rev. ed.). Berkeley: University of California Press, 1996.

Ettorre, B. "Religion in the Workplace: Implications for Managers." *Management Review,* 1996.

Fuller, M. "Workplace Guideposts." *Los Angeles Times,* April 5, 1998.

Nash, L. *Believers in Business*. Nashville, Tenn.: Nelson, 1994.

Sample, T. *U.S. Lifestyles and Mainline Churches*. Louisville, Ky.: John Knox, 1990.

# SHAPING THE CENTER WITH WISDOM FROM THE EDGES

*David Trickett*

David Trickett is president of The Jefferson Circle, Fairfax, Virginia. He facilitates individual and organizational renewal in his international teaching consultancy with governments, corporations, and nonprofit organizations. He speaks and writes frequently for academic, business, and popular audiences.

_____ o _____

THE PREVIOUS CHAPTER raised one of the most potentially divisive issues in the workplace: restrictions on expressing one's deepest faith convictions and values. The bifurcation between our personal and public lives prevents us from being whole people in our workplace relationships and responsibilities. Nevertheless, inappropriate sharing of these convictions and values only compounds deep fissures that already exist in the workplace by adding religion to the list of all that delineates us into separate categories. Instead of specifically addressing other potentially divisive issues (such as race, gender, and ethnicity), this chapter goes behind the issues and into the area of personal and organizational life from which they stem, exploring the shadows around the edges of our ways of relating and operating at work. In so doing, this chapter, it is hoped, will deepen this volume's discussions of community, trust, wholeness, and integrity.

Organizations are all about communication and relationships. For all the attention we give to performance-based outcomes, it is the more elusive human infrastructure that makes or breaks an organization. It is at this level that leadership operates, whether in a business, a governmental agency, or a nonprofit group. Leadership has more to do with inner dynamics than with status or position. The styles of leadership in an organization shape its tone and performance; what deserves further examination is how much the organization includes a genuine diversity of perspectives and abilities rather than simply focusing on a narrower pool of intellectual capital. In short, what is at stake is how we see the world, how our worldviews affect the ways in which we communicate with and otherwise relate to others, how able we are to spot obstacles to our organizations' progress, and what we can do to weave a cohesive whole out of distinctive parts. Leadership is all about making connections.

## Organizational Ecology

A helpful way to view an organization is as an ecological system. As such, its elements may be in harmony, but the system itself may often be out of balance. The organization, in order to pursue its mission effectively, needs all its people to be committed to a shared vision of its purpose and of how that purpose should be fulfilled. Really good leaders can be found in many positions in an organization. Wherever they may be, they are able to discern how things fit together and where they don't, and they can help bring greater balance to the institution's social ecology. A custodian is unlikely have the same impact on a company as its chief executive, but a thoughtful custodian whose insights are valued does have a vital role in shaping the tone and performance of the entire organization. Usually, though, professional managers are the ones from whom basic insights and decision making flow. For this reason, I will focus on the two primary styles of leadership—inclusive and exclusive—that may be found among this group of people.

Many of us pride ourselves on our accomplishments as professionals. Years of study, investment in education, and graduate degrees make us experts in certain areas. My own field is organizational ethics. I began to realize a long time ago that the more I learned about my field, the fewer people there were with whom I could speak about it in depth or at length. Have you ever watched lawyers speaking with doctors, engineers with MBAs, or clergy with laity? There is often a profound language gap that separates us from one another and that can upset the creative balance of an organizational ecology; the same languages, attitudes, and behaviors that shape us into experts also lessen our capacity to cross boundaries and forge meaningful links with our colleagues, and the results tend to be distrust, then fear, and, finally, subterfuge and cynicism. For example, I was once asked to work with a unit of the U.S. Department of the Treasury, to help the people in that unit understand and creatively address problems that they perceived as having to do with questions of diversity. They were thinking largely in terms of ethnic issues, but the real diversity-related challenges had more to do with two other issues: with the lack of a meaningful connection between the Department of the Treasury's Washington headquarters and the regional field officers, and with the inability of this unit's lawyers, economists, and bank examiners to understand one another's professional worlds and work well with one another.

In this kind of setting, a certain form of leadership is required. I like to call it *penumbra management*. The word *penumbra* denotes the area that is in partial shadow around what can be clearly seen. The term *penumbra* may be an unfamiliar one, but it helps us realize that leadership basically has to do with discerning factors that are not transparent or highlighted but that are nevertheless crucial to the ethos and functioning of an institution. Penumbra management has to do with bringing these factors to light in a way that creates an environment where very different perspectives can be brought together and mediated. In addition to perspectives that we willingly talk about, it must include such issues as the hurt feelings in a time of downsizing that tempt us to engage in organizational espionage, or our rage over the fact that our years of effort for a company have not brought us the corner suite after all. In volatile situations, good leaders are able to identify strengths in their people that can sustain an organization into the future.

We don't see much of this kind of leadership, however, because it tends to be counterintuitive; too often we suffer from blind spots. For example, I once headed up a consortium of ten graduate schools. Among the combined faculties were several dozen women and men who were focusing on issues of ethical responsibility in organizations. At the beginning of every year we had a celebration, and on those occasions we convened our faculties into either discipline-specific or cross-disciplinary clusters. Because I had been vexed by the difficulties that our graduates were having in connecting their respective fields of expertise with the varieties of people they served, I was keen to launch a new leadership initiative in our schools. Therefore, I asked our ethics specialists to talk about their fields of inquiry—law, medicine, business, theology—but they talked about their work in a way that paralleled the dead ends our graduates were having. I then asked them, "What have you found is the best way to conduct dialogues with specialists in fields other than your own?" Their answers were disappointing. Many were uncomfortable even thinking about interacting with nonacademics, even with those whose fields of expertise overlapped with their own. There was a basic breakdown in understanding of how to communicate with people unlike themselves.

Whenever I have had the opportunity to teach as a visitor in medical, business, and law schools, I have noticed the same kind of functional disability. Is it any wonder, then, that the graduates of a host of fine professional schools can't connect their learning with their work? This is a major leadership challenge, and it demonstrates the need for what I call *penumbral discernment* and whatever actions flow from it. We simply must find a way to span the dividing lines and take ourselves beyond our own special expertise, whatever it may be. Penumbra management is boundary management; it reflects a deep faith in embracing rather than fearing otherness, whether that embracing takes place in an organization or in life generally. This is a stance that resonates strongly with a Christian point of view, in which there is a profound overcoming of sexual, racial, and national boundaries (see Eph. 2:13–22).

## Professional Blinders

Most models of leadership, even those that acknowledge its fundamentally social nature, don't get to the core of our current situation: the question of identity. We want sharp edges in our definitions of roles, and we like measurable objectives and criteria for evaluating them. But reality is more complex, and if we stay bound by our professional formation, which places things into neat categories, then we will be in trouble.

At a meeting some years ago, for example, I was talking with an acquaintance, a representative from one of the largest U.S. financial institutions, about the need to pursue global planning and complex change management, and about styles of doing that. To illustrate a point, I related my experience of consulting with a multinational petrochemical company on ways of focusing and measuring the company's values and beliefs by formulating a matrix, which distinguished between perspectives favoring inclusion of diversity and those favoring exclusion of diversity, each perspective having particular ramifications for organizational planning and leadership.

"I've faced the same kind of issue in my organization," my acquaintance said, "but when I try to get my senior colleagues to take the issue of diversity on, they tell me I'm trying to force them to do what ought to be done on Sunday at church. I've been stymied. My peers and superiors regard my efforts as either an irrelevance or a threat. They don't see the connection between diversity and the mission driving our bank."

The blinders of this bank's senior managers were actually putting the bank at risk, for these managers did not really know how best to serve the bank's customer populations. They would have been able to discover how to do that by exploring the hidden areas of their customers' beliefs, aspirations, and values, but many of the managers regarded this information as belonging strictly to the realm of the personal. We should not pry into people's deepest and most private concerns, of course, but what is private and what is personal are not the same thing, even though we too often confuse them.

There is a rich intellectual and religious tradition, going back thousands of years, that focuses on this basic insight. The very makeup of the universe, not to mention human existence, is social and shared rather than individualistic and private. This insight is at the core of the whole Judeo-Christian worldview and has some thoughtful modern exponents, among them Mead (1932), who stresses that to be at all is to be part of a larger whole. This idea meshes with what I have said about organizations as, ideally, balanced social ecologies. Perhaps many of the failings of people in leadership roles can be attributed to their never having seen that living relationships, not merely roles, accountability structures, or chains of command and control, make the organizational world go around.

It is lamentable but true that clear, basic convictions and commitments —what the religious community speaks of as faith—are still not enough to equip people to see the inextricably social nature of reality. Witness the colleagues of my banking acquaintance, who were united in wanting to keep Sunday's concerns apart from Monday's. To persist in the face of such a wall of resistance is more than many of us feel we can do; it is fraught with risk and derision at every step. But here, precisely, is a key to effective leadership, whatever the position occupied by the person who provides it. Moving the minds and hearts of people in complex organizations involves reframing situations afresh and learning how to connect the dots anew. To do so, we must be willing to cross boundaries and bring to light what is in the shadows.

This path requires courage, for it leads to much misunderstanding and many obstacles. My experience suggests that those who have a real advantage here are people who have spent some time in intercultural and interfaith dialogue. Our vocation has pushed us outside the safety zone of disciplinary expertise; we reside in the shadow, or "between," where insight can be found. We hear the voice of wisdom beckoning in the core insights of those who have traveled the same path. Consider, for example, Tillich (1967), who gave us the phrase "on the boundary"; or Morton (1985), who said that "the journey is home"; or Drucker (1997), who offers the "confessions of a bystander"; or Autry (1996), whose own "confessions" are those of an "accidental businessman"; or Bateson (1994), who speaks of "peripheral visions." What do we learn from boundary spanners like these? We come to recognize that people speak with increasing openness about a disconnection between their sense of what it is to be a person and what is expected of them in the workplace. What is the underlying issue? What is to be done about it?

## Roots of the Problem

The basic problem is the conceptual split that has long pervaded the developed nations and is now gaining ground in developing nations, and at a frightening pace. This gulf is not merely between oneself and one's work; it is much deeper and wider.

### Self-Alienation

Over the past several centuries, a number of thinkers, Descartes foremost among them, have driven a wedge between mind and body or, more generally, between inner and outer experience of the world. This wedge was driven deeper by the impact of the scientific and technological revolution. One unfortunate result has been people's growing sense of alienation from themselves. It is not uncommon today to hear people saying that they would rather not have to leave their "selves" at the door when they enter their offices. Something basic has been sundered. We need to identify what it is and why this sundering has happened, and to help those who are willing to take the courageous steps toward discerning a path that leads to healing and renewal. This is a cardinal task of leadership today, and it requires a deeply inclusive exercise of power.

### Transactions Versus Relationships

A second contemporary factor that has been deepening the rift within ourselves is the trend of confusing transactions with relationships. Transactions dominate in most of our waking lives today. Even in areas once thought sacrosanct—marriage, doctor-patient relationships, and interactions between a pastor and a church member—we find indications of contractual rather than covenantal bonds. This move from more organic to more conditional, regulated bonds lies behind the phenomena of pre- and postnuptial agreements, cost- and process-based health care, and stewardship drives that focus chiefly on the meeting of the financial targets. A relationship holds the possibility of mutual transformation and may not involve a tangible net gain for the parties involved; a transaction tends to involve material benefits, and even in the much heralded win-win transaction there is always a winner and a loser. A transactions also tends to leave untouched the deeper level of human experience, where dreams, fears, and convictions reside. This deeper level tends to be the birthing ground of what so many of us desperately seek—real insights, practical breakthroughs, creative innovations. But we hardly ever reach this level in the workplace, nor, more and more, do we reach it in any place at all. We are confused, and the price of our confusion is peril, not least to those of us who yearn to find a way of connecting our deepest wellsprings of belief with how we spend our days at work. But even as we persist in ignoring this peril, we cry out for enhanced performance, higher productivity, and better morale in the workplace.

## Self-Focused Individualism

A third factor in perpetuating the rift within ourselves and one that works against the integration of conviction-based values and performance in the workplace, is the extraordinary contemporary first-person-singular focus, particularly in the United States. Perhaps it is the residue of the great westward expansion of the eighteenth and nineteenth centuries; in those times, individualism was viewed as the only way to survive in a violent environment (a point of view that completely ignored some of the basic tenets of the Native Americans, who saw a deep interconnection between themselves and the earth).

The preoccupation with getting ahead is not the only manifestation of the first-person-singular focus, however. There is also the so-called imposter syndrome (first identified in such professional populations as attorneys and physicians), whereby, as we gain professional expertise, we are held accountable to high expectations. We may realize that we ourselves don't know a great deal, but our peer group enforces a taboo against our saying so, and we keep looking over our shoulders, hoping that no one will discover our vulnerable spots, only some of which we ourselves perceive. As we know, however (see Chapters Three and Five), vulnerability is a key to effective leadership, and humility should be a core trait of the faith-based leader. Nevertheless, most signals sent through organizations today, especially among professionally educated populations, indicate that vulnerability is a chink in one's armor, a sign of weakness, a sure indicator of failure at some point.

Another reflection of self-focused individualism may appear at first to be an expression of conviction-based leadership: stereotypical or narrowly focused efforts to "share faith" in the workplace (see Chapter Ten). Such sharing is generally well meant, but it can be off-putting and hurtful to those who don't have the same deep passions and commitments, and even to some who do. Niebuhr (1963, 1989) has addressed this issue by explaining the difference between what we affirm (about which we are often right) and what we refute or deny (about which we are often wrong, especially with respect to belief systems differing from our own). In both affirmation and denial, however, there is a danger of idolatry, for we tend to make too much of what means most to us and to vilify what gets in its way. There is also a close link between what we don't like and what we don't understand, which is why, in our high-minded eagerness to share our precious convictions with others, we often succeed only in distancing ourselves from them: we haven't figured out how to communicate our most strongly held beliefs in a way that doesn't divide the world into two camps. This confusion is disastrous for anyone who seeks to exercise leadership, for it perpetuates and, perhaps, worsens the disconnection that many of us already experience in the workplace. Separation remains, even when the goal is communion. Niebuhr (1989) encourages us, as we share our core convictions, to think less in terms of what is right or wrong and more in terms of what is fitting and balanced. He forces us to take seriously the fact that an insight, if it is to affect a person's life with any significance, must first be put into language that connects it with the person's concerns.

## Community and Shared Convictions

One barrier to the exercise of faith-based leadership in organizations is the fact that few of us really know those with whom we work. My wife, who is English, has helped me perceive the North American habit of calling perfect strangers by their given names, as if they were friends. This kind of pseudofamiliarity can deflect us from realizing that we are a society of strangers acting as if we were in community.

Because we don't know others, we don't trust them—but trust, as we have seen (Chapter Three), is required for the effective transmission of conviction-based values in any setting, not just a corporation but also a house of worship, where shared practices that could be life-enhancing rituals may become little more than choreographed performances, instrumental rather than personal.

For all our talk about community, we are not willing to invest the time and energy it takes to make the commitments that could help us overcome our disconnection from others. The work environment is largely corrosive of the spirit that makes such commitments possible. We remain separate from one another, even in our increasingly networked world.

## Answers from the Edges

Many of us believe that there must be a better way, but we are unclear about what it is or how to find it. We are looking for answers to the most deeply vexing questions that we bring to our life and our work: How do we find value while we seek to add value? How do we count for something in the midst of what seems ephemeral?

Sometimes these questions are posed with unexpectedly great feeling, even by apparently hardened men and women. Whenever they are voiced, I am reminded of three things: Jesus lamenting over the people of Jerusalem, saying that he would like to gather them up as a mother hen does her chicks, but that they are not receptive (Luke 13:34); Chinen's marvelous studies (1989, 1993a, 1993b, 1996) of folk and fairy tales, one haunting theme of which is those who have lost their way and do not know the way home; and a photograph, snapped from inside the Black Forest cottage of Martin Heidegger, in which, through the window above Heidegger's desk, a maze of eventually intersecting paths through the deep forest can be discerned, but only very faintly. Moving from continual disconnection to reconnection is like going home, but home may no longer look familiar, and the path may not be easy to follow. We must be able to read its signs; discernment is crucial. We must know how and where to make the connection between the conviction-based values that are central to us and the conviction-based values held by others. And we must know the difference it makes to establish these links without losing anything essential. Dialogue is critically important, for the paths that people tread are multiple; we must know how to translate from one to another, faithfully, in order to grow a community of shared commitment. I believe we do this work best by attending to what is in the penumbra rather than to what is in bright light or total darkness.

The penumbra is home to the heart's language. Of all the abilities a leader requires, the art of listening to and speaking this language, of seeing what is at the edges, is perhaps the one closest to the core of the leader's effectiveness. The ability to find the path for communicating faith-based values with grace and power, thus engaging the aspirations of others

so that everyone can take the practical steps required to make the organization a community of shared commitment: this is the ability that will
distinguish the type of leader whom we must nurture in the coming millennium, the type of leader who can help to develop the relationships that
will ground all transactions, who can discern the gifts and possibilities
that people with diverse convictions bring to the organization. Leaders
who focus only on direct, tangible goals (whether these involve the bottom line or not) will miss the mark by failing to see that the most effective way of hitting that target is to develop a group of people who know
themselves to be genuinely valued, trusted, and respected. A leader actually can do little more than help to generate a vision and catalyze an environment where this kind of nurturing and growth can take place, and that
will be the chief contribution of those gifted with penumbral vision.

Lest we believe that this vision is unattainable, we should note some
experiments that are now under way in a variety of settings; I shall mention only a few of which I have firsthand knowledge:

○ The Center for Global Ethics has undertaken a worldwide survey
  of what people in many cultural and organizational contexts
  believe may be our shared values.

○ A cluster of large and small corporations, under the aegis of the
  Hitachi Foundation, has begun to focus on a new and more
  significant face for corporate social responsibility. Several
  membership organizations, such as the World Business Academy,
  the Prince of Wales Business Leaders Forum, and Business in the
  Community, as well as the Caux Round Table, are developing a
  rich base of practicable core values and commitments for nurturing
  community.

○ Some exciting cross-sector partnership models are being birthed, as
  reflected in the convergence of the worlds of government and
  business in the development of the Waterton-Glacier International
  Peace Park at the border between the United States and Canada.

We can gain something important from each of these experiments, but
perhaps what is most important is that we learn ever more effective ways
to translate the commitment and value bases from which people approach
their work.

At this point, too few of us have found a way of listening with discernment in order to connect values with performance and leadership. We
spend too much of our time defending our own narrow views of what
counts as value, thereby contributing to the divisiveness we see in the

marketplace. We urgently need a cadre of people who can focus on convergence, on making connections that develop an inclusive community of shared commitment and behavior.

Many specific things can be done if we attend to weaving together the varied threads that we all bring to any social context. Some of these things will have an impact on formal education for management and leadership, whether it takes place in universities, business schools, or corporate learning environments. Most of these things simply have to be tried out in organizational planning and decision making. Whatever we do, we must remember the importance of being inspired and encouraged to leave the comfort zone of our deep convictions, for only by doing so—by going into what may seem to be a wilderness, with dangers lurking everywhere—may we have a chance of finding the reconnection we so earnestly seek.

When all is said and done, the whole matter of seeking to include or exclude, connect or disconnect, is itself a reflection of conviction and perspective, of attitude and faith. Faith-based leadership in the next millennium, if it is to be authentically true to its calling, must be freed from its myopic attempt to defend what is not its to defend and to erect barriers, with good intent or bad, where walls should actually come down. The deep insights of biblical faith point us in this direction: the self, others, and the organization are absolutely interdependent. It is our task to watch the edges, to focus on the penumbra. By doing so, we can discern powerful ways to grasp and apply these profound insights.

## Conclusion

One of our difficulties in sharing conviction-based values in the workplace is that we have no agreed-on systemic support for integrating beliefs and values. We need people who can lead us in forging positive points of connection with our fellows. The keys to opening up the semihidden, penumbral side of life are the principles of listening with discernment and engaging in discerning dialogue. When these principles are understood and practiced, leadership does not shrink from the shadows; it provides the impetus in an organization for the incubation of creative reflection, and for action in pursuit of reconnection.

REFERENCES

Autry, J. *Confessions of an Accidental Businessman: It Takes a Lifetime to Find Wisdom.* San Francisco: Berrett-Koehler, 1996.

Bateson, M. C. *Peripheral Visions: Learning Along the Way.* New York: HarperCollins, 1994.

Chinen, A. B. *In the Ever After: Fairy Tales and the Second Half of Life.* Wilmette, Ill.: Chiron, 1989.

Chinen, A. B. *Beyond the Hero: Classic Stories of Men in Search of Soul.* New York: Putnam, 1993a.

Chinen, A. B. *Once Upon a Midlife: Classic Stories and Mythic Tales to Illuminate the Middle Years.* New York: Putnam, 1993b.

Chinen, A. B. *Waking the World: Classic Tales of Women and the Heroic Feminine.* Los Angeles: Tarcher, 1996.

Drucker, P. F. *Adventures of a Bystander.* New York: Wiley, 1997.

Mead, G. H. *The Philosophy of the Present.* La Salle, Ill.: Open Court, 1932.

Morton, N. *The Journey Is Home.* Boston: Beacon Press, 1985.

Niebuhr, H. R. *The Responsible Self: An Essay in Christian Moral Philosophy.* New York: HarperCollins, 1963.

Niebuhr, H. R. *Faith on Earth: An Inquiry into the Structure of Human Faith.* New Haven: Yale University Press, 1989.

Tillich, P. *On the Boundary.* London: Collins, 1967.

## ADDITIONAL READINGS

Whitehead, A. N. *Adventures of Ideas.* Cambridge, England: Cambridge University Press, 1933.

Whitehead, A. N. *Modes of Thought.* Cambridge, England: Cambridge University Press, 1938.

# 12

# RECOGNIZING LEADERS' HIDDEN BELIEFS

*Stephen Pattison*

Stephen Pattison has worked as a health service manager in the British National Health Service and as a senior lecturer in the School of Health and Social Welfare at the Open University. He is currently a professor in the Department of Education at the University of Wales, Cardiff. His special interests in ethics, management, and public theology are reflected in his book *The Faith of the Managers: When Management Becomes Religion.*

———○———

LEADERSHIP, ALTHOUGH OFTEN not expressly connected with faith, is nevertheless supported by assumptions and beliefs that shape a fundamental view of the world and of reality, and that influences leadership's active expression. Religious and quasi-religious beliefs permeate the leader's realm. There are even so-called secular leadership principles that are held as tightly as any religious tenet. To find the hidden forms of faith among leaders, it is necessary to evaluate both categories.

My approach to this chapter stems from my perspective as a British theologian with a long-term interest in leadership in the public sector. From this vantage point, I consider the religious styles of leaders, particularly those in corporate organizations; in many ways, leadership in that context parallels leadership in a religious cult. I also raise questions about the underlying worldviews of leaders and the assumptions of faith that are made with respect to the nature of reality. There follows a discussion of a salient, religionlike aspect of leadership style—namely, the use of language, of such words as *vision* and *mission*—because the power of language deserves close scrutiny. This discussion in turn is followed by a critical consideration of some quasi-religious rituals that pervade organizations and may function, at a deep level, as expressions of faith.

In the early 1980s, just as North Americans were beginning to lose faith in certain methods of management and leadership (Locke, 1996), the same problematic methods were being introduced into the United Kingdom. "New wave" theories, such as those of the management guru Tom Peters, were readily accepted as gospel in mainstream British universities, social service agencies, public utilities, and health service agencies (Peters and Waterman, 1982; Huczynski, 1996). Services and organizations that had been professionally led and administered (rather than managed) were suddenly blessed with the benefits of business-style leadership and management.

The change was unmistakable and profound. In the British National Health Service (NHS), for example, chairs of health authorities, directors of finance and personnel, community physicians, nurse managers, general managers, and aspirants to management listened to the prophets of this new order. Influential business professionals, pioneering administrators, reforming researchers, and members of the new NHS management board outlined their dream, a vision that was both organizational and moral. According to Strong and Robinson (1990, p. 3), "this was not just another way of restructuring the health service, it was also a crusade. The vast, million-strong organization was being remolded along new and highly radical lines."

It was shortly after these types of pervasive transformations, in 1988, that I started to work full-time for the NHS as a health service manager. My background was in practical theology, as a university theology professor and part-time hospital chaplain. I signed up at the local university for a course in public sector management and started to learn about management and leadership.

It was not long before I began to realize that, having left one arena, in which belief was overtly important, I had stumbled into another, in which it was just as significant but apparently much less conscious (Pattison, 1991). This realization led me to study the unrecognized faith and beliefs of business leaders (Pattison and Paton, 1996; Pattison, 1997).

Let me say here that I do not see belief as a fanciful substitute for knowledge: all social life and human action depend on provisional assumptions about the nature of reality; beliefs of some kind are essential to living, whether these beliefs are essentially religious or not. Moreover, although I recognize differences in emphasis and function between management and leadership, managers in the British public sector are often called on to exercise leadership, and so in this chapter I seek to provide a balanced use of both terms. The beliefs of managers in the British public sector are similar to those of North American business leaders; indeed, the latter, through both the deliberate and the unwitting export of their ideas and practices, have shaped many of the beliefs and practices of the former (Locke, 1996). My hope is that the perceptions outlined in this chapter will illuminate the unrecognized beliefs and practices that are often found in leadership, whether in the public sector or the private sector, and whether in Britain or in United States. It may be easier, in fact, to recognize such beliefs as faith-based assumptions by examining them in a context other than the one in which they are normally encountered.

## Leadership and the Context of Belief

Probably no society, culture, group, or individual can survive without beliefs and assumptions of some kind, and leaders are no exception to this rule. Fundamental religious needs, and desires for meaning, efficacy, belonging, and security, may change from one era or culture to another, but they do not go away. In our postmodern, millennial era, certainty and security are in short supply. Therefore, it is not surprising that some people, seeking a sense of control and security, turn to the solid-looking techniques and theories of management and leadership. As they do, they may find themselves unwittingly but perhaps gladly imbibing a unique and unrecognized system of faith.

It is often argued that the Enlightenment emancipated human beings from religion by giving them the freedom of reason and providing the impetus for the process of secularization. It can also be argued that human beings still tend to need to believe in something, even if they have less faith than before in formal Christian religious institutions. The practice of management and leadership offers a socially credible system of faith in our secular age. Perhaps business leaders' recent overt expressions of interest in spirituality demonstrate the continuing importance of active, inhabited faith in modern society.

It should not be assumed that Christianity is without influence in the contemporary world. The United States remains a country with high rates of participation in formal religion. Protestant Christianity and business in North America have been influencing each other since the middle of the nineteenth century. This explains, in no small part, the overtly

Christian cast of some management beliefs and practices. If we believe that secularization is just one moment within the larger history of Christianity in the West, we can argue that management represents a transmutation or a new manifestation of Christianity in the modern world.

It is also worth noting that some influential, foundational leadership theorists have always seen management beliefs and practices as having significance beyond their pragmatic organizational functions. For example, according to Beatty (1998), Peter Drucker has expressed a strong interest in the nineteenth-century philosopher and theologian Søren Kierkegaard, and Drucker himself (1974, p. 261) has articulated a high moral doctrine of management as "the keeper of society's conscience and the solver of society's problems"—that is, as a global guardian of freedom and decency, against totalitarian forces such as those that drove him from his native Austria. This kind of function was traditionally played, at least in part, by religion. Other theorists, although they do not express any kind of overtly Christian faith or commitment, have drawn extensively on religious styles and methods of persuasion to gain sway in the business world (Pattison, 1997).

## "Religious Styles" in Leadership

As preachers know all too well, beliefs are truly significant only if they find embodiment in behavior and practice. I first began to suspect that the model of leadership and management being imported to Britain from the North American business sector was built on a quasi-religious belief system when I noticed the following similarities and parallels between behavior and assumptions in the business world and in some radical, often sectarian, Christian groups (see, for example, Hill, 1973):

○ Radical commitment from every member of the organization, regardless of position

○ Corporate identity that is intensely prized and jealously guarded, with members of the organization required to be loyal and to adhere to a common set of values

○ Attention to such distinctive features of the organization as its values and identity (with the organization itself deemed good, virtuous, beneficent, salvific, and altruistic, whereas other, similar organizations and the world outside are either damned or ignored)

○ Abundant dualistic language of apocalypse and mysticism in such concepts as vision, mission, and doom scenarios

- Conversion of people to the aims, values, and practices of the organization as the means by which they will find a sense of purpose, community, and belonging

- Seeking of perfection, in the form of excellence or quality, on the part of all organizational members, to ensure that consumers aren't lost

- Prizing of personal experiences and stories (rather than theory, analysis, reading, and research) as resources for understanding and action

- Values of obedience and conformity, despite rhetoric of empowerment and liberation

- Fear and insecurity, as encouraged by the use of short-term contracts, reinforced with the threat of rapid dismissal, to ensure conformity (compare the place of hell, damnation, and exclusion from the community of salvation in some Christian groups)

- Evangelization within the organization and its client base, with the requisite emphasis on what are enigmatically called *communication skills*

- Clear, simple, indisputable theories and statements about the organization

As for how leadership is exercised in such organizations, other kinds of parallel behavior are also often noticeable:

- A rhetoric of communal and individual empowerment, but with a leadership style that is often directive, and with leadership from above

- Rather than an elaborate hierarchy of leadership, a flattened structure that is distinct and definite

- Leadership based essentially on charismatic authority rather than on professional training or knowledge, with qualifications embodied primarily in personality, gifts, competence, and experience

- Assessment of leaders according to performance, or outcomes (as other charismatic figures are also assessed), even though the features essential to leadership may be vague or disputed

- Requirement that leaders (particularly senior-level leaders) exercise personal asceticism, devote themselves to their organizations, and view their commitment as a kind of vocation that takes precedence over other demands and relationships

o Unique positioning of leaders, because of their charismatic gifts and authority, to create visions that their organizations should pursue

o Leaders' periodic attendance at conferences (rallies or revivals) where traveling evangelists (such as Tom Peters) uplift them with heartwarming personal stories of managerial success (Crainer, 1997), thereby helping them reinforce their authority and confirm their identity, vision, and inspiration (business leaders may prefer convention centers to old-fashioned revival tents, but the means used by such conferences, and the messages they convey, are similar to those found among successful Christian evangelists, and these conferences often appeal more to the hearts than to the minds of those who attend them)

The parallels just outlined do caricature somewhat the style and nature of the business leadership that was introduced into British public service (and I think these parallels apply to the North American context as well). Despite this stereotypical condensation, however, most people will find, for better or for worse, a large measure of truth in these descriptions.

## Examples of Leaders' Worldviews

All kinds of human activity, behavior, and practices express fundamental views and beliefs, or assumptions, about the nature of the world. These assumptions often remain implicit, for they constitute everyday reality; they are essentially invisible and unquestionable. They are embodied in deep metaphors and images that condition, perhaps unconsciously, people's views of reality and of the nature of the world.

Almost every popular book on leadership presents a set of techniques and concepts that, if followed (it is claimed), will transform an organization and guarantee its success. This is particularly true of the books produced by any of the so-called gurus. These books are characterized by a sense of forward-looking optimism about the possibilities in a changing world (Peters, 1987; Handy, 1995). In many ways, theorists and consultants are selling faith, hope, and meaning as much as specific knowledge or techniques. The kinds of belief systems or action-informing worldviews that they are propounding often embody, to a greater or lesser extent, the following assumptions:

o People, as long as they have the right techniques, can largely control the world and effectively colonize the future.

o Clear goals and objectives can be set for the future, and they can and will be attained.

- Customers or consumers should be able to have exactly what they want, when they want it.

- Everything that is significant can and should be measured objectively.

- The greatest good is the prosperity and flourishing of the organization.

- Well-motivated organizations and their employees can do no harm.

In many ways, the unspoken faith or belief system is laid bare in these assertions. Most of them are open to fundamental criticism, question and dispute, particularly from the perspective of Christian theology.

For example, Christian theology would affirm the importance of human activity in the world and does not oppose creative thinking about the future. It is obvious, however, even to those who do not work within the paradigm of Christian thought, that people cannot and will not be able to control major events and factors in the future, in all or even in most respects. Utilitarians have discovered, to their embarrassment, that things seldom work out as they are expected to. The hope of colonizing the future is a myth. It looks as if this theory, although it has ingested from the Judeo-Christian tradition the importance of human creative activity and responsibility, has also lost, unfortunately, the corresponding aspect of that tradition, which emphasizes the limits and fallibility of human activity and suggests that the future is ultimately not in the hands of mortals.

Similar comments can be made about the practices of setting goals and objectives and assuming that the future will be better than the present. This forward-looking optimism finds some of its roots in Christian eschatology, where the promise of humankind's liberation is expected to find fulfillment in the future Kingdom of God, with the return of Christ. In Christianity, however, there are also substantial warnings that what the Second Coming will represent for some is a time of judgment, condemnation, and woe; the future lies in God's hands and will not necessarily be worked out according to human desire, all of which throws the notion of unthinking optimism into question. And this skepticism is entirely congruent with everyday experience, in which objectives are often quickly dated, strategic plans look unrealistic after only a short time, and nothing quite works out as it was expected to.

Most people have enough experience of negative and unexpected outcomes to realize that things are as likely to get worse as they are to improve; if we are lucky, there is a balance as some things get better while others get worse. Ultimately, business leaders and their organizations cannot know whether their goals, objectives, and values will produce a better future. Like all believers, they must assume that a better future is forthcoming, and like the rest of the population, they must wait and see. The only thing that can be expected with any confidence is the unexpected.

As for the sovereignty of the customer, it is one of the principal themes of business leadership theory, and it has crept into all parts of life. For example, Drucker (1974, p. 67) argues that the main aim of business is "to create a customer." Moreover, what lies at the heart of Total Quality Management is the ideology that everyone is the customer of everyone else inside and outside the organization, and that customers' true needs and requirements are sacrosanct. It is laudable that people are considering the interests of others. It is questionable, however, that the richest, most adequate model of human relationships should be the model of customer and supplier—not least because many people on earth will have only very limited access to the money required to be an effective "customer" in the first place. Furthermore, the notion that individuals can have exactly what they want, when they want it, is profoundly false. No moral imperative in the natural order suggests that people should always have what they want and should have constant access to an ever-available, inexhaustible supply of goodies. One of the most interesting aspects of life and of education is the discovery that, although we have not received what we thought we wanted, we can make use of different, unpredictable, and unexpected types of goods and experiences. Learning to see the benefits of not getting our way, finding treasures in the very experiences we normally shun, is in fact a spiritual practice.

Another important assumption of leadership thinking is that everything worth doing can and should be quantified in some way. Drucker (1974) sees objective setting and measurement as two of the five main management tasks, whereas Handy (1996, p. 137) relates that as a junior manager he was taught, "If you can't count it, it doesn't count." This kind of thinking is very dominant in Britain's public sector organizations: because resources are limited, results and optimal effectiveness are all-important. But this is a reductionist approach to the nature of existence. Many of life's important aspects are actually intangible and cannot be measured; the relational aspect of work is but one obvious example. There may be intrinsic value (in terms of friendship and creativity) in going to work, as well as intrinsic benefits (for example, access to health and happiness) in being employed. Nevertheless, some theorists' advocacy, on the basis of shared commonsense experience, of the notion that everything worth doing can be predicted and objectively measured is an absurd distortion.

Many businesses and their leaders have recently become more conscious of their social context and their inherent responsibility to it;

attention to business ethics flourishes as the conscience of organizational life. Most leaders continue, understandably, to see the productivity and profitability of their organizations as an unquestionable first priority and unchallengeable good, and arguments can certainly be cited in support of this assumption; for example, an unproductive and unprofitable organization is unlikely to supply secure employment for its staff. A broader social perspective, however, may lead to the belief that robust organizational growth is not always the greatest good.

It seems probable that no group of individuals and no organization, however morally dubious it may appear to an observer, can cope with the notion that its effect on the world and those around it is fundamentally negative. People need to feel that they are doing good and useful work, at least in their own eyes. This need, combined with the recent emphasis on organizations' being value-led and having clear aims and ethical standards, has conspired, perhaps, to reinforce a fundamental belief in "organizational goodness": because we have clarified our aims and enunciated clear values, and because we are well-motivated, decent people, it can be assumed that our organization benefits humankind and does no harm.

But we don't need the protests of ecologically concerned groups, or of consumers harmed by some commercial product, in order to recognize that most leaders and organizations do harm as well as good. This is the nature of the human condition, and it has to be accepted and lived with, not denied or ignored. On the whole, organizations of all kinds, together with their leaders, are very poor at acknowledging the harm that they do and seeking to make real amends for it—what Christians would call *repentance,* making restitution and seeking reconciliation. Perhaps the capacity for corporate repentance should be seen as a necessary social virtue, not just an optional religious one.

The beliefs I have been describing may be necessary and basically immutable among leaders in the world as we currently know it, but that should not be a facile excuse for leaders not to acknowledge these beliefs and take more responsibility for them. When we are unaware of the beliefs to which we (tacitly) assent, we become their possessions rather than their possessors, and our power to make much-needed changes is limited.

## Mystical Metaphors

The use and manipulation of language is perhaps the main tool that leaders use in their influential roles. According to Mangham (1986, p. 82), "Language is the currency of interaction at all levels of encounter and its manipulation is a key feature of persuasion. . . . Organizations are created, maintained and changed through talk." The unrecognized beliefs of leaders are often most vividly displayed and implied by the use of words and concepts. I have been fascinated by leaders' acceptance of words and concepts that have overtly religious resonances, and that are used in important ways to obtain commitment and legitimacy in organizations. Nevertheless, leaders and managers often seem oblivious both to the provenance of their vocabulary and to the hidden and secondary meanings that might be implicit in it. Two of the most prominent of such concepts are those of the organizational "mission" and the organizational "vision." The organizational vision is what is supposed to motivate an organization—to give it a sense of ultimate direction and even ultimate meaning. The organizational mission, often embodied in a short mission statement, points to what the organization intends to do in order to realize its vision.

The concept of the mission has positive connotations: clarity of purpose, urgency, outer-directedness, and the need for change. But it also has more negative connotations, evidenced in the history of religious and other ideological movements: unquestioning response to a command "from above," dualism, a view of the world as a hostile place that needs changing, and a perception of those outside the organization as alien or even demonic "objects" needing conversion or elimination. Christian missions have often been aggressive, violent, exploitative, and colonial (hence also the utility for the military of the concept of the mission). Those who use this concept in leadership need to be aware of its negative as well as its more positive associations and underlying meanings. Similar observations can be made about the concept of the vision. On the one hand, it has connotations of changing things for the better, not accepting an unsatisfactory present, and thinking about the future. On the other, it can be associated with arbitrariness, fending off challenges (after all, who challenges a vision?), top-down planning, and obedience and passivity in the face of an authority that cannot be questioned.

I do not mean to suggest that leaders should refrain from using powerful, motivating concepts that embody important beliefs about the nature of reality. I am simply suggesting that there may be something to be gained from recognizing the nature of our beliefs and the effects that they may be having on us, our organizations, and our wider social context.

## "Religious" Rituals

A belief system is seldom if ever merely a free-standing collection of abstract ideas and assumptions. It usually comes with a matching set of practices and rituals, which, like the belief system they support, may not be as instrumental and rational, at first sight, as they appear.

In the case of contemporary organizations, many practices have the quality of rituals. In this context, I use the term *rituals* to mean activities that are symbolically important but that do not necessarily have the direct instrumental function that they may be assumed to have. In the Christian Church, for example, the Eucharist is a ritual act because, although it is a meal, people do not actually partake of it to gain nutrition. Strategic planning is a good example of an activity that is undertaken by many organizations with great seriousness, and at great expenditure of effort. There are exceptions, but the typical strategic plan is irrelevant almost as soon as it has been completed: the internal and external environments change so quickly that the information used to formulate the plan is already outdated. Unfortunately, this fact does not necessarily stop planners from sitting down and repeating the planning exercise all over again.

What is going on in this situation, where this kind of activity can be thought of as essentially futile? Cleverly (1971) suggests that strategic planning functions as a means of coping with anxiety in the face of an unknown and threatening future. This is a classic use of ritual, and Cleverly likens it to the Roman practice of killing birds and examining their entrails in order to predict the future in times of crisis and war: the greater the threat, the more birds were sacrificed. In a similar way, strategic formulation or implementation that does not reckon with variables that are actually shaping the future allows people to feel as if they are in control, as if they are doing something to gain mastery (an illusory sense of mastery) over the unpredictable future. There are many other practices in leadership and management that are more ritualistic and symbolic than rational and functional. The importance accorded to leadership itself, and the dominance of the mythical "bottom line," are two further examples of phenomena whose significance may be different from the meaning actually ascribed to them by their protagonists (Grint, 1995).

Here again I must reiterate that I am not suggesting the jettisoning of practices and ideas supported more by faith and assumptions than by measurement and empirical evaluation. Rather than live without faith and beliefs of any kind, the point is for us to recognize and critically assess our inhabited systems of faith, our beliefs, and our rituals.

## Conclusion

Belief- or faith-free leadership is probably not realistic or even desirable in the contemporary world. Leadership is, to a large extent, a creative and aesthetic activity. It contains important symbolic, nonrational, and even spiritual elements (Alvesson and Willmott, 1996). It is easy to ignore or deny them, but instead they can be usefully acknowledged, befriended, and owned.

Instead of aspiring to become free of faith or beliefs, leaders might become more critically aware of their basic beliefs and assumptions. This awareness would allow them to engage in more careful assessment of the nature, content, effects, and desirability of their beliefs. It could also help them positively choose or change their beliefs. In this way, it would become possible for managers to possess their faith systems more clearly rather than be possessed by them. They would then have a critical, questioning faith.

## REFERENCES

Alvesson, M., and Willmott, H. *Making Sense of Management.* Thousand Oaks, Calif.: Sage, 1996.

Beatty, J. *The World According to Drucker.* London: Orion Business Books, 1998.

Cleverly, G. *Managers and Magic.* White Plains, N.Y.: Longman, 1971.

Crainer, S. *Corporate Man to Corporate Skunk: The Tom Peters Phenomenon.* Oxford, England: Capstone, 1997.

Drucker, P. *Management: Tasks, Responsibilities, Practices.* Portsmouth, N.H.: Heinemann, 1974.

Grint, K. *Management: A Sociological Introduction.* Cambridge, England: Polity, 1995.

Handy, C. *The Empty Raincoat.* London: Arrow Books, 1995.

Handy, C. *Beyond Certainty.* London: Arrow Books, 1996.

Hill, M. *A Sociology of Religion.* Portsmouth, N.H.: Heinemann, 1973.

Huczynski, A. *Management Gurus.* London: International Thomson Business Press, 1996.

Locke, R. R. *The Collapse of the American Management Mystique.* New York: Oxford University Press, 1996.

Mangham, I. *Power and Performance in Organizations.* Oxford, England: Basil Blackwell, 1986.

Pattison, S. "Mystical Management: A Religious Critique of Management in the Public Sector." *Modern Churchperson,* 1991, *33*(3), 17–27.

Pattison, S. *The Faith of the Managers: When Management Becomes Religion.* London: Cassell, 1997.

Pattison, S., and Paton, R. "The Religious Dimensions of Management Beliefs." *Iconoclastic Papers,* 1996, *1*(1).

Peters, T. *Thriving on Chaos: Handbook for a Management Revolution.* New York: Knopf, 1987.

Peters, T., and Waterman, R. *In Search of Excellence: Lessons from America's Best-Run Companies.* San Francisco: Harper San Francisco, 1982.

Strong, P., and Robinson, J. *The NHS—Under New Management.* Buckingham, England: Open University Press, 1990.

## ADDITIONAL READINGS

Flanagan, H., and Spurgeon, P. *Public Sector Managerial Effectiveness.* Buckingham, England: Open University Press, 1996.

Fleming, S., Bopp, K., and Anderson, K. "Spreading the 'Good News' of Quality Management." *Health Care Management Review,* 1993, *18*(4), 29–33.

Stewart, R. *Leading in the NHS.* Old Tappan, N.J.: Macmillan, 1996.

## PART FOUR

# FAITH-BASED LEADERSHIP IN ACTION

# 13

# LEADERSHIP AND LEGACY

## ONE LEADER'S JOURNEY IN FAITH

---

*John D. Beckett*

John D. Beckett is president of R. W. Beckett Corporation, a manufacturer of oil burners for residential and commercial heating. He is
the author of *Loving Monday: Succeeding in Business Without Selling
Your Soul*.

---○---

FOR NEARLY FOUR decades, I have been on a life-changing journey in the
development of my personal faith. The growth in my faith has paralleled
my professional development as president of a manufacturing business in
northern Ohio. So intertwined have been these two facets of my life that
I would be hard pressed to delineate between them, for they have indeed
gone hand in hand.

I fully realize that my experience is uniquely my own and may not be
directly related to the development of your own faith. But personal lessons
learned, I have found, often have broader applications, if only to encourage, affirm and inspire.

## Can We Succeed Without Faith?

I've observed over the years that effective leaders are those who have
developed a sturdy faith. That kind of faith has taken those leaders
beyond a narrow, self-serving perspective and to the realization that they

are a vital part of God's greater strategy—uniquely endowed, vested with purpose, and reliant on divine wisdom. For these people, faith has become an essential ingredient of the capacity to lead.

"But," you may protest, "don't we see leadership without faith every day?" Indeed we do: in the self-made business owner who, through grit and determination, has built a thriving enterprise; in the politician who garners sufficient favor among constituents to be returned to office after each election; in the superstar athlete who flaunts a questionable lifestyle. How do we explain these anomalies?

It is possible to achieve much, at least in terms of this world's measures, without an active faith. How can we fail when we are equipped with high-powered education, boundless information, technology, storehouses of conventional wisdom, and reason (including that reliable old standby, common sense)? We see nations governed, fortunes amassed, and empires built without any reference or deference to God.

The pivotal question, however, is this: Can we leave a lasting legacy without deliberately involving God in the process? The writer of the New Testament book of Hebrews contends that we cannot— "Without faith, it is impossible to please Him" (Heb. 11:6 )—and the apostle Paul is even more emphatic: "And whatever is not of faith is sin" (Rom. 14:23). These statements suggest that if we are simply operating by our own logic and energy instead of actively employing faith in the exercise of our responsibilities, we are actually placing ourselves at a distance from the Lord and, ultimately, conducting our efforts in opposition to Him. How many leaders are in exactly this position, choosing human modalities rather than embracing a faith-based approach?

Is there a better way? On the basis of my experience, I suggest that there is. My journey in faith has led me to invest my efforts in building carefully on "that foundation already laid, which is Jesus Christ," and my desire intensifies each day to produce results that endure, symbolized by "gold, silver and precious stones," instead of results that are temporal and superficial, symbolized by "wood, hay and stubble," which in the final judgment will be unceremoniously consumed (1 Cor. 3:11–15).

## Four Keys to a Growing Faith

I have learned that faith does not develop overnight, although crises can often catapult us to new levels of trust in God. Faith develops progressively as we are properly focused, and as we learn from life's challenges through the willingness to change and embrace the process that all growth requires. Four areas have proved pivotal for me:

1. Understanding who God is, and who we are
2. The link between faith and God's word
3. Faith for our calling
4. The release of faith in our work

## The "Who" in Our Faith

Most basic to the development of faith is an understanding of who God is and who we are. As we all well know, there is a world of difference.

One of the least common phrases in the Bible is "I saw the Lord." The few who did see God in all His splendor were left completely awestruck. After catching sight of God "high and lifted up," Isaiah could say only, "Woe is me, for I am ruined . . . for my eyes have seen the King, the Lord of Hosts" (Isa. 6:1–5). Similarly, when Job was in the midst of his suffering, God addressed him out of the whirlwind (Job 38), demanding answers to such questions as "Where were you when I laid the foundations of the earth?" Overwhelmed by the impact of this encounter, Job answered, "I have heard of Thee by the hearing of the ear; but now my eye sees Thee; therefore I retract, and I repent in dust and ashes" (Job 42:5,6).

The irony is that this omnipotent God—who spun the universe from His fingertips, who collected a scoop of dust from which to fashion the first human being, whose breath held back the waters of the Red Sea and the Jordan River, who did so much more than even the Bible fully recounts—actually takes note of us, dealing with us so personally and intimately, even numbering the very hairs of our heads. David captures this truth in the Psalms: "O Lord, our Sovereign, how majestic is your name in all the earth. . . . When I look at your heavens, the work of your fingers. . . . What are human beings that you are mindful of them, mortals that you care for them?" (Ps. 9:1,3–4). How remarkable that God, who superintends the universe, is also involved in every detail of our lives.

An early lesson in my business career taught me something of God's nature and infinite care. My father passed away after I had been working with him for only a year in our small family business. At the age of twenty-six, I felt woefully ill-prepared to take the helm of the R. W. Beckett Corporation. Dad, forty years my senior, had worn all the hats in our business, and I clearly lacked his talents and vast experience. Therefore, I immediately set out to hire a capable colleague to assist me, particularly in the area of marketing.

My first step was a logical one. I began to contact former college class-mates and business acquaintances who I thought might be interested—all to no avail. It seemed our fledgling company was too risky a prospect for them. At that stage in my life, I was only beginning to understand the power of prayer; but, faced with the urgent need for help in running the company, I began to pray in earnest. My prayer was a simple one: that God would send the right person for the job.

The answer came quickly and unexpectedly. Bob Cook, a marketing executive for one of our customers, was traveling with me on a business trip to evaluate a potential supplier. As we conversed on the plane, Bob began asking about our company's future. To my surprise, he expressed interest in coming to work for us. It was soon apparent that he had exactly the skills I was looking for and was ready to take on the challenges we were facing. Here was God's answer to my prayer—not in the files of an executive-search firm, but comfortably seated next to me on a business trip.

That providential discussion with Bob marked the beginning of a thirty-five-year working relationship that continues to this day. But, more important, it marked for me the beginning of a new understanding of the primacy and effectiveness of consulting God first on any matter pertaining to my company. It built my faith, especially as I began to understand the Lord's desire for personal involvement in matters pertaining to my work.

## The Object of Our Faith

Faith needs an object, but for many, sadly, faith is invested merely in the future, or in the free enterprise system, or in democracy, or in natural law, or even in their own personal abilities. By contrast, Jesus told His followers, "Have faith in God" (Mark 11:22). How wonderful that God so clearly invites us to have faith in Him! How remarkable to have God as the sole object—actually, a very living subject—of our faith! Our faith, if it is true faith, must be in God and in God alone.

## Dependence on Ourselves or on God?

The great King David cried out, "But I am a worm" as he considered himself relative to the holy awesome God (Ps. 22:6). We must ultimately decide whether our faith is in God or in ourselves. Self-confidence, where it is legitimate at all, must be in the context of what God imparts.

But there's a wrestling match here. I am sobered as I realize how far I will go into an activity or a project while depending solely on my own skills and abilities, never bothering to invite God's perspective or to lean into His wisdom and His ways. Over the years, I have come to understand that my most responsible posture is not to see how much I can inject of my own will, my own ways, and my own self into the equation but rather to humble myself and acknowledge my utter dependence on God. Only when we look up are we able to see how reliant we are on the Lord for everything of true and lasting value.

## The Mind-Set of a Servant

Paul wonderfully describes this state of mind in his letter to the Philippians. "Let this mind be in you," he says, and he goes on to describe Christ's own mind-set as He laid aside his divine prerogative and completely humbled Himself. Here is the full rendering of this idea:

> Let Christ Jesus be your example as to what your attitude should be. For he, who had always been God by nature, did not cling to his prerogatives as God's equal, but stripped himself of all privilege by consenting to be a slave by nature and being born as mortal man. And, having become man, he humbled himself by living a life of utter obedience, even to the extent of dying, and the death he died was the death of a common criminal [Phil. 2:5–8]

Here is the most vital lesson in leadership I can give to a business leader or professional person seeking to walk in faith: make it a lifelong habit to embrace the mind-set of a servant. Despite some contemporary attempts at "servant leadership" (Greenleaf, 1977; Spears, 1995), the world's way of thinking largely revolves around rulership—imposing authority, lording it over others. This approach may appear to be effective, and it may actually produce worldly success, but results like these are not the ones we should seek, nor are they the ones that reflect the character of Christ.

Our posture of humility and dependence is also the catalyst to earnest prayer. As we pray, we are acknowledging God as the source of all strength, all wisdom and insight, all grace and mercy. Through our "dialogue" in prayer, we draw from His infinite storehouse and gain the perspective and fortitude—and, yes, the faith—to function in our callings.

The man or woman who walks in humility, prayerfully staying dependent on God, will by no means be ineffective, but the standard will be different. Such a person will reflect God's love, reaching people's hearts, not just their pocketbooks. With such an approach, we will actively resist wrong thinking and wrong activities, not just tolerate them. In humility, we will forgo the quick fixes that bypass the deeper lessons God is trying to teach us. And, because He has promised to do so, God will in due time exalt us.

Thus this is a call for a different way of thinking, whereby God is at the very center of our faith. As we acknowledge Him as majestic Lord, and as we, like Christ, take on the role of a humble servant, God's ways and life-giving energy are practically woven into the fabric of our lives and attitudes. We can relax, resting in a dependence on God for everything of true value. From our repose begins to emerge the kind of solid faith required for effective leadership.

## Faith and God's Word

Our first responsibility, then, in the development of personal faith is to apprehend the overwhelming greatness of God and our need for humble and complete reliance on Him. Next, I would point to the Bible, God's word, as an essential catalyst to the development of personal faith. The apostle Paul describes the connection between faith and God's word this way, in his letter to the church at Rome: "So then faith comes by hearing, and hearing by the word of God" (Rom. 10:17). Hearing biblical truth produces faith.

For nearly thirty years, it has been my practice to read the Bible each day. My decision to do this came initially in response to a challenge put forth by a speaker at a Christian teaching conference. He asked the attendees to commit themselves to reading the Bible daily for at least five minutes. I like challenges, and I took this one. At first it was sheer discipline, but as I dutifully continued my daily Bible reading, the discipline gradually became a delight. Almost imperceptibly, I began looking at things differently as ideas and concepts from the Scriptures began reshaping my thoughts and attitudes.

From that regular practice, faith began to blossom in me as I read the examples of those whose life accounts are recorded in the Old Testament. What faith it took for Noah as he stood alone in his generation and built a strange ship far from the ocean's shore; for Moses as he confronted Egypt's pharaoh and then led a nation out of bondage; for David as he waited patiently for God's timing in the fulfillment of his prophetic destiny to be king; for Daniel, in the vulnerable position of a civil servant to foreign kings, as he stayed unflinchingly true to God.

Scripture's examples also helped me understand the breadth and versatility of faith. As Tozer has so aptly said ([1961] 1996 ), "Faith in one of its aspects moves mountains; in another it gives patience to see promises afar off and wait quietly for their fulfillment."

We can learn much from biblical role models about how to build dependability into our character, a steadfastness that will not be deflected by opposition. The Bible is replete with examples of faith for all seasons. By emulating this kind of faith, God's people can build godly enterprises, lead nations to their righteous destinies, and in the process, inherit an eternal reward.

## Faith, the Fuel for Our Calling

"Come now, therefore, and I will send you to Pharaoh, that you may bring my people, the children of Israel, out of Egypt" was God's clear call to Moses (Exod. 3:10). We see many others in the Bible who were uniquely called: Joseph, Nehemiah, Ruth, and Esther, for example. Each of them at some point encountered God's direction, in a way that clarified their callings. From that point on, their faith developed and held firm as they walked out their calls.

Not all of them succeeded, for it is always left to the individual to obey or disobey God's call. Saul's faith weakened to the point where he sought assistance from a necromancer. Esau, driven by physical hunger, forfeited his faith, his calling, and his birthright for some food. Mark, weakened in faith, decided not to go with Paul on a dangerous mission into central Asia. Jesus prayed for Peter before his act of betrayal, "that your faith should not fail" (Luke 22:32), but Peter, despite his protests to the contrary, found out within hours how weak his faith could be. Perhaps this is why he later wrote to his fellow saints that they should "be even more diligent to make your calling and election sure," prescribing for them several qualities of character that, if embraced and sustained, would keep them from stumbling—and foundational to the connection between those qualities and their callings was faith (2 Pet. 1:5–11).

## Finding Our Way and Our Calling

The development of my capacity for faith has been inextricably linked with my call to business. For many years, it was far from clear that a career in business was God's call for me. Toward the end of high school, as I was considering where to attend college, I struggled with whether to pursue some recognized form of ministry. I had grown up in the Episcopal denomination, and I wondered whether pastoral ministry might be right for me, so I applied to Kenyon College, which had an adjunct Episcopal seminary.

But my heart was elsewhere. My father had trained as an engineer, and, deep down, I wanted to be an engineer, too. So I also applied to the Massachusetts Institute of Technology (MIT), reasoning that the outcome of my application process could also bring clarity to my choice of career.

A letter of acceptance arrived from Kenyon, and I wondered whether it meant that I was headed toward a pastoral vocation; a rejection from MIT would confirm this direction. I waited for what seemed like an eternity, although it was just weeks. And then came the hoped-for letter of acceptance from MIT. It meant that the way had opened toward a vocation in engineering and business; it was as though an invisible hand were steering me.

Later, in college, I went through a similar process, this time wondering whether I should undertake a stint as a military chaplain. Again, this choice sounded more "worthy," a higher calling than simply plunging into a business career. I took counsel with the rector of the Episcopal church I was attending in Boston and was given the straightforward advice that I shouldn't pursue an ecclesial vocation unless I was sure I had a clear call. I couldn't say that I did have one, and when an offer came for me to work as an engineer in an aerospace firm, I again concluded that an invisible hand was pointing me in the direction of business. But the nettling issue of whether I was missing the highest calling for my career was still unsettled.

The question of calling arose again not long after I had been thrust into the leadership of the family business. I took stock. Our business was doing very well. I loved my work. Our family was developing wonderfully. My faith was growing. And yet I was nagged by doubt. Was I really where God wanted me, or was I in business more through personal preference? This time I prayed earnestly about the matter, my mind wrestling week after week, but with no clear answer. But then I felt that I was the one being asked a probing question: Would I be willing to completely give up my family business, change careers, and follow God in a different direction, wherever and whenever?

Finally, I made one of the most difficult decisions of my life. I said, "God, this business can't be yours and mine at the same time. I give it, myself, and my career totally over to you. I will follow you wherever you want me to go." What I heard in response was unexpected but unmistakably clear. I sensed the Lord saying, "John, I needed to know you were completely willing to follow me, and not put other things, including your work, ahead of me. But you are exactly where I want you to be. I have called you to business. For you, there is no higher calling." This understanding was accompanied by a tremendous sense of peace, more than I had ever known. A decades-long struggle was over. I knew I was where God wanted me, and I could pursue business with the same zeal and sense of call that I would have felt in any other kind of ministry.

That decision was made over thirty years ago, and I can now look back on how God has faithfully confirmed this direction for me. My work, heading up a manufacturing company, has been a calling in which I have been able to achieve much that I never could have achieved in a more traditional form of ministry, for one principal reason: I am where God wants me to be. Out of this firm conviction has come the faith to function in this calling. Instead of facing day-to-day situations in timidity and fear, I have my faith, which has instilled boldness, courage, and confidence—not in myself but in Christ. I have found that faith accompanies the call—faith that, by His grace, is always sufficient. A friend of mine once said, "You can't be righteous in Dallas if God has called you to be in Philadelphia," and the converse is equally true and profound, especially in the context of having faith: if we know beyond a doubt that we are where God has called us to be and doing what we've been called to do, then we will have faith to function boldly and effectively, producing results that count for eternity (Diehl, 1987).

## Faith at Work

The full development of one's personal faith never takes place in isolation from the "real" world. God puts us into families, communities, and institutions that become unique classrooms where faith is forged, tested, refined, and enlarged. Sparks has addressed this process:

> You notice that the Apostles got their revelation for the Church in practical situations. They never met around a table to have a Round-Table Conference, to draw up a scheme of doctrine and practice for the churches. They went out into the business and came right up against the desperate situation, and in the situation which pressed them, oft-times to desperation, they had to get before God and get revelation. The New Testament is the most practical book, because it was born out of pressing situations.

Events, relationships, challenges, problems, even crises—the things that continually unnerve and stretch us—are not happening outside the purview of God. They are not random. They are not arbitrary. God is at work in them, pressing us closer into divine purposes.

This pattern was evident even in Jesus' life. He lived in total harmony with the Father, and yet, time after time, things happened that were unplanned and unanticipated. They happened while he was "on the way"—the encounter with the woman at the well, the nighttime visit by Nicodemus, the meeting with the woman who touched the hem of His garment, the call for help from the blind man, the encounter with a tax collector. How did Jesus respond to all that the Father placed before Him? In every situation, Jesus saw His Father at work; then, by faith, He joined in, achieving all that He could redemptively: "'My Father is still working, and I also am working,' Jesus said to them. 'Very truly, I tell you, the Son can do nothing on his own, but only what he sees the Father doing; for whatever the Father does, the Son does likewise'" (John 5:17,19).

Faith is the means by which we see the purposes of God in each situation. Through faith, we step out of the narrow perspective that attends mere human endeavor and reach for the divine insight hidden from our natural view. We are looking for God at work. In faith we join in, and as we employ faith, it grows. The analogy to the muscles in our bodies applies: what is exercised strengthens; what is not, atrophies.

## Practical Outworking of Faith

In my experience, work and faith are continually intersecting. I recall a time when I was baffled by a technical problem. I had worked most of a Saturday in our development lab, trying to find a solution to a combustion problem with one of our products. With no solutions forthcoming, I decided to leave work and swim with my family, saying a quick prayer as I left our factory that I might somehow soon find the answer.

The key insight into the solution came while I was swimming laps, and it came so clearly that I knew this solution would work. Later that afternoon, back in our lab, I was able to test out the concept I had seen through faith. It was perfect, and I learned a valuable lesson: to think much more broadly about how God wants to be involved in our everyday affairs.

Faith also became the essential ingredient in a business decision some years later, during an international oil crisis, when an embargo in the Middle East threatened to shrink the market for our products by at least half. To add to our worry, we had just completed a major expansion of our plant facilities, putting a strain on our financial resources. Our competitors were taking drastic action. They were cutting sales activity, and some were scaling back and downsizing their entire operations.

After much consternation—and, this time, more systematic prayer—our senior managers and I came to a decision: rather than pull back to a safe position, we would take the opposite course. We would be bold and aggressive and look beyond the current disruption to the long term. To others in our industry, we probably looked somewhat foolish, but faith quite often does. (Remember Noah?) Our strategy turned out to be exactly right, and when the energy crisis abated, the company was in a stronger position than ever. Our expanded facilities had become necessary, more than we had ever imagined.

## Reversing the Sequence: Having Faith Early

One of the most important lessons I am learning about faith in the "school of Christ" is the principle of having faith early instead of waiting for a crisis that requires me to exercise faith in an extraordinary way. My tendency is to let faith come into play only when I have exhausted my own resources. I do what I can on my own strength, and if I don't get the needed results, then I turn to God in faith—when I reach the end of my rope. But the irony, and the flaw, in this out-of-sequence application of faith is my perception that the more capable I am, the less I need God. After all, why pray if I can handle the situation myself? Why not save the faith walk for when I really need help?

I am endeavoring to reverse this sequence. God's desire, I believe, is that we exercise faith early instead of putting forth our best efforts first and turning to Him only in desperation. With most of us, God has very graciously tolerated this back-to-front sequence, but there is a better way. That better way is to see faith intertwined with every dimension of life and to engage faith from the start. It is to see faith as a vital strand in a robust cord, integrally joined with and supporting our God-given gifts and abilities. That way, we don't come to the end of our rope and only then call for help. Faith becomes an active ingredient in every step along the way.

This is easier said than done, especially for leaders. We often think we are superbly competent, but if we hold to the traditional view of crisis faith in desperate situations instead of undertaking each event of each day in faith, we will stall out in the "school of Christ." Even the mundane things—having our morning toast and coffee, driving to work, greeting people at the office, setting our schedules and priorities for the day, holding meetings, making decisions, letting ourselves be interrupted—can be done in faith, in God's presence, where we find the heart of God and our real reward: our continually increased sense of God's presence and involvement in our lives.

# Conclusion

Several times, Jesus chided His followers for having so little faith—for example, when His fearful disciples woke Him during the raging storm, and when doubt ended Peter's walk toward Jesus on the Sea of Galilee (Matt. 6:30, 8:26, 14:31). "You of little faith," Jesus said. (My own faith flags before I even get into the boat!)

Fortunately for us, the development of faith is progressive. By using the words "little faith," Jesus is telling us something very significant: faith can grow, no matter where we are on the growth curve. The disciples, realizing the smallness of their faith, appealed to Jesus directly: "Increase our faith" (Luke 17:5). Jesus responded with the analogy of the mustard seed, the smallest of seeds: faith even that small, he said, could move everything from mulberry trees to mountains, "and nothing will be impossible for you" (Luke 17:6; Matt. 17:20). Likewise, we can ask God to increase our faith to deal with whatever mountains are before us.

I have found four key principles of personal faith, and I want to share them here with other leaders:

1. *Faith is instilled in us as we see God in His vastness, His greatness, His majesty, and His dominion and glory.* It further develops as we humble ourselves and let ourselves be embraced by the oceanic depths of divine love, reminding ourselves how desperately we need God day by day and moment by moment. Truly, without God, we are nothing.

2. *The word of God is the seedbed of true faith.* No investment will bring greater return than study of and meditation on God's word. It is a prime catalyst for faith, and it is worthy of our best attention. It is a life source that endures forever.

3. *Faith helps us make our calling sure.* God's call is unique for each of us. If we are not where God has called us to be, we will have an uphill battle to receive faith in facing our day-to-day challenges. But when we are in God's calling for us, he will be pleased, even zealously eager, to give us faith in every situation.

4. *Our work is a classroom for the development of our faith.* Faith is manifested as we are "on the way." It is dynamic, lively, relevant to where we are. We need to begin in faith and stay in faith instead of expending our best human efforts, hitting the wall, and only then turning to God.

The ultimate reality is that this faith we speak of really isn't our faith at all: like everything else of true value, it is a gift from God. It is bestowed, imparted, given abundantly by the One who is always full of faith: faithful.

## REFERENCES

Diehl, W. *In Search of Faithfulness: Lessons from the Christian Community.* San Francisco: Harper San Francisco, 1987.

Greenleaf, R. K. *Servant Leadership: A Journey into the Nature of Legitimate Power and Greatness.* New York: Paulist Press, 1977.

Spears, L. (ed.). *Reflections on Leadership: How Robert K. Greenleaf's Theory of Servant Leadership Influenced Today's Top Management Thinkers.* New York: Wiley, 1995.

Sparks, T. A. *The School of Christ.*

Tozer, A. W. *The Knowledge of the Holy: The Attributes of God: Their Meaning in the Christian Life.* New York: Walker, 1996. (Originally published 1961.)

# 14

# CREDO AND CREDIBILITY

## MANAGEMENT SYSTEMS AT SERVICEMASTER

*Joseph A. Maciariello*

Joseph A. Maciariello is Horton Professor of Management at the
Peter F. Drucker Graduate School of Management, Claremont,
California. He is a coauthor of the well-known book *Management
Control Systems* and has been involved recently in examining
U.S.-based multinational corporations whose management systems are
based on Judeo-Christian values.

○

A RECENT PUBLICATION (Murphy, 1998) presents eighty ethics statements
from well-known U.S. businesses, including exemplary statements that
"are worth holding up as examples for others to follow" (p. xiii). There
are values statements, credos, and codes of conduct; one company has
both a values statement and a corporate credo. A number of positive values are accentuated in these statements: commitment, fairness, fun, the
golden rule, honesty, integrity, openness, quality, respect, responsibility,
teamwork, and trust. Certain negative practices to be avoided are speci-
fied as well: false advertising, bribery, the giving of inappropriate gifts,
exploitation of workers in foreign countries, unethical sales practices, and
sexual harassment. In view of the values expressed and the practices
restrained, it would be easy to conclude that these are indeed exemplary
statements. But a nagging question remains: Do these companies live these
beliefs, or do they merely espouse them? This chapter describes how one

U.S.-based multinational firm, the ServiceMaster Company, has effectively implemented Judeo-Christian values by deeply embedding them into the firm's management systems and the behaviors used in managing the firm. The purpose of this chapter is to demonstrate that in order for a corporate credo to be implemented and negative conduct prevented, an organization's management systems must actually be designed to encourage positive values and discourage negative practices. Unless management systems are designed in this way, it is not certain that the organization is making a genuine attempt to bring congruence to the values it espouses and the values it expresses in action.

## ServiceMaster's Management Systems

This chapter's discussion of ServiceMaster presents an approach to the design of management systems that is compatible with the wisdom that can be gleaned from the Bible regarding the management of work in light of the nature of humankind. For more than half a century, ServiceMaster has been demonstrating that this approach can be used to produce outstanding results, both morally and economically. If we are observing "a shift from an instrumental view of work to a sacred view of work where people seek the intrinsic benefit of work," and if "the ferment in management will continue until we build organizations that are more consistent with man's higher aspirations beyond food, shelter and belonging" (Senge, 1990, p. 5), then we would do well to learn from the example of companies like ServiceMaster.

The values of ServiceMaster, and the approach that the firm has taken to the design of its management systems, can be applied to any organization. But the starting point is the formulation of the credo, which begins with executives who are committed not only to believing the values that they have enumerated but also to living them. Indeed, if executives do not attempt to live the values expressed in their credos, values, and ethics statements, then they will not implement these values in their management systems, and this failure of implementation will be, in effect, a denial of their stated beliefs. This is the lesson from ServiceMaster. The company is a very encouraging example of what is possible when the people who belong to an organization make a long-term commitment to live their beliefs.

## ServiceMaster's Operations

ServiceMaster is a public corporation whose shares are traded on the New York Stock Exchange (the company's symbol is SVM). Incorporated in 1947, ServiceMaster became a public corporation in 1962 and completed fifty years of corporate operations in 1997. As of early 1999 the company employed more than fifty thousand people, had operations in forty-two countries on six continents, and served more than 10.5 million customers.

ServiceMaster offers an array of services through its two major operating units: consumer services and management services. These units include the following services:

○ Pest control

○ Cleaning of residential and commercial buildings

○ Lawn care

○ Home appliance warranty and inspection

○ Maid service, plumbing, and furniture repair

○ Facility maintenance and management for customers in healthcare, education, and business

○ Management for long-term care facilities

○ Special disaster and restoration services (such as cleanup after the 1995 bombing in Oklahoma City)

For the year ending December 31, 1998, ServiceMaster had annual operating revenues of $4.7 billion. The company has achieved an 18 percent annual compounded rate of growth in earnings per share for the past twenty-five years and has increased revenues, profits, and cash distributions to shareholders for twenty-eight consecutive years. The experience of ServiceMaster shows that a very profitable corporation can become so without pursuing as its only purpose the maximization of profit and shareholders' wealth. This long-term performance illustrates that an organization can pursue socially worthwhile values without being a shark to employees, customers, stockholders, vendors, or the community.

## ServiceMaster's Key Beliefs and Values

The value system that operates at ServiceMaster can be understood through the firm's four objectives:

1. To honor God in all we do
2. To help people develop
3. To pursue excellence
4. To grow profitably

The value system inherent in these objectives allows the people who work for the company to pursue their own interests as their positions dictate. Nevertheless, people's individual goals and objectives are also supported by widely shared understandings, which take account of the morality of individual behavior and of the impact that individual behavior has on the interests of ServiceMaster as a whole.

The value system starts with the assumption that each person has been created in God's image and therefore has inherent value, worth, and dignity. Treating people with dignity and respect honors God's image in people and therefore honors God. The logic of these objectives can be seen in the following formulations:

- *To honor God in all we do:* This value follows from the biblical counsel to honor and glorify God in all that is done (1 Cor. 10:31). How is this value enacted at ServiceMaster? Moral standards are applied to all the organization's activities. There is also an effort to reinforce the ability to see in all the firm's stakeholders the image of God. Further, giving honor to God is what provides the motive for all work undertaken by the company, and this motive in turn provides the standard by which the firm's activities are assessed.

- *To help people develop:* God is honored when people are respected, developed, and served.

- *To pursue excellence:* This value entails faithful stewardship and is derived from the first objective: ultimately, all resources come from God. Using resources—human, financial, and physical—in the most productive manner honors God.

- *To grow profitably:* Profitability becomes a good indicator of how effectively the company is managing to fulfill society's wants while also honoring God, helping people develop, and pursuing excellence.

ServiceMaster considers the first and second objectives to be ends, whereas the third and fourth are considered to be means. As we have seen, ServiceMaster sets a high priority on applying godly standards to all its activities and on developing people; the first objective provides the faith and energy for carrying out the second with conviction. As a result, people's capabilities are enhanced, and their likewise enhanced capacity for excellence leads to the company's profitability, which in turn provides resources for people's further development. Thus, on an ever-broadening scale, satisfaction of the third and fourth objectives continues to provide the means of satisfying the first and the second. These four objectives define the spirit (or culture) of the organization and have a pervasive influence on the design of ServiceMaster's management systems.

## Design of ServiceMaster's Management Systems

The firm's management systems comprise a set of formal and informal subsystems designed to assist executives in steering the organization toward the achievement of its purposes by bringing unity out of the diverse efforts of individuals and units in the firm. These systems are distinct yet also so highly interrelated that they are often indistinguishable from one another, as the reader should bear in mind during the discussion and descriptions that follow.

The formal management systems permit the delegation of authority and impose standards of accountability. They make explicit the structure, policies, and procedures to be followed. Just as Barnard (1938, p. 115) defines the informal organization as "the aggregate of personal contacts and interactions and the associated groupings of people," so can the informal management systems at ServiceMaster be said to consist of interpersonal relationships, not shown on the formal organization chart but instrumental in getting the work done. Thus the informal management systems complement the formal management systems in a manner similar to the way in which the informal organization complements the formal organization.

Figure 14.1 illustrates a generic set of five management subsystems, useful here for describing both the formal and the informal aspects of ServiceMaster's management systems:

1. The subsystem comprising the organization's infrastructure

2. The subsystem comprising the organization's management style and philosophy

3. The subsystem comprising the organization's mechanisms for coordination and integration

4. The subsystem comprising the organization's distribution of rewards

5. The subsystem comprising the organization's planning, resource allocation, and reporting processes

The formal and informal systems are best viewed as being symmetrical while embodying the same values, the same management style, and

Figure 14.1 Generic Set of Management Systems.

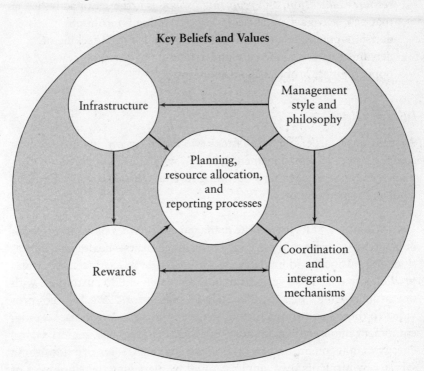

the same philosophy:

1. The informal counterpart of the formal *infrastructure* is the set of emergent roles in the organization, or informal relationships and responsibilities that emerge on the basis of expertise and trust. Emergent roles build cooperative norms through the development of informal contacts, which promote compatibility among personnel and encourage people's willingness to serve organizational purposes.

2. The informal counterpart of the formal *management style and philosophy* is the manner in which executives relate to their associates as they seek to implement the values, objectives, and goals of the firm.

3. The informal counterpart of the formal *mechanisms for coordination and integration* (such as committees and chartered teams) is the network of cooperative relationships that emerges as a result of people's socialization and mutual adjustment.

4. The informal counterpart of the formal *reward* subsystem is recognition.

5. The informal counterpart of the formal subsystem for *planning, resource allocation, and reporting processes* is the set of activities that people engage in, as necessary, in making nonroutine decisions concerning the realignment of goals or the seeking of new information to increase understanding of potential new opportunities, problems, and solutions.

## Infrastructure

As mentioned earlier, ServiceMaster's two major operating units are consumer services and management services, which account for more than 90 percent of ServiceMaster's operating revenues and practically all of the company's operating profits.

MANAGEMENT SERVICES. The management services division provides outsourcing services to three large business segments—healthcare, education, and business and industry. At the end of 1998, ServiceMaster was providing management services to approximately 2,000 customers, with operating revenues of approximately $2 billion for 1998. Services provided to these institutions include general maintenance, housekeeping, equipment maintenance, laundry, grounds maintenance, materials and energy management, and food services. ServiceMaster provides these services by hiring its own employees and by managing the employees of customers' organizations.

CONSUMER SERVICES. The consumer services division of ServiceMaster is a group of companies that provides services to more than 10.5 million consumers (ServiceMaster, 1998), mostly households, through a network of more than 7,000 service centers. Of these companies, three have become household names in the United States: Terminix, the market-share leader in termite and pest control; TruGreen–ChemLawn, the dominant commercial lawn care provider in the United States; and ServiceMaster Residential/Commercial (Res/Com), which provides carpet and upholstery cleaning for homes and businesses, small-scale janitorial services in commercial buildings, and heavy cleaning services, including disaster cleanup. Res/Com includes more than 4,500 distributors and franchisees; many of the franchisees belong to distributors that are not company-owned. These three companies provided operating and franchisee revenues of more than $2.5 billion in 1997.

In addition, the consumer services division includes Merry Maids, primarily a franchised service, providing housekeeping services for approximately 225,000 homes (Merry Maids has approximately 40 percent of the organized market for housecleaning services); American Home Shield, which sells warranties for the repair and maintenance of home appliances and for heating and plumbing systems; Furniture Medic, for furniture repair through 550 franchise locations; Rescue Rooter, the nation's second leading provider of plumbing and drain-cleaning services; and AmeriSpec, acquired by ServiceMaster in 1996 and integrated within American Home Shield, a leading home-inspection service for buyers, sellers, and agents that operates through 257 franchise locations (its services are marketed by American Home Shield through real-estate offices, buyers and sellers of homes, and independent repair contractors).

SYSTEM FOR THE SELECTION, TRAINING, AND EVALUATION OF SERVICE WORKERS. Taken together, the selection, training, and evaluation processes of the management services and consumer services divisions of ServiceMaster constitute a dynamic process for training and developing people. These processes have led to the transformation of thousands of entry-level employees into people with high levels of responsibility and self-esteem. The selection, training, and evaluation system has four components: the STAR system, service partner recruiting, service partner training, and service partner evaluation.

*The STAR system.* STAR is an acronym for the selection, training, assessment, and recognition process at ServiceMaster. Strictly speaking, only selection and training fit into the infrastructure subsystem, as depicted in Figure 14.1; assessment is part of the reporting processes, and recognition is part of the formal reward and informal recognition subsystems. Training also belongs to those activities that help to integrate the tasks performed by the various organizations, because of the opportunity to help people understand the company's values and how their own tasks fit into the work of the entire organization. From the four key objectives at ServiceMaster follows the company's "theory of the business" (Drucker, 1994): ServiceMaster is in the business of training and developing people, and the company's people-service systems reflect this emphasis. This theory also provides the major focus for the planning, resource allocation, and reporting processes of the organizations.

*Service partner recruiting.* In the selection of service partners, the management services division looks for attitudinal variables, especially the attitudes of prospective employees toward work and toward service. The company believes that if people bring the right attitudes to work, other appropriate aptitudes can be taught through formal and on-the-job training.

The service partner selection tool that is used in the management services division is based on the attributes of the most successful service partners. This tool is the product of a management process in which division managers simply ask, "What are the personal characteristics that our most successful service partners have brought to the job?" With these attributes in mind, the company looks for new service partners who possess characteristics that closely match those of the most successful service partners. These characteristics include a good work ethic, a sense of responsibility, trustworthiness, and a desire to provide service. The division is looking for people who want to become professionals and who are seeking to grow as individuals.

ServiceMaster takes risks with people during the selection process, and the company sometimes makes mistakes. But the company will take a person with a rough demeanor if it appears that the person will demonstrate a sense of responsibility for the work to be done, and if it appears that the person wants to grow. ServiceMaster is seeking people who are likely to be responsive to managers and to organizational training processes whose purpose is to develop people. ServiceMaster hopes that a listening, caring, and compassionate attitude on the part of management, coupled with formal training, will tap the inner motivational attributes of service partners. Managers hope that this process will lead in turn to the development of responsible and productive service providers.

The company has seen people from very disadvantaged backgrounds respond to this form of recruitment, caring, and personal development. Many of these people have later moved on to supervisory positions in the company. In fact, ServiceMaster, in its management services division, seeks to fill 20 percent of its supervisory positions from the pool of service partners. It should be said, however, that managers are selected for a variety of types of competence, and not all are equally good at developing this class of service worker. Nevertheless, this is the ideal for company managers.

The company tends to persevere with newly recruited employees and go the extra mile until it is clear that employees themselves have given up. This practice reflects the corporate values. Because the organization is committed to honoring God in all it does, and to developing people, it tends to stay with marginal service partners until it is absolutely clear that the situation is irremediable.

*Service partner training.* Once a service partner is recruited, the company turns to the training process. The overall purpose of training at ServiceMaster is to foster dignity, maturity, growth, and development in its service partners.

The first step in the training process uses a checklist of activities for the first day of employment. This checklist is meant to provide a basic orientation to the company and to the specific work assigned to the service partner. The second step involves one-to-one training with the partner's immediate supervisor and with the manager of the unit.

After the service worker has been performing the job for a time, refresher training is carried out according to a prescribed schedule. Managers are held accountable for this training, which is scheduled in advance. This training consists of skill development for relatively new partners and recognition activities for partners who have been performing their jobs for a number of years. Skill training is devoted to improving the processes for work in which the partners are already engaged and to ensuring that the partners are following the right work procedures.

Beyond refresher training, there are monthly team meetings in which the teams review lists of potential problems that may occur on a job. Included is an analysis of the partners' potential to perform more effectively. Also included in these monthly meetings are scheduled discussions of such issues as on-the-job safety. Monthly meetings are also are used by ServiceMaster to provide training in "life skills," which have to do with personal development. Such training may include classes in preparing income tax forms, instruction in English as a second language, or instructions for obtaining a library card.

Many of the managers at ServiceMaster have a strong value orientation toward training and believe that every opportunity to train should be used. They also believe that before service partners are made aware of how much a manager knows, they should be made aware of how much the manager cares.

*Service partner evaluation.* Service partners' performance is evaluated according to the quality of their work. Supervisors use standardized inspection forms to assess quality. Inspections are carried out at regularly scheduled intervals; the service partner being evaluated does not know the precise date.

Absenteeism, a major problem for this category of worker, and one that has obvious ramifications for evaluation, varies on an account-by-account basis and depends on the quality of the management servicing the account. A related issue is turnover. At John F. Kennedy International airport in New York, where ServiceMaster provides cabin-cleaning service for Delta Airlines and other carriers, the turnover rate went from 100 percent down to 5 percent as a result of management-initiated programs. These programs included English-language training and arrangements for vans to transport service partners to and from work. The turnover rate for service partners averages about 25 percent in the management services division, but this turnover rate is only a fraction of what is experienced by the industry in general, and it is very much a function of the particular manager in charge of a facility. It has been ServiceMaster's experience that if managers demonstrate that they care for service partners and want to foster their development, and if, in the process, they help partners become professionals, then both absenteeism and turnover rates drop sharply.

## Management Style and Philosophy

At the heart of the management systems at ServiceMaster are its objectives. The leadership philosophy of the executives follows directly from their objectives and influences the design of the entire system of management.

Although executives, managers, and service partners may espouse a diverse range of personal faiths or have no professed faiths, the philosophy of management at ServiceMaster is based on the example of Jesus Christ. As a result, servant leadership is the dominant management style. Servant leaders are those who are leading in such a way as to put others ahead of themselves. The servant leadership management style is the embodiment of ServiceMaster's first objective: to honor God in all that is done.

The servant leadership style has five key distinctive features:

1. Serving the best interests of all stakeholders, and exhibiting compassion for those served (it is tough and results-oriented but also compassionate)
2. Leading by example, and seeking to exhibit a servant's heart toward those served (by, among other ways, display a willingness to do the most menial tasks, thus giving added dignity to all work)
3. Giving recognition to those who need it, even at one's own expense
4. Accepting, empathizing, and listening to all constituents
5. Coaching and teaching (a style in which the leader is easy to please but hard to satisfy completely)

Is this approach effective? Greenleaf (1977, pp. 13–14) suggests that the best test of servant leadership is embodied in the following questions: "Do those served grow as persons? Do those served grow healthier, wiser, freer, more autonomous, more likely to, in turn, become servants? And what is the effect on the least privileged in society?" Although I have no concrete indicators, I believe that the servant style of leadership practiced at ServiceMaster has a positive influence on its employees in all sectors of the business.

## Coordination and Integration

The alignment of individuals' and subunits' goals with the values and objectives of the larger organization is an important task of management. Fitting the diverse parts of the organization into a harmonious whole is demanding. The four objectives have a profound influence on the effectiveness of this task. Together, the clearly articulated value system, the company's vision ("to be an ever-expanding and vital market vehicle for use by God to work in the lives of people as they contribute to others"), and its theory of the business ("we are in the business of training people") provide a common standard.

The ends-related objectives, to honor God and to develop people, put the needs of the company and of others ahead of narrow self-interest. They facilitate the process of aligning individual goals and actions with the goals and actions of the larger organization. It is this alignment process that is so crucial to overall coordination and integration, and it is right at the heart of the task of designing the management systems. Any organization that can accomplish this alignment also creates a significant source of competitive advantage through its people by a wholesale reduction in the internal costs of transacting business.

Procedures for conflict management and conflict resolution are enhanced as people ask, "What is the God-honoring solution to this problem?" The emphasis shifts from who is right to what is right. Trust in leaders' motives is enhanced if associates know that leaders have the best interests of the organization in mind. This knowledge in turn enhances openness because it encourages personnel to speak out and question management's decisions whenever such questioning is appropriate.

The values at ServiceMaster encourage associates to integrate the secular with the sacred, and business life with family life. This kind of integration makes it possible for the company to employ the whole person, thus improving not only the quality of employees' motivation but also the quality of the community. As the firm supports family life, it tends to reap the benefits of having more effective workers, and so alignment between people's efforts and corporate purposes is enhanced. Moreover, because the pressures on the traditional family have become overwhelming, one hope for the family is for it to become socially tied to companies, and this is where ServiceMaster's policies of nurturing the integration of family and business life offers a good example for the rest of corporate America.

In handling its people, ServiceMaster emphasizes the principle of unity in diversity. This means hiring a person for her or his strengths and covering any weaknesses with the strengths of others. Thus diversity in recruiting and placement decisions is emphasized and becomes a major tool for creating unity.

As mentioned earlier, the prominent place of training at ServiceMaster allows service partners to understand their roles in the overall organization as well as the importance of their work in providing value to customers. Moreover, the high degree of training activity affords the company a vehicle for transmitting and maintaining its values in the face of rapid expansion. In the company's mechanisms for coordination and integration, it is not difficult to see the role played by building trust, using inclusive leadership, and performing vocational mentoring.

## Rewards

At ServiceMaster, evaluation leads to rewards, which are for what a person does. The company's values lead to recognition, which is for who a person is.

Increases in salary and responsibility come with promotion into supervisory positions. Promotion opportunities exist in terms of moving up the hierarchy at a customer facility or moving within the wider organization. In some cases, a ServiceMaster customer employs a person who was initially hired by ServiceMaster.

In the management services division, the possibility of moving a service partner beyond the minimum wage depends on the partner's productivity. Nevertheless, the idea behind service partners' employment is to honor God and develop people, and so the company believes that it has fulfilled these two objectives if it is able to have a positive effect on the life of a person who is willing to grow into a more responsible position, either at ServiceMaster or with another company. If a manager genuinely cares about a service partner, is seeking to develop his or her talents, and is seeking his or her growth in responsibility, then the manager hears fewer gripes about the minimum wage. A service partner earning the minimum wage also knows that somebody in the company cares about him or her.

The employees who have trouble in this environment are those who are not treated respectfully. Upper-level managers often find that service partners are eager to share their experiences, and that they are especially sensitive to being treated disrespectfully by supervisors. If a manager snubs a service partner, his or her action provokes attitudes of defiance and statements like "I never want to see that supervisor again." Treating service partners with respect improves motivation and leads them to deal respectfully with others in their turn.

Not all rewards at ServiceMaster involve monetary compensation. For example, work processes are devoted to conveying dignity to service partners and to building their self-esteem. The processes and equipment used by ServiceMaster add to the people's development, and this in itself is a substantial reward. Standardized, technical work processes are designed to make jobs simpler and more productive. In housekeeping, service employees are provided with lightweight, easy-to-use tools, and the provision of these tools speaks volumes to people who are providing basic services. As a result, service partners feel better about themselves; they have more self-respect and dignity.

For example, a middle-aged service partner is arthritic. She must work because she is divorced and has two children in college. ServiceMaster provides her with a lightweight vacuum cleaner that fits on her back, to facilitate her vacuuming the staircases in a hospital, a business, or the concourse of an airport. If she expresses her gratitude for this modern tool, and if her manager explains that it was given to her to make her job easier and thereby promote the organization's objective of excellence, then a connection is made between the values of the company and this partner's becoming a more productive, loyal, and motivated employee, one who is treated with dignity. The occasion becomes a teachable moment in which the company infuses her with its values around a vivid personal illustration. Values espoused and values in action become one for this employee. Similarly, a short person may be given a short mop; a lawn technician may be given a twin hose so he doesn't have to walk as far to accomplish the lawn-feeding job and can care for more lawns. The idea is to link technology and the work to the four objectives to which ServiceMaster is committed.

ServiceMaster is not unusual in the formal rewards that it provides, but the company takes rewards one step farther by finding ways to say to employees, "You are worth something. You are created in the image of God and have inherent dignity." In other words, "Life can be what you make it." These efforts are all directed toward building self-esteem in service employees, and ServiceMaster thinks of these efforts as recognition activities. For some services, managers are required to schedule regular "pride days" at customers' facilities. On these days, employees wear flowers as they go about their regular duties. Representatives of customer companies normally also participate in pride days, taking time to express their appreciation to service partners on behalf of their organizations. These activities, too, are intended to impart the values of ServiceMaster and to be sources of self-esteem for the service partners.

## Planning, Resource Allocation, and Reporting Processes

There is a high degree of balance between the formal and informal planning processes at ServiceMaster. For example, there is a belief that excessive measurement activity and formal control hurt the spirit of the organization, and that excessive monitoring betrays a counterproductive lack of trust in subordinates' competence and behavior. Therefore, the approach toward planning and reporting at ServiceMaster is not to rigidly regulate behavior but to use measurement in promoting learning and development, on both a personal and an organizational basis.

Strategic planning at ServiceMaster has to do with creating competitive advantage in a particular business. The strategic planning process has a strong focus on growth; each of the autonomous units at ServiceMaster seeks double-digit growth in revenues, and the company as a whole is seeking to double its size every five years. These goals mean an objective of 15 percent growth in sales every year, a goal that has very important implications for helping people develop: the faster the growth, the greater the leap in personal development that is required. Without growth, however, there could be an increase in emotional tension and politics, and thus in destructive pressure brought to bear on the company's value system.

Planning for executive succession is crucial to the continuation of the corporate objectives and values. The responsibility for this area rests primarily with senior managers because they reinforce or change the existing values. The promise of continuity also stems from strong informal planning for management succession. The values of the company are applied in the recruitment, appraisal, and promotion of all personnel, and the recruiting principles themselves tend to place emphasis on the candidate's propensity to serve and on his or her respect for the dignity of others, knowledge of right and wrong, and orientation to customer service.

At ServiceMaster, plans for executive succession focus on forty promotable leaders in each division. Senior management monitors the accomplishments and background of each leader and identifies a suitable plan for that leader's training and development. This process, which has been successful for more than fifty years, is designed to produce executives for the future who will provide continuity with the company's values, strategy, and operations management. Nevertheless, values are continually tested as the company grows, especially in periods when growth comes primarily through acquisitions.

The overall vision of ServiceMaster is to be the world leader in providing incremental service value. This vision has a significant influence on the activities undertaken in the firms' planning, resource allocation, and reporting processes. The influence of this vision is clearly seen, for example, in the drive for acquisitions (which include foreign acquisitions) and the planning for growth that pervades the planning and control processes.

ServiceMaster's mission is stated in terms of ministry. It is noteworthy that the very name "ServiceMaster" is a play on words: "master of service" and "service to the master." The company implements its mission through the planning, resource allocation, and reporting processes by implementing its four objectives.

As already mentioned, ServiceMaster's "theory of the business" is that training is the core of its success. Typically, ServiceMaster employs standard systems for the delivery of the services it provides, and training is integral to the execution of these work systems. These standard systems entail five steps:

1. Studying the nature of the task to be performed
2. Designing equipment and materials for accomplishing the task
3. Developing a hierarchy of jobs, along with appropriate incentives, for getting the task accomplished
4. Developing educational and training programs appropriate to the task and the jobs
5. Developing databases and other productivity-improvement tools in order to establish a competitive advantage

Reengineering is a continuous process at ServiceMaster. The company's fundamental approach is to take basic processes and attempt to improve them. While reengineering a job, ServiceMaster seeks not only to improve the process but also to enhance the dignity of workers by developing tools and procedures that improve their circumstances. Innovation at ServiceMaster starts from the premise that every person has been created in the image of God, with value, worth, and dignity and with the potential to be creative. In planning and reporting, innovative activity is separated from ongoing operations. Nevertheless, clear targets for measurable results and accountability exist for innovation activities.

A high level of openness and trust and a strong commitment to a shared vision facilitate the informal planning and problem-solving processes at ServiceMaster. In the words of one executive, "If you don't share the vision, you don't stay with the company very long."

## Conclusion

A look at the design of ServiceMaster's management systems should have convinced the reader that the company has effectively implemented its objectives and values. Moreover, as ServiceMaster makes clear, it is one thing to prepare a formal credo; it is quite another to design a company's values into its management systems.

Values at ServiceMaster influence the design of every management subsystem. One can only admire the thought and effort that the company has put into moving its credo into the domain of credibility. Given the realities of competitive corporate life, ServiceMaster's credo and its implementation may seem utopian, but they do represent the "ServiceMaster Way," and the company's remarkable financial returns have been consistent for more than half a century.

REFERENCES

Barnard, C. I. *The Functions of the Executive*. Cambridge, Mass.: Harvard University Press, 1938.

Drucker, P. F. "The Theory of the Business." *Harvard Business Review,* Sept.–Oct. 1994, pp. 95–104.

Greenleaf, R. K. *Servant Leadership: A Journey into the Nature of Legitimate Power and Greatness*. New York: Paulist Press, 1977.

Murphy, P. E. *Eighty Exemplary Ethics Statements*. Notre Dame, Ind.: University of Notre Dame Press, 1998.

Senge, P. M. *The Fifth Discipline*. New York: Doubleday, 1990.

ServiceMaster Company. *1997 Annual Report*. Downers Grove, Ill.: ServiceMaster Company, 1998.


ADDITIONAL READINGS

Bellah, R. N., Madsen, R., Sullivan, W. M., Swindler, A., and Tipton, S. M. *Habits of the Heart* (rev. ed.). Berkeley: University of California Press, 1996.

Maciariello, J. A., and Kirby, C. *Management Control Systems: Using Adaptive Systems to Attain Control*. Old Tappan, N.J.: Prentice-Hall, 1994.

Pollard, C. W. *The Soul of the Firm*. New York/Grand Rapids, Mich.: HarperBusiness/Zondervan, 1996.

# RESOURCE: ANNOTATED GUIDE TO RELEVANT ORGANIZATIONS, VIDEOS, AND PUBLICATIONS

## Key Organizations in the General Marketplace

Center for Business, Religion, and the Professions
Pittsburgh Theological Seminary
616 North Highland Avenue
Pittsburgh, PA 15206–2596
(412) 362–5610, ext. 2195
www.pts.edu
jcraig@pts.edu

Offers forums on issues of public interest. Cooperative professional master's degree programs with Pittsburgh Theological Seminary and Carnegie-Mellon University, Duquesne University, and the University of Pittsburgh enable students to earn dual degrees in theology, law, business administration, public management, social work, information and library science, music, and healthcare administration.

Christian Vocation Research Project
c/o Memorial Episcopal Church
1407 Bolton Street
Baltimore, MD 21217
(410) 669–0220

Provides resources for discerning call in community; offers parish support for ministries and resources for accountability in ministry.

Coalition for Ministry in Daily Life
800 Hausmann Road
Allentown, PA 18104
(610) 706–0493

Through provision of resources to equip believers, helps Christians advocate the ministry of the whole church. Offers events, research, and

sharing programs and maintains a network to enable talk about ministry
in daily life to become a reality.

Fellowship of Companies for Christ International
4201 N. Peach Tree Road, Suite 200
Atlanta, GA 30341
(770) 457–9700
www.fcci.org
linda@fcci.org

Brings together companies and businesspeople endeavoring to operate
overtly on Christian principles. Also offers videos and organizes seminars
and conferences.

Ministry in Daily Life
Evangelical Lutheran Church in America
8765 W. Higgins Road
Chicago, IL 60631–4195
(773) 380–2870, (800) 638–3522
www.elca.org
info@elca.org

Provides a wide variety of resources to encourage and support the ministry of the laity.

Ministry of the Laity in the Workplace
American Baptist Churches
P.O. Box 851
Valley Forge, PA 19482–0851
(610) 768–2000

Supplies a range of resources related to the ministry of the laity.

National Center for the Laity
(708) 974–5221
Contact: Bill Droel

Publishes the newsletter *Initiatives* as well as a variety of other publications to facilitate the ministry of the laity, especially in the Roman
Catholic Church.

Strategic Careers Project
Open Church Ministries
1624 S. 21st Street
Colorado Springs, CO 80904
(719) 471–9455

Helps Christians in the marketplace and elsewhere who are considering changes in vocation to identify and move into occupations where a Christian presence is most needed in our society.

The Vesper Society
384 Embarcadero West, Suite 200
Oakland, CA 94607
(510) 444–1114

Dedicated to helping individuals and organizations throughout the world increase their ability to serve (especially the underserved) and emphasize the relationship of moral and ethical values to the structures of society.

## Key Leadership-Specific Organizations

De Pree Leadership Center
135 N. Los Robles, Suite 620
Pasadena, CA 91101
(626) 578–6335, (626) 578–0918 (fax)
www.depree.org

Seeks to emphasize the spiritual, relational, and ethical dimensions of leadership. Affirms leaders in their influential roles, which shape learning and caring organizations. By encouraging leaders to become faithful servants, entrusted with the mission of developing the full potential of those around them, promotes a whole-person approach to organizational life and leadership. Develops programs that cultivate the character of the leader and encourage the integration of faith with public life.

The Robert K. Greenleaf Center
921 E. 86th Street, Suite 200
Indianapolis, IN 46240
(317) 925–2677, (317) 259–0560 (fax)

Works to improve the caring and quality of institutions through a unique approach to leadership, structure, and decision making. Offers many educational materials and service aids for transforming the leadership of Christians.

Trinity Forum
210 Lyngate Court, Suite B
Burke, VA 22015–163
(703) 764–1070, (800) 585–1070
www.ttf.org
rwo@ttf.org
Contact: Richard Ohman, executive director

"Academy without walls" that helps leaders engage the leading issues of our day in the context of faith. Hosts executive seminars across North America and around the rest of the world.

## Film and Video Resources for the General Marketplace

*Called to the Marketplace*
InterVarsity Christian Fellowship
P.O. Box 7895
Madison, WI 53707–7895
(608) 274–4823
www.ivcf.org

Examines Christian roles in paid occupations in secular society. Four videocassettes, each 20 to 30 minutes.

*Day by Day*
Religious Film Corporation of America
P.O. Box 4029
Westlake Village, CA 91359

Employs the film-within-a-film method to present a series of vignettes in which actors explore the ministry of everyday life. One episode concerns an employee who is not working to capacity.

*God and Profit? Building a Large Corporation on Biblical Values*
Christian College Coalition
329 Eighth Street, N.E.
Washington, DC 20002–6158
(202) 546–8713
www.gospelcom.net/cccu
coalition@cccu.org

Discussion of Christian corporate goals and their implementation at ServiceMaster, Inc. One videocassette, 30 minutes.

*March 25—A Day in the Life of Catholic Laity in America*
Office of Publicity and Promotion Services
U.S. Catholic Conference
1312 Massachusetts Avenue, N.W.
Washington, DC 28005–4105

Portrays laypeople working out their faith in diverse contexts, including banking, social work, and the military. Of interest to Protestants as well.

## Leadership-Specific Film and Video Resources

*The Miracle of Pittron*
Value of the Person Consultants
Pittsburgh, PA

Story of Wayne Alderson's Christian efforts to overcome labor-management tensions at Pittron Steel Corporation. Film, 16mm; 58 minutes.

*Leaving a Legacy*
De Pree Leadership Center
135 N. Los Robles, Suite 620
Pasadena, CA 91101
(626) 578–6335, (626) 578–0918 (fax)
www.depree.org

Examines the role of leaders in terms of leaving a legacy in organizations, communities, and families. Videocassette, 25 minutes.

## Publications for the General Marketplace

*360° Views*
De Pree Leadership Center
135 N. Los Robles, Suite 620
Pasadena, CA 91101
(626) 578–6335, (626) 578–0918 (fax)
www.depree.org

De Pree Leadership Center newsletter. Addresses issues pertinent to leaders in both the business and religious communities.

*Advocate*
Evangelicals for Social Action
10 East Lancaster Avenue
Wynnewood, PA 19096
(610) 645–9390
www.esa-online.org
esa@esa-online.org

Addresses issues of law and public policy from a Christian perspective. Includes some business and economic articles and references.

*At Work—Stories of Tomorrow's Workplace*
155 Montgomery Street
San Francisco, CA 94104
(800) 929–7006

Inspires integration of faith and work by providing new ideas and practical guidance.

*The Christian Businessman*
Carlson Communications
7001 SW 24 Avenue
Gainesville, FL 32607–3704
(888) 858–5905, (352) 332–4917

Equips and empowers working men with the tools they need to become successful spiritually, personally, and financially while advancing the gospel of Christ. Offers inspiration and encouragement from the lives of leading Christian businessmen and authors.

*The Christian Working Woman—A Ministry for Marketplace Christians*
P.O. Box 1210
Wheaton, IL 60189
(708) 462–0552

Bimonthly publication based on ideas of nationally acclaimed author and speaker Mary Whelchel. Provides profiles, resources, and conference information.

*Contact Quarterly—The Magazine for Business Today*
P.O. Box 3308
Chattanooga, TN 37404
(800) 566–CBMC (566–2262)

Christian Business Men's Committee publication. Contains articles, book reviews, stories, and quotations to help equip Christian men in the marketplace.

*Faith@Work*
160 E. Broad St., Suite B
Falls Church, VA 22046–4051
(703) 237–3626
Fthatwrk@aol.com

Popular magazine featuring regular columns, Bible studies. Filled with practical applications and other encouragement for Christian business-people integrating their faith with their workplace activities.

*Faith in Business Quarterly*
Dr. Ian Groves
4 Broughton Road, Ipswich, Suffolk
IP1 3QR
UK 01473–257344
Isgroves@iee.org

Quarterly journal of the Ridley Hall Foundation. Explores Christian faith and values in the business world. Provides a forum to promote the application of Christian faith and values to businesses, the professions, and public and voluntary service.

*Faith Works*
(888) 715–9403
www.faithworks.com

New publication containing a good Generation X presentation. Explores application of faith to all areas and aspects of everyday life, including school, medicine, business, violence, culture, and children.

*Initiatives—In Support of the Christian in the World*
National Center for the Laity
(708) 974–5221
Contact: Bill Droll

Newsletter of the National Center for the Laity in Chicago. Rich content, access to Roman Catholic resources and programs. Helpful insights into parish initiatives and Protestant aids for ministry in daily life.

*Laynet*
Joan Irving
565 Corley Brook Way
Lawrenceville, GA 30045–6496
(770) 513–1020
jcirving@juno.com

Compiles and discusses items from other publications on Christian approaches to work and other areas of responsibility in a secular environment.

*Leader to Leader*
Jossey-Bass Inc., Publishers
350 Sansome Street
San Francisco, CA 94104–1342
(415) 433–1767
www.josseybass.com
dfalcone@jpb.com.

High-quality publication from the Peter Drucker Foundation, aimed especially at nonprofit organizations. Contains occasional articles by Christians in the marketplace.

*Leadership Insights—Applying Biblical Principles to Career Challenges*
Career Impact Ministries
8201 Cantrell Road, Suite 330
Little Rock, AR 72227

Regular one-page fax created by the Leadership Network. Contains thought-provoking questions and helpful Scriptural references to equip Christian workers.

*Life @ Work: Blending Biblical Wisdom and Business Excellence*
Life@Work Company
P.O. Box 1928
Fayetteville, AR 72702
(501) 444–0664

Provides Christians with examples of people who are integrating biblical wisdom and business excellence in their lives at work.

*Marketplace—A Magazine for Christians in Business*
2501 Oregon Pike, Suite 2
Lancaster, PA 17606
(204) 944–1995

Rooted in the Mennonite tradition of faith in all of areas of life. Examines ethics, lifestyles, and relationships from a biblical perspective in order to promote economic justice. Contains quotations, comments, resources, and reviews from a wide range of sources in the marketplace.

*Ministry of Money—Growth in Discipleship, Compassion for the Poor, Global Stewardship*
MOM
11315 Neelsville Church Road
Germantown, MD 20876–4147
(301) 428–9560

Church of the Savior publication. Seeks to transform Christians from the bondage of money to the ministry of money. Examines local and overseas missions.

De Pree Leadership Center monograph series (various titles)
De Pree Leadership Center
135 N. Los Robles, Suite 620
Pasadena, CA 91101
(626) 578–6335, (626) 578–0918 (fax)
www.depree.org
depree@fuller.edu.

Explores innovative leadership skills and tactics necessary for influence as a leader in the world.

*Christians in Business International*
2125 Smith Avenue, Suite 202
Chesapeake, VA 23320
(757) 523–4890, (757) 523–6600 (fax)
www.cibint.com
104115.221@compuserve.com.

Publication of a global alliance of marketplace ministries that provides resources and information for the purpose of equipping individuals to be more effective in the marketplace.

*Vocatio*
Regent College Foundation
P.O. Box 33276
Seattle, WA 98133
(800) 663–8664, (604) 224–3245

Features contributions on the ministry of Christians in the workplace. Reflects the context of its Christian graduate school, adding thoughtful analysis.

*Zadok Perspectives*
P.O. Box 289
Hawthorn, Victoria 3122
Australia
(03) 9819–5450, (03) 9818–3586 (fax)
www.vicnet.net.au/~zadok

An Australian publication that promotes informed theological reflection, by people from all walks of life, on contemporary issues in Christianity and brings Christian perspectives into public debate.


## Additional Groups for the General Marketplace

Business Enterprise Trust
204 Junipero Serra Boulevard
Stanford, CA 94305
(650) 321–5100
www.betrust.org

Center for the Study of Values in Public Life
Harvard Divinity School
45 Francis Avenue
Cambridge, MA 02138
(617) 496–3586, (619) 496–3668 (fax)
csvpl@div.harvard.edu
Contact: Dr. Laura Nash

Center for Spiritual Transformation
Marble Collegiate Church
1 W. 29th Street
New York, NY 10001–4596
(212) 686–2770
www.marblechurch.org
staff@marblechurch.org

The Drucker Foundation
320 Park Avenue, Third Floor
New York, NY 10022–6839
(212) 224–1174
www.pfdf.org
info@pfdf.org

Institute of Worklife Ministry
7100 Regency Square, Suite 210
Houston, TX 77036
(713) 266–2456
www.worklifeministry.com
www.worklifeinstitute.com
info@worklifeinstitute.com

Intercristo (division of Christian Ministries)
19303 Fremont Avenue N.
Seattle, WA 98133–3800
(800) 426–1343
www.jobleads.org
hrg@crista.org

Laity Lodge
P.O. Box 670
Kerrville, TX 78029–0670

Marketplace Network
1 Park Street
Boston, MA 02108
(617) 227–4226

The Mentoring Institute
11316 Ravenscroft
Sidney, B.C. V8L5R4
Canada
(250) 655–0325
www.mentor-u.com
mentor@uniserve.com.

Ministry in Daily Life
InterVarsity Christian Fellowship
P.O. Box 7895
Madison, WI 53707–7895
(608) 274–4823
www.ivcf.org

Mockler Center for Faith and Work
Gordon-Conwell Theological Seminary
130 Essex Street
South Hamilton, MA 01982
(978) 468–7111, (978) 468–6691 (fax)
www.gcts.edu
info@jcts.edu

Professional Women's Fellowship
1013 8th Avenue
Seattle, WA 98104
(206) 382–7276

Reformed Christian Business and Professional Association
970 Bonnieview Avenue
Burlington, Ont. L7T 1T5
Canada
(416) 524–1203

Regent College
Marketplace Program
5800 University Boulevard
Vancouver, BC V6T 2E4
Canada
(604) 224–3245, (800) 663–8664
Contact: Wayne Heaslip, associate registrar

Workplace Ministry
St. Andrews-Wesley Church
1012 Nelson Street
Vancouver, BC V6E 1H8
Canada
(604) 683–4574

## Additional Leadership-Specific Groups

Center for Creative Leadership
One Leadership Place
Greensboro, NC 27410
(336) 288–7210
www.ccl.org

Center for Ethics and Corporate Policy
637 South Dearborn Street
Chicago, IL 60605
(312) 922–1512

Kellogg International Leadership Program and Kellogg
National Fellowship Program
W. K. Kellogg Foundation
One Michigan Avenue East
Battle Creek, MI 49017–4058
(616) 968–1611

The Leadership Institute
University of Southern California
University Park Campus
Los Angeles, CA 90089
(213) 740–4318
Contact: Professor Jay Conger

National Hispaña Leadership Institute
1901 North Moore Street, Suite 206
Arlington, VA 22209
(703) 527–6007

## Web Sites

Center for Faith and Scholarship
www.puk/ac/za/sywwww

Center for the Study of Religion & American Culture
www.iupui.edu/it/raac
Center for the Study of Values in Public Life
divweb.harvard.edu/csvpl

Christian Business Faculty Association
www.geneva.com@edu

Faith at Work
www.scruples.org/faith_at_work_toc.htm

National Association of Christians in Social Work
www.nacsw.org/inside.html

# INDEX

Expectations: hopes versus, 13; for perfection, 173; for perfection in leaders, 128–129, 163; for perfection in subordinates, 12–13; for success versus failure, 52–53

Expediency, compromise and, 30

Face-to-face meetings, value of, versus electronic communications, 16, 44

Failings, human, 25–26

Failure: constructive use of, 53–54; expectations for success versus, 53–54

Faith, 3–17; actual versus professed, 65; belief and, 4, 64–65; confidence and, 46–48, 51–60; constructivist view of, 48, 49, 50; defined, 4, 81, 82; development of, 186–195; developmental view of, 48, 49; disjunction of faithfulness and, 3, 4–7; faithfulness and, 3–17; as gauge for the future, 134–135; in God, 50–51, 58–60, 187–189; God's Word and, 190–191, 196; as heart of leadership, 63–65; individual, movement toward, 5–6, 141–142, 157; influence of, in leadership styles, 169–181; journey in, case story of, 185–197; keys to growing, 186–195; as leadership factor, 185–186; meanings of, 4, 7–9, 48–51; object of, 188; popular understanding of, 3–4, 46; power sharing as expression of, 93–108; practical outworking of, examples of, 194–195; principles of personal, 196; proactive, 195; as a reality map, 132–137; risk taking and, 55–58, 59–60, 134–135; servant mind-set and, 189–190; sharing, in the workplace, 140–156; silent expression of, 6; as source of wisdom, 82–83; traditional religious view of, 4, 48–49, 50; transformative nature of, 50; trust and, 4, 35, 49, 55, 130–132; vision and, 64–71; as vocational direction, 135–137, 191; for the vulnerable, 129–137; the "who" in, 187–188; at work, 140–156, 193–195, 196

Faith-based leadership. See Leadership

Faith-based mentoring: examples of, 116–119; qualities of, 112–115. See also Mentoring

Faith in Business Quarterly, 220–221

Faith of the Managers: When Management Becomes Religion (Pattison), 169

Faith Works, 221

Faithfulness, 3–17; biblical understanding of, 9; components of, in leaders, 14–15; direct approach to developing, 15–16; disjunction of faith and, 3, 4–7; faith and, 3–17; indirect approach to developing, 15; in leadership, benefits of, 16–17; in leadership, expressions of, 9–14; in leadership, nurturance of, 14–16; nature of, 4, 7–9; popular understanding of, 4, 7–8; principles and, 8–9; promises and, 11–12; relationships and, 9, 15; role modeling of, 15–16; tolerance of mistakes and, 12–13

Faith at Work, 220

Family life, valuing of, 209–210

Farley, M. A., 5, 18

Farson, R., 80, 92

Fear: darkness of, 99, 101–103; of expressing faith in the workplace, 155–156; as obstacle to finding purpose, 85; technique for dealing with, 103; two faces of, 85

Fellowship of Companies for Christ International, 151, 216

Fidelity, in corporate names, 4

Fidelity, promise keeping and, 11

Film and video resources, 218–219

Financial gain, preoccupation with, 7, 176–177

Fixations, 72

Flanagan, H., 181

Fleming, S., 181

Folk and fairy tales, 165

Followers: confiding in, 130; expectations of, 128–129; perceptions of, 40, 54–55; preferences of, for leaders, 124, 126; unconscious identification of, 54. See also Employees

Fowler, J. W., 48, 50, 60, 64, 66–67, 75

Fred (faith-based mentoring case example), 116–117

Long-term perspective, vocation and, 136

Lopez, I. O., 79

*Los Angeles Times,* 152–153

Lou Harris & Associates, 38

Love: acknowledgment of sin and, 26; Jesus' commandment to, 64, 86–87; in mentoring, 110, 113; as source of serving others, 81, 86–87

*Loving Monday: Succeeding in Business Without Selling Your Soul* (Beckett), 185

Loyalty: decline in, 5, 13; faithful leadership and, 17; faithfulness and, 5, 7; faithfulness to employees and, 13–14; to professional guilds versus particular organizations, 125

Lu (faith-based mentoring case example), 117–118

Luke: 6:38, 87; 13:34, 165; 17:5, 6, 196; 22:32, 191

Luke, the apostle, 142

Luther, M., 136

Lutheran church, 143

Lutheran Church of the Holy Spirit, Emmaus, Pennsylvania, survey of, on expressing faith at the workplace, 145–151

Maciariello, J. A., 198, 214

Madsen, R., 141, 156, 214

"Majority rules" position statement, 70

Management: Christian-influenced practices of, 171–178; Christian-influenced practices of, in Service-Master case example, 198–214; parallels between, and radical Christian groups, 172–174; penumbra, 159–160, 165–166; quasi-religious rituals of, 178–179; theories and fads of, 86, 170, 171, 174–178

*Management Control Systems* (Maciariello), 198, 214

Management gurus, 170; assumptions of, 174–175; Christian influences on, 172; as evangelists, 174

Managers: in British public sector, 171; leaders and, 34; mentoring of, in case example, 119; occupational

ethics of, 27; trust between subordinates and, 34–45

Mangham, I., 177–178, 180

Manipulation, risk of, while sharing faith at the workplace and, 144–145, 148–149, 156

*March 25—A Day in the Life of Catholic Laity in America,* 218

March to End the Silence, 94, 95, 106–107

Mark 11:22, 188

Mark, the apostle, 191

Mark the Ascetic, St., 69

*Marketplace—A Magazine for Christians in Business,* 222

Maslow, A. H., 134, 139

Massachusetts Institute of Technology (MIT), 192

Masterplanning Group International, 111, 120

Material rewards, 49–50

Matthew: 5:21–28, 24; 6:30, 196; 7:16, 65; 8:26, 196; 11:29, 72; 14:31, 196; 17:20, 196; 18:2–4, 71–72; 18:6, 73; 23:27, 24; 28:19–20, 142

Maxwell, R., 21

McCann, D. P., 123

McKibben, M. T., 62, 63, 65, 66, 69, 75, 76

McLoughlin, M., 33

Mead, G. H., 161, 168

Mead, M., 103

Meaning: faith as process of making, 48–50; hunger for leadership with, 47–48; in work, 49–50

Measurement, belief in, 176

Media, and leader vulnerability, 128

*Mein Kampf* (Hitler), 21

Mentees: as God's resources, 115; qualities to look for in, 110

Mentoring: accountability in, 115; aspects of, 110; being helpful versus, 112; case examples of, 116–119; faith-based, examples of, 116–119; faith-based, qualities of, 112–115; goals of, 114; God as initiating force of, 115; for leadership development, 109–120; models of, 110–111; motivation in, 113; versus other forms of leadership

Tillich, P., 161, 168
Time demands, 84–85
Tipton, S. M., 141, 156, 214
Titus 2:15, 30
Total Quality Management, 176
Tozer, A. W., 190–191, 197
Training, employee, at ServiceMaster, 206–207, 210, 213
Transactions versus relationships, 15, 162–163
Transcendent leadership, 47–48, 50–51
*Transforming Leadership: A Christian Approach to Management* (Higginson), 19
Trickett, D., 157
Trickster face of fear, 85
Trinity Forum, 217–218
Trueblood, E., 141
TruGreen-ChemLawn, 204
Trust, 34–45; advertisement of, 4; betrayed, 38, 44; Christian theological perspective on, 35, 36, 39; confidence and, 35, 36, 55; decline of, 5, 35, 38–39; development of, suggestions for, 41–44; faith and, 4, 35, 49, 55, 130–132; faithful leadership and, 17, 34, 130–132; in God, 35, 131–132; knowing others and, 164; longing for, 42; between managers and subordinates, 34–45; popular understanding of, 36; rebuilding, 44; as risk taking, 35–36, 37–38, 43–44; as social capital, 36–38; sources of, 39–41; that support will be provided, 102, 106
Truth: belief and, 170–171; faith as reality map for, 132–137; relative, 133
Turnover: employee, at ServiceMaster, 207–208; leadership, frequency of, 123–124
Tyrannical leaders, 21

United Auto Workers, 125
U.S. Department of the Treasury, 159
Unpredictability: global, as source of leader vulnerability, 126–127; trust and, 35–36, 37–38
Uprightness, 23–24

Utilitarians, 175

Vesper Society, 217
Virtual networks, for leadership development, 16
Virtues, resurgent. *See* Resurgent virtues
Vision, 62, 65–71; alignment of organizational with religious, 57; Christian, 65–71; Christian versus secular, 68–69; confidence and, 54, 56; definitions of, 65–66; faith and, 64–65, 67; of Holy Trinity, 65, 66, 67–69; of Kingdom of God, 63, 66, 67–68, 75; language of, 170, 178; local, 67, 68; organizational, 69–71, 75, 178; personal, integration of, into shared organizational, 70–71; reality and, 135; role of, in people's lives, 66; shared, 69–71; as source of implementation, 65–71. *See also* Purpose
Vision statements, 65
Visualization, 66
*Vocare,* 135
*Vocatio,* 223
*Vocatio,* 135
Vocation: career versus, 6, 136; community involvement in, 137; faith and work as, 49, 50–51, 135–137, 191–193, 196; hearing God's summons for, 135–137, 191–193. *See also* Purpose
Vulnerability, 123–139; confidence and, 46; decision making and, 128; expectations for perfection versus, 128–129, 163; external environmental sources of, 126–128; faith for dealing with, 129–137; internal organizational environments as sources of, 124–126; in leaders, 42–43, 47, 123–139; leadership turnover and, 123–124; sources of, for leaders, 124–129; trust and, 42–43, 130–132

Ward, B., 68, 69, 75, 76
Ware, K., 76
Warner, C., 103, 108
Washington, J. M., 61
Waterman, R., 170, 181